Using the Internet Safely For Seniors For Dummies

P9-CDC-791

Eight Tips for Becoming Safer Online

➡ **Create stronger passwords.** Create passwords that aren't easy to guess, and don't share them with others. See Chapter 3 for more about this.

➡ **Don't expose personal information.** Be aware of how much of your personal or financial data you might be sharing with strangers on social networking sites, through e-mail, and on special-interest sites. See Chapter 7 for more information.

➡ **Don't fall for e-mail scams.** Online criminals may use e-mail to get your personal information for ID theft. Or an e-mail might entice you to click a link that takes you to a bogus site or downloads malware (malicious software) to your computer. Read Chapter 5 for more advice about using e-mail safely.

➡ **Know who you're doing business with.** It's quick and easy to create a Web site that looks legit, but not all Web sites are. See Chapter 4 for information about identifying trusted sites.

➡ **Be cautious with e-mail attachments.** Attached files may contain malware, which can damage your computer — or it may install code that can track your activities. See Chapter 5 for more about dealing with e-mail attachments.

➡ **Use software to avoid malware.** Chapter 15 outlines several types of software products you can consider using to spot and avoid viruses, spyware, and objectionable online content.

➡ **Create safe e-mail aliases and usernames.** Whether creating an e-mail account or a user account on a social networking or special-interest site, be careful how much information you give away. See Chapter 8 for information about creating safe names and profiles in social networking sites.

➡ **Find out how others might expose you.** Even if you never go online, your information is probably out there. Learn to identify your exposure and stop others from revealing personal information in Chapter 7.

For Dummies: Bestselling Book Series for Beginners

Using the Internet Safely For Seniors For Dummies®

Cheat Sheet

Great Senior Safety Web Sites

➤ www.ilookbothways.com: The authors' company Web site offers blogs and step-by-step procedures to help you stay safer. Keep up with the latest online risks and gain skills to be a safer online consumer. The Ask Linda feature lets you ask safety questions at any time for expert advice.

➤ www.ftc.gov/bcp/edu/microsites/idtheft: Fighting Back Against Identity Theft is a site from the Federal Trade Commission that guides you through the process of deterring ID thieves, detecting ID theft, and defending yourself against it.

➤ www.fraud.org/internet/intinfo.htm: The National Fraud Information Center's site lets you look up the latest online scams, under the theory that knowledge is power. It also has an online complaint form that you can use to inform them of bad experiences you've had with online spammers or scammers.

➤ www.bbb.org: This is the site of the Better Business Bureau, a good place to start in identifying online stores that are safe to do business with.

➤ www.sec.gov: The U.S. Securities and Exchange Commission site is a good place to get information to help you protect your investments and access investment calculators.

➤ www.cnet.com: CNET is a good site for reading reviews of products from their editors and users before making your online purchase. There is a strong focus here on electronics and technology, so if you're thinking of buying a computer, this is a good source of information.

For Dummies: Bestselling Book Series for Beginners

Using the Internet Safely For Seniors

FOR DUMMIES®

by Linda Criddle and Nancy Muir

WILEY

Wiley Publishing, Inc.

Using the Internet Safely For Seniors For Dummies®

Published by
Wiley Publishing, Inc.
111 River Street
Hoboken, NJ 07030-5774

www.wiley.com

Copyright © 2009 by Wiley Publishing, Inc., Indianapolis, Indiana

Published by Wiley Publishing, Inc., Indianapolis, Indiana

Published simultaneously in Canada

For general information on our other products and services, please contact our Customer Care Department within the U.S. at 877-762-2974, outside the U.S. at 317-572-3993, or fax 317-572-4002.

For technical support, please visit www.wiley.com/techsupport.

Wiley also publishes its books in a variety of electronic formats. Some content that appears in print may not be available in electronic books.

Library of Congress Control Number: 2009922969

ISBN: 978-0-470-45745-0

Manufactured in the United States of America

10 9 8 7 6 5 4 3 2 1

WILEY

About the Authors

Linda Criddle is an internationally recognized expert in online safety and teaches extensively in schools and universities. Linda is the author, along with Nancy Muir, of the award winning book *Look Both Ways: Help Protect Your Family on the Internet* (Microsoft Press, 2006). She has also developed an online course titled *Internet Safety for Educators* being offered through Washington State University and The University of Alaska. Linda has worked with governments, law enforcement, and companies around the world and is a frequent speaker at Internet-safety related conferences worldwide. Her company, LOOK**BOTH**WAYS, Inc., develops software, consults with companies, governments, and law enforcement on Internet safety, and writes educational curriculum. Learn more at their Web site, www.ilookbothways.com.

Nancy Muir has worked with Linda Criddle on Internet safety-related projects for the past three years, co-authored two books with Linda, and developed and taught an online course. Nancy has written over fifty technology and business books, and produced video programming for major corporations such as IBM and Symantec. Prior to her writing career Nancy was a publishing executive with several major technology book publishers including John Wiley & Sons, Inc., and MacMillan Publishing. Nancy has taught technical writing at Purdue University/Indiana University, and holds a certificate in Distance Learning Design from The University of Washington. She currently oversees content development for LOOK**BOTH**WAYS, Inc.

Authors' Acknowledgments

The authors wish to thank project editor Blair Pottenger for his able stewardship of this project and his flexibility in working towards the best book possible. Thanks also to Katie Mohr and Greg Croy, acquisitions editors for the book, for believing in the need for a safer online world and this book. A tip of our hats also to Joyce Nielsen, technical editor, for an eagle-eyed review, and to copy editor Heidi Unger, whose wordsmithing skills kept our writing literate.

A special thanks to Linda's mom and dad, Richard and JoAn Criddle, for their prodding to get this book written, and for the inspiration and guidance they gave along the way.

Dedication

The authors wish to dedicate this book to all the brave 50+ folks who are jumping online to discover all the Internet has to offer and helping to make the online world a safer one through vigilance and good online citizenship.

Publisher's Acknowledgments

We're proud of this book; please send us your comments through our online registration form located at `http://dummies.custhelp.com`. For other comments, please contact our Customer Care Department within the U.S. at 877-762-2974, outside the U.S. at 317-572-3993, or fax 317-572-4002.

Some of the people who helped bring this book to market include the following:

Acquisitions and Editorial

Project Editor: Blair J. Pottenger

Executive Editor: Greg Croy

Acquisitions Editor: Katie Mohr

Copy Editor: Heidi Unger

Technical Editor: Joyce Nielsen

Editorial Manager: Kevin Kirschner

Editorial Assistant: Amanda Foxworth

Sr. Editorial Assistant: Cherie Case

Cartoons: Rich Tennant (`www.the5thwave.com`)

Composition Services

Project Coordinator: Katie Key

Layout and Graphics: Sarah Philippart

Proofreader: Nancy L. Reinhardt

Indexer: Broccoli Information Management

Publishing and Editorial for Technology Dummies

    Richard Swadley, Vice President and Executive Group Publisher

    Andy Cummings, Vice President and Publisher

    Mary Bednarek, Executive Acquisitions Director

    Mary C. Corder, Editorial Director

Publishing for Consumer Dummies

    Diane Graves Steele, Vice President and Publisher

Composition Services

    Gerry Fahey, Vice President of Production Services

    Debbie Stailey, Director of Composition Services

Table Of Contents

*T*he Internet seems to have become an integral part of our lives in the blink of an eye, and in a sense, that's true. It's been only about 20 years or so since its beginnings, and now many people couldn't live without it. We use it to check news stories, watch movies, balance bank accounts, buy any number of things, and communicate with others.

If you realize that you can't avoid using the Internet, but you worry about some of the risks it harbors, this book will help you understand what's going on out there, help you acquire skills that can keep you safer, and show you how to enjoy your online time with greater peace of mind.

About This Book

This book is specifically written for mature people like you, folks who are relatively new to using a computer and want to discover how to use the Internet safely. In writing this book, we've tried to take into account the types of activities that might interest a senior citizen who's either discovering computers for the first time or discovering how to use them more safely.

Foolish Assumptions

This book is organized by sets of sections and tasks. These sections and tasks start from the very beginning, assuming you know little about computers and online safety, and they

Introduction

Conventions used in this book

This book uses certain conventions to help you find your way around, including the following:

➡ When you have to type something in a text box, we put it in **bold** type. When you have to take action, such as clicking a button or link, we put the name of the item you have to act upon in **bold** type. Whenever we mention a Web site address, we put it in another font, `like this.`

➡ When we introduce a term that you might not be familiar with, the term appears in italics, followed by a plain-English definition of the term.

➡ For menu commands, we use the ⇨ symbol to separate menu choices. For example, you might see this instruction: Choose Tools⇨Internet Options. The ⇨ symbol is just our way of saying "Open the Tools menu and then click Internet Options."

➡ Callouts for figures draw your attention to an action you need to perform. In some cases, points of interest in a figure might be identified. The text tells you what to look for, the callout makes it easy to find.

 Tip icons point out insights or helpful suggestions related to tasks in the step list.

 Warning icons indicate online behaviors that might put you, your information, your loved ones, or your pocket book in jeopardy.

guide you through, from the most basic steps in easy-to-understand language. Because we assume you're new to computers, the book provides explanations or definitions of technical terms to help you out.

All computers are run by software called *operating systems,* such as Windows. Because Microsoft Windows–based personal computers (PCs) are the most common type, the book focuses mostly on Windows functionality. Specifically, we use Windows Vista and Internet Explorer in most of our examples. But rest assured that the majority of the advice in this book about staying safe online works no matter whether you use a Mac, a Windows-based PC, or a Linux machine.

Why You Need This Book

You've probably decided it's time to go online to take advantage of all the Internet has to offer, but you hesitate to take the plunge because you hear all these stories about predators, scams, and spam. Well, here's a shocker: Even if you've never gone online, your information is out there from a variety of sources, and you are at risk. By going online and doing so safely, you may be able to mitigate your risk while learning your way around. You may also discover how to help protect your family online.

With the simple step-by-step approach of this book, you can get up to speed with the Internet and learn the ins and outs of smart, defensive computing.

You can work through this book from beginning to end, or you can simply open up a chapter to solve a problem or help you learn a new skill whenever you need it. The steps or bulleted lists in each section get you where you want to go quickly, without a lot of technical explanation. In no time, you'll start picking up the skills you need to become a safer Internet user.

How This Book Is Organized

This book is conveniently divided into several handy parts to help you find what you need.

➡ **Part I: The Foundation of Using the Internet Safely:** This part helps you understand what's going on out there that puts Internet users at risk, including the predators' activities, e-mail scams, ID theft, and more. You find out how the financial model online makes information about you — your interests, location, shopping habits, and more — into a very valuable commodity. Chapter 3 helps you get much safer right away by modifying some typical risky behavior quickly and easily.

➡ **Part II: Use the Internet While Dodging the Risk:** In these chapters, you begin to explore the Internet, starting with the basics of navigating with an Internet browser, such as Internet Explorer. You discover the ins and outs of safe e-mailing, how to post photos and videos safely, and how to protect your personal information online.

After you have the basics about getting around and posting safely, you get to explore the fun side of the Internet, safely. These chapters cover the world of social networking and blogging, online games, virtual worlds, and entertainment, and how you and your grandkids can have fun online together.

➡ **Part III: Your Wealth and Your Health:** The Internet isn't all games and videos. You can use your computer to shop, manage your money, and get advice about your health. Of course, the trick is to do all these things without putting yourself at risk, and that's what the chapters in this part help you do.

➡ **Part IV: Being Proactive:** Besides modifying your behavior online, you can use technology tools to block computer viruses and spyware and push back on companies and the government to work to make you safer. The two chapters in this part give you the tools you need to protect your computer, report abuse, and make a difference in making the Internet safer for us all.

➡ **Glossary:** The Glossary is your place for quickly finding the meaning of common Internet and safety terms.

Get Going!

Whether you're somewhat computer savvy but need to find out how to be safer online or you're just starting to use the Internet, working your way through this book will help you become even savvier than your grandchildren or the kid next door.

Think of that!

Part I
The Foundation of Using the Internet Safely

The 5th Wave   By Rich Tennant

"Before the Internet, we were only bustin' chops locally. But now, with our Web site, we're bustin' chops all over the world."

Understand What's Going On Out There

Chapter 1

Throughout this book, we point out again and again what a great tool the Internet is. Why? Because you hear a lot of hype about what a dangerous place the Internet is, and that hype sometimes causes people to miss out on a wealth of information, entertainment, communication, and opportunity.

Do Internet risks exist? Yes, just as risk exists every time you step out your front door, climb behind the wheel, or cross a street. But you haven't stayed in your house your entire life; you've learned how to stay relatively safe while exploring the world all these years.

You can stay just as safe online. First, you need a basic understanding of how Internet risks occur so that you can place any Internet safety advice in context. Once you know the nature of online risks, you can then begin to acquire skills to stay safer.

This chapter explores the landscape of risk online; in the process, we show you which risks are real and which are largely myth, look at the financial model that drives the Internet and the factors that allow abuses to occur, and show you how your own behavior can sometimes put you in harm's way.

Congratulations: You're the Most Sought-After Generation Online

With millions of seniors going online and expanding their Internet activities, service providers see folks over 50 as a critical new target audience (see **Figure 1-1** from AARP) . . . and so do online criminals.

Every age group has unique vulnerabilities in addition to general Internet risks, and seniors are no exception. Few entirely new types of crime are created to target seniors; instead, existing crimes are tailored specifically to exploit older Internet users.

For example, while an online scam targeting minors promises trips to Disneyland or cool toys, scams aimed at seniors are more likely to offer discount medications and low-cost insurance. *Phishing scams* are e-mails that frequently target seniors with fake bank notices or official-looking fake government documents.

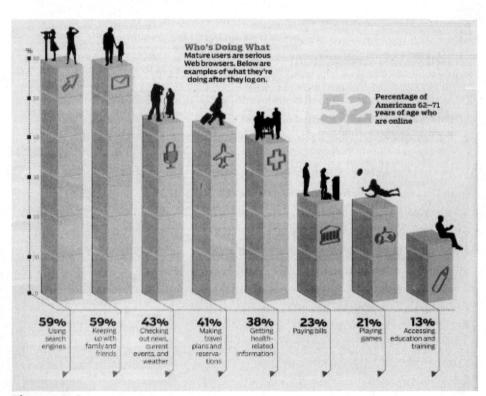

Figure 1-1

In addition to being targeted for different types of crime, seniors may share characteristics that make them especially vulnerable online. Here are some of the major factors that make seniors vulnerable:

➠ **Lack of computer skills.** Although many seniors are very computer savvy, many more aren't. They may not understand technologies such as firewalls and anti-spyware that they can use to protect their data.

➠ **Lack of Internet skills.** Though many seniors are cutting-edge users of Internet services, most are beginners when it comes to interacting with others and doing business online. You have a wealth of experience in judging the character of people you meet in person, but you have probably developed fewer skills for assessing the character of the people and companies you meet online.

Lack of exposure to technology can make you more vulnerable. Understanding how content you place online (an activity called posting) might be misused, how criminals try to deceive you, or how to determine the trustworthiness of a site, for example, actually has little to do with how well you can use a computer. See the section "It's Not Always about Technology, It's Often about Behavior," later in this chapter, for more about this key concept.

➠ **More trusting.** Seniors are typically more trusting and respectful of official-looking material than younger generations, so seniors are more apt to fall for scams. And you're more worried about notices that claim that there's a problem with your information that might somehow sully your good name or threaten your life savings.

Roads Have Rules, The Internet Doesn't

The Internet began as a tool for university researchers to share information. When it took off with the general public, nobody was in charge, nobody owned the Internet, and no rules governed what you could and couldn't do online. Today, this is largely unchanged.

In addition, because of its global nature, the Internet lets us all cross borders — for good, and for bad. Some governments have regulations about Internet use. But with an international population using the Internet, it's hard to enforce the laws of a single country — and it's easy for people to fly under government radar. For example, in the United States, gambling online can be illegal, yet the casino in **Figure 1-2** actively solicits U.S. customers.

Figure 1-2

In essence, we have a very sophisticated and powerful tool existing within a frontier culture — something akin to giving Jesse James and his gang laser guns. The current state of affairs is the result of a lot more than bad guys armed with technology. In fact, six factors contribute to the current online situation:

➡ **Lack of knowledge.** Consumers of every age and at every level of technical expertise lack broad online safety education. This lack of knowledge isn't limited to seniors, but extends to the general population, including computer specialists who may not know any more than others about online predatory behavior.

➡ **Carelessness.** Even when we know better, we make mistakes. Usually, we make those mistakes when we're tired, rushed, or don't have a complete understanding of the risks involved. This is especially true when we see no obvious cause and effect to help us correct our behavior. When you post information and a month later criminals use that information to rob your home, you aren't likely to recognize a connection between the two events. In fact, the vast majority of victims of online crime never recognize that an action they or someone else took online made them vulnerable to a criminal act.

➡ **Unintentional exposure of (or by) others.** It may be a grandchild, friend, employer, or volunteer organization that provides publicly accessible information that exposes you. Perhaps your own computer (or mobile phone, or other connected device) has been compromised with spyware that enables criminals to collect your personal information. Maybe when a friend's computer or other Internet-enabled device was lost or stolen, your information fell into the wrong hands.

➠ **Technology flaws.** Online products and services can expose consumers — either because the companies that offer them fail to secure their customers' data and are hacked, or because a company fails to build adequate safeguards and safety messaging into their product to protect consumers.

➠ **Holes in consumer protection standards.** Right now, most of the burden of online safety is on consumers. Because of the rapid growth of the Internet, governments have not yet been able to create a full set of standards and laws.

➠ **Criminal acts.** Placing the word *cyber* in front of -criminal, -thief, -robber, -molester, or -predator only changes the criminal's tools, not his motivations or goals. Criminals still want to steal your money, dominate or abuse, or destroy property. The Internet didn't create crime, and sadly, it won't abolish it. But it does offer some powerful tools for criminals to take advantage of.

The first five issues in this equation create an environment in which criminal and malicious acts can flourish. What's new is that the Internet gives criminals broader access to more people and information than ever before. Predators are generally equal-opportunity offenders, happy to target victims of any age. Young people represent only one segment; adults and seniors are equally at risk, although the motivation for exploitation of older consumers is more often for financial gain than for emotional or sexual gratification.

Online Anonymity

Although you may think you are anonymous online, you may not be. Online companies may have exposed you. For example, some e-mail programs display your full name in every e-mail you send, even if you've come up with a clever e-mail alias. If you join a social networking site such as MySpace or Eons (a senior-focused site), your publicly viewable profile might give away your name, location, and gender (see **Figure 1-3**), even if you set your page to private.

Though you may not be as anonymous online as you think, criminals are very good at staying anonymous or pretending to be someone or something they aren't. Offline, no one can build a fake bank or store on some street corner for a few days, so you don't have to worry about whether the bank or store is real. When you enter, you quickly get a sense of whether it's a reputable business. If you have a problem with a purchase, you can march right back through the door and demand service.

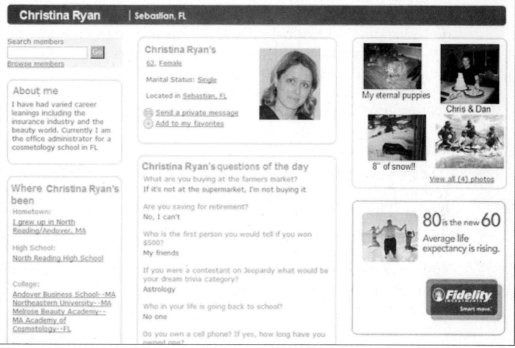

Figure 1-3
© 2008, Look Both Ways LLC

On the Web, those physical attributes and clues are all gone. Anyone can build a Web site that looks official and legitimate for very little money. They can trick search engines to make their Web sites show up as one of the first results when someone runs a search. Anyone can copy the look and content of any other Web site. This means that the fakes are sometimes very, very hard to identify, no matter what your age.

It's Not Always about Technology; It's Often about Behavior

Ironically, people who are computer savvy are sometimes more at risk online because they believe that being computer savvy means they are Internet savvy. In reality, Internet safety is often more a matter of understanding human behavior than understanding technology.

Think about your average phishing scam. This particular form of e-mail spam appears to come from your bank, investment company, or another site where you do financial transactions. (See **Figure** 1-4.) The e-mail will claim some "reason" why they need to verify your account number or password or credit card, Social Security Number, and so on (or all of the above!). The e-mail looks official, and it provides links for you to visit their site and verify your identity. But the site is as fraudulent as the e-mail and any information you provide is in the hands of financial predators. These e-mails may even display a prominent safety and privacy message meant to help convince you that the site is legitimate. However careful study of the message reveals several red flags once you know what to look for (see **Figure** 1-5).

Technology makes it possible for somebody to make a scam e-mail look authentic right down to using the legitimate company's logo, and send it to you. But what's putting you at risk isn't technology, it's the danger that you'll fall for the bait — hook, line, and sinker. If you're savvy, you'll know that the link to the site might take you to a mocked-up site that may look like your bank, but it isn't. Be suspicious of any e-mail that wants your bank account number or other sensitive information. Don't click on links! Instead, look up your bank's phone number (don't call the number provided in the e-mail, which could also be false), call, and report the scam.

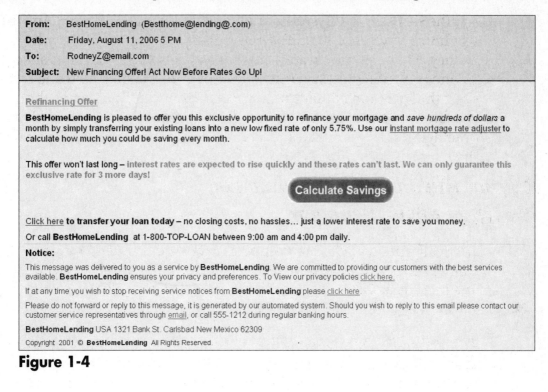

From: BestHomeLending (Bestthome@lending@.com)

Date: Friday, August 11, 2006 5 PM

To: RodneyZ@email.com

Subject: New Financing Offer! Act Now Before Rates Go Up!

Refinancing Offer

BestHomeLending is pleased to offer you this exclusive opportunity to refinance your mortgage and *save hundreds of dollars* a month by simply transferring your existing loans into a new low fixed rate of only 5.75%. Use our instant mortgage rate adjuster to calculate how much you could be saving every month.

This offer won't last long – interest rates are expected to rise quickly and these rates can't last. We can only guarantee this exclusive rate for 3 more days!

Calculate Savings

Click here **to transfer your loan today** – no closing costs, no hassles… just a lower interest rate to save you money.

Or call **BestHomeLending** at 1-800-TOP-LOAN between 9:00 am and 4:00 pm daily.

Notice:

This message was delivered to you as a service by **BestHomeLending**. We are committed to providing our customers with the best services available. **BestHomeLending** ensures your privacy and preferences. To View our privacy policies click here.

If at any time you wish to stop receiving service notices from **BestHomeLending** please click here.

Please do not forward or reply to this message, it is generated by our automated system. Should you wish to reply to this email please contact our customer service representatives through email, or call 555-1212 during regular banking hours.

BestHomeLending USA 1321 Bank St. Carlsbad New Mexico 62309

Copyright 2001 © **BestHomeLending** All Rights Reserved.

Figure 1-4

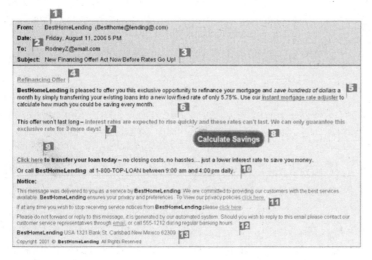

Figure 1-5

Red flags:

1. Company you haven't heard of.

2. The e-mail is not "To:" you.

3 and 6: Financial transaction under time pressure.

4. The e-mail doesn't acknowledge who you are.

5 and 8: Encouraged to enter financial information.

7. Legitimate offers contain specific dates.

8. Doesn't go to a site called "besthomelending".

9 and 12 More "click here" links that do not go to the purported site.

10. Doesn't specify the time zone.

11. Not an 800-number.

13. An Internet mapping site shows there is no such address.

Hit or Myth: Online Information Exposure

Having your information exposed online is one of the greatest risks you face, but seniors generally buy into a few myths about how their information is exposed online.

The first myth is that if you don't use a computer or go online, you aren't exposed online. False. Just because you didn't put information online doesn't mean it isn't there — virtually everyone has information online.

Here are a few examples:

➡ Publicly available government records show if you own a home, vote, have a criminal record (or speeding ticket), and much more.

➡ Your location (including photos in most cases) is listed online through any Internet mapping service like the one shown in **Figure 1-6**.

➡ Unless you've been very careful to ensure your phone number isn't in any phone book, or taken care to have never entered it in a sweepstakes or other contest, it's online. Even if you have been careful, you should check to see. Type your home phone number (with area code and hyphens) into any search engine and see if it brings back your information — chances are that it will.

➡ If you donate to a charity without doing so anonymously, the charity's Web site probably lists you as a donor as a way to thank you.

➡ If you volunteer with an organization, belong to a church group, sports group, action committee, and so on, chances are you are listed on its Web site.

Figure 1-6

➠ If your grandchild has a *blog* (an online journal), or has registered for her wedding or a new baby, your name, location, and other information may appear there.

➠ If a relative enjoys genealogy, you and your relatives' names, birth dates, wedding dates, death dates, locations, and more may be posted on a genealogy site.

The second myth is that if you haven't fallen for an Internet scam, you won't be the victim of an Internet crime. The truth is that you may never know what the Internet connection is (or even if there was one) in most crimes. For example, online public records may give a criminal the information and means to rob your home or steal your identity.

The third myth is that only people you know are going to look at the information you post online. Everything on the Internet is copied and indexed — constantly. Even if you take your information off the Internet, a copy of it may still be out there, although you can reduce exposure by removing personally identifiable information from anything you or family members post online.

Keep Your Information Private

Sharing personal information with the wrong people is one of your biggest risks online. Before you provide personal information, be sure you're comfortable with how it will be handled. Table 1-1 lists some common pieces of personal information, along with the risk of exposing this data online.

Table 1-1	Information Exposure Risks
Information	**Risks of Abuse**
Address and phone number	Makes the user a target for home break-ins, junk mail, and telemarketers, and provides a stronger persona in identity theft cases.
Names of husband/wife, father, and mother (including mother's maiden name)	Provides access to even more confidential information in public records, this data is also often used for passwords or secret question answers; and it may expose additional family members to ID theft, fraud, or personal harm.
Information about your car, including license plate numbers; VIN (vehicle identification number); registration information; insurance carrier; loan information; and driver's license number	Can lead to car theft, insurance fraud, and access to more of your confidential information.
Information about work history and credit status	Helps criminals take over your identity and gain more access to your financial records.
Social security numbers	Enables ID theft, fraud, and access to additional information about you.

How Information Accumulates

Every detail you share online about your life and the extended group of people you interact with is stored *somewhere*. Understanding the way this information accumulates is critical.

Many people are very casual about giving out personal information online because they fail to fully understand the ramifications of doing so. Think of each piece of information as a drop of water. Today, each drop of information posted online is collected into personal virtual buckets. The information rarely disappears; rather, it accumulates, slowly building a comprehensive picture of your identity and life. Small details about your appearance, where you live and work, where you went to school, your financial status, emotional vulnerabilities, and the lives of those close to you all add up in a smart predator's mind.

People post resumes that include hobbies, past employers, past addresses, and professional associations. People post highly personal and identifiable information in online journals called *blogs.* On travel sites, you may reveal your excitement about an upcoming trip. Perhaps you are exposing friends and family's e-mail addresses by forwarding e-mails. (See **Figure 1-7**.)

Exposed e-mail addresses

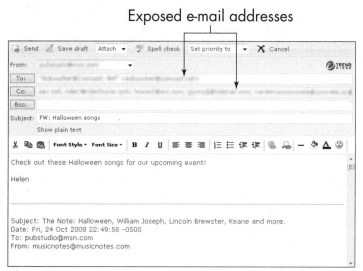

Figure 1-7

The good news is that you can begin to control the information you expose about yourself, and even ask friends and family members to limit how they expose you. Just keep in mind that you, your friends, and family aren't the only ones sharing information, so remember to

periodically search the Web for information and then, if you find
something you don't want shared, ask the site owner to remove the
information:

➡ **Employers need to consider the level of information they share about current and former employees.** Consider carefully what information is
appropriate to include in an employee bio that is
posted on your company Web site. How much
should be visible to other employees on your
intranet (your internal company "Internet")? When
you attend a conference, is the attendee list shown in
online conference documents? Teach employees to be
careful about the information they leave in out-of-
office messages; saying 'taking the grandkids to
Disneyland' also says 'our home will be empty' and
potentially makes them a target for burglary.

➡ **Organizations should be cautious about exposing
volunteer information on their Web sites if the
general public can view those sites.** Posting photos
and identifying volunteers or staff by last name can
place people in harm's way. Posting schedules of club
activities along with information about what activities an individual participates in provides a criminal
with the physical location and time where he can
find that person.

 Consider who can see your information before you
post it. It is your choice how much personal information you post online in publicly viewable sites, how
much you share on private sites, and what you
choose not to share online at all. Schools and companies can restrict access to parts of their sites to make
information available to those who need it, but not
to anyone outside of your organization. See Chapter
8 for more about social networking site settings.

Online Information Is Forever

One of the reasons information exposed online puts you at such great risk is because, once it's out there, it stays out there. Comments, actions, or images posted online may stay online long after you delete the material from your site or request that a friend delete your information from his or her site. You won't know who else has downloaded what you wrote or what search engine crawled (automatically searched the Internet) and stored a photo. You can't know who else sees your comments and judges you by them, nor will you have the opportunity, in most cases, to explain. (See Chapter 7 for more about sharing information safely online).

Another aspect of information permanence is the difficulty it presents when you want to distance yourself from something in your past or go in new directions. Perhaps you no longer want to be associated with an old relationship, but the information remains online to haunt you and for anybody to come across.

Anyone — with good intentions, as well as those with intent to do harm — can dip into your public virtual bucket and search for your information years from now. It may be the new pastor at your church, a potential employer, a new friend, or your grandchildren who discover something you'd rather keep private. Or it could be an identity thief, any other kind of predator, or anyone in your life who wants to lash out at you to cause harm.

What seems like a good idea at the time may come back to bite you in a variety of ways, so think before you post. It's far easier to think twice and refrain from posting than it is to try to take it back. By doing so, you can control your information exposure and privacy while staying safer online.

How the Internet Views You

Chapter 2

*I*f you want to avoid a pickpocket in a crowded marketplace, it helps to know that the world has such things as pickpockets, that they hang out in crowded marketplaces, that they use certain tactics, and that they want to steal money and other valuables from you (hence, you know which pocket to protect).

The online analogy (you knew there'd be one) is that you have to understand what types of activities go on online, what you have that has value, who wants it, and how companies and individuals use what they take. We explore these things in this chapter, and when you understand them, you're much better able to traverse the online world with your finances, privacy, and reputation intact.

Understand the Online Financial Model

In the early days of the consumer-based Internet (about 1995 or so), some Web companies set about selling subscriptions to their sites. You would pay $29.95 a year to subscribe to AOL, for example, for which you got an Internet connection and this large portal of news, an e-mail account, access to chat rooms, and so on.

At some point, right around the `.com` crash in the late 1990s, Web companies realized that most people weren't really willing to pay for services. That's when everybody's high-tech stocks took a dive and many online services and sites essentially became free. Browse the Web today and you'll find free e-mail accounts, free news, free mortgage calculators, free recipes, and on and on (see **Figure 2-1**).

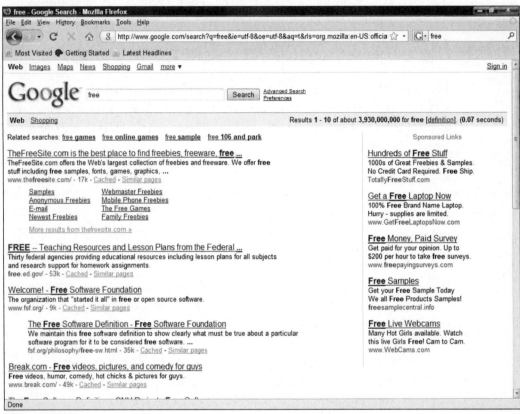

Figure 2-1

This begs the question, how do these companies make money? Ask most people how free online services and sites make money, and they'll answer in one word: advertising.

In reality, the primary way most free services tend to make money isn't by selling advertising space to other companies. What they sell, depending on their terms and conditions, is *access to you and your information* to advertisers, marketers, researchers, and others who want your information for a wide variety of ethical, unethical, or entirely illegal purposes.

In fact, you're still paying for these services, but what's changed is the currency — you no longer pay in dollars; instead, you pay in loss of privacy.

As you provide information online, it's important that you consider which parts are sold, bought, or simply taken, and you should understand how that information may be used to create potential outcomes. Then you can select your comfort level and act accordingly.

What Information Do Others Want, and Why?

Just about every piece of information about you has value: which soft drink you buy, what kind of car you drive, your income bracket, your medical information, your musical tastes, and even what kind of mood you're in today.

Some of this information is useful for

⟹ Making the service better for you.

⟹ Selling you products or services.

⟹ Scoping out the user demographics of sites, again with the goal of designing and targeting products or services more successfully to consumers. (See **Figure 2-2**.)

⟹ Employers or insurers who want to check your background or search your medical history, for example. They may search (or hire a company to search) for your information, unbeknownst to you.

Some people feel that more targeted advertising simply makes sense — you avoid seeing ads for things that are useless or even offensive to you. However, there's also the seedy side of the Internet, which includes criminals who compile catalogs of information about people who just bought expensive electronics. They can sell this information to thieves.

Figure 2-2

 Information about you and your Internet-connected devices is collected from a variety of sources. Some is information that you've posted to sites, some comes from other people who know you, and some is placed online by companies, organizations, and the government. See Chapter 7 for more about protecting your information online and understanding how others may expose you.

How Posted Information May Be Used against You

Every piece of information you or others post about you and every action you take online has commercial value to someone. That isn't necessarily a bad thing, if it simply helps companies target your interests and preferences, but your information may be used in negative and sometimes criminal ways. For example, it might be used by

➠ Someone who wants to embarrass or bully you.

➠ Plagiarists who want to claim your content as their own.

➠ Criminal organizations or individuals building profiles of people to scam, steal identities from, hijack computers, find interesting homes to break into or cars to steal, target people to physically harm, and so on.

➠ Companies who want to use your information in ways that act against your interests. Consider these examples:

  • Insurance companies may use information posted on blogs to deny coverage of medical claims, car accident claims, and so on.

  • A potential employer may reject your job application based on information about you online. Or your current employer may find reasons to fire you.

Set Boundaries for Information Exposure

Where you set your own boundaries for information exposure is an entirely personal choice, but here's a quick overview of what you should consider in making your choices. If a site requires personal information, you should recognize the differences in these types of data:

➠ **Information that an organization *has to collect* before you can use its Web site:** Many services have to collect some information from you in order for them to interact with you. Online shopping Web sites, for instance, need to have your name and address, among other data, for financial transactions. (See **Figure 2-3.**) They need to know certain things about your computer, such as your *IP address* (this stands for Internet protocol, which is a unique identifier assigned to devices, such as your computer, that connect with the Internet) to route information to and from you. They check which Internet browser you use (such as Internet Explorer or Firefox) and whether you use a Windows or Mac operating system (and which version) to best display their Web pages on your monitor. If you've been to the site before, they may have put a cookie on your computer that identifies you when you visit again and provides your preferred experience automatically.

A *cookie* is a small piece of code that's downloaded to your computer. This code contains information about you and your browsing or purchasing habits. Sites such as Amazon.com might download a cookie, for example, so that they can greet you by name and recommend books or music you might like, based on which items you've looked at or purchased. Browsers offer the option of choosing whether to block the download of cookies or to specify sites you trust and want to allow to download cookies.

➡ **Information that *isn't essential* but that you're comfortable sharing:** A company may ask how you heard about its site, or it may ask you to rate products so they can make other recommendations, for example. This exchange of information is relatively harmless, unless the sells your preferences to others to *spam* you (send you unsolicited offers). Still, providing these pieces of information shouldn't be mandatory, as they aren't required to complete a transaction or interaction, in most cases.

➡ **Information that you *aren't comfortable* sharing:** For example, if you're buying a book and the store asks for your gender and income bracket, that's highly personal information that isn't required to complete the transaction. If this information is optional, don't provide it. If it isn't optional, you shouldn't do business with that site. Period.

Web sites require personal information for financial transactions

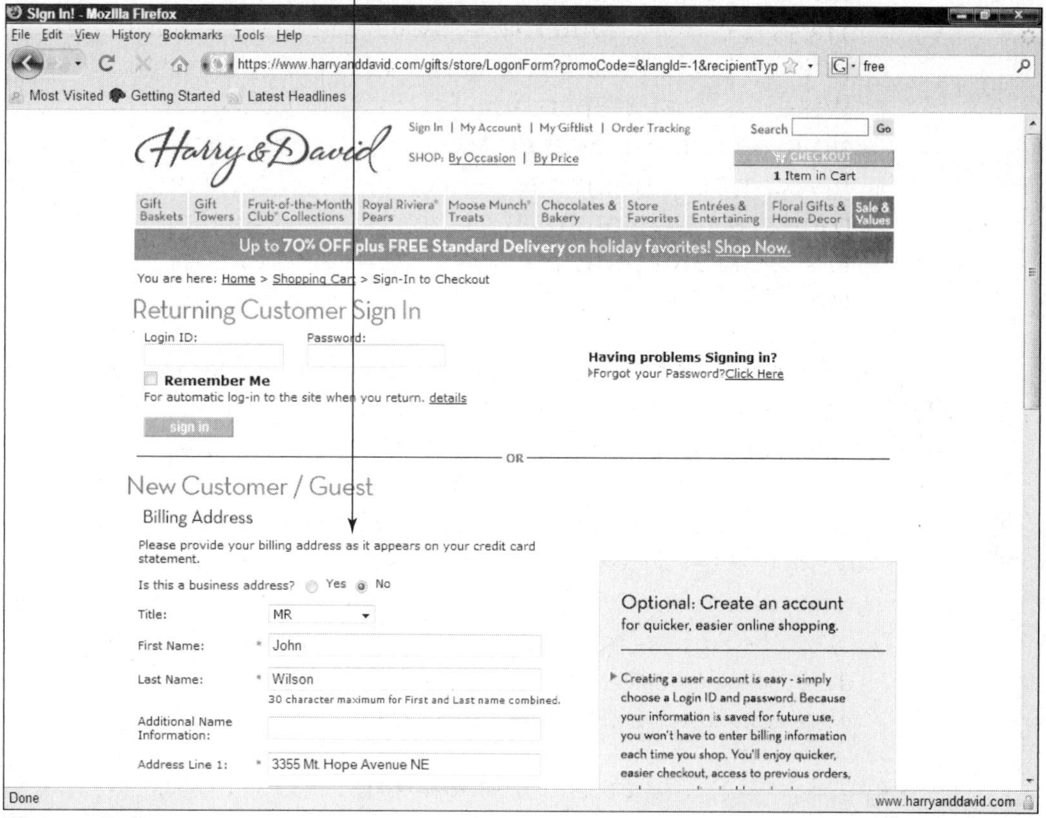

Figure 2-3

How Web Sites Use Demographics

Web sites typically need information — for a variety of reasons —
about the people who visit. They have the ability to do the following:

➡ Capture a set of information that they may use for
better matching your interests or for marketing/infor-
mation reselling purposes.

➡ Monitor how long you stayed on their site and which
articles/pages you visited while there.

➡ Track which Web site you were on before coming to
their site and which site you go to after you leave
their site. (See **Figure 2-4**.)

Web sites can track your online activity

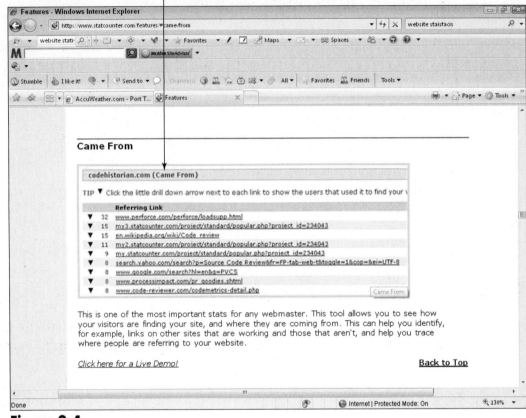

Figure 2-4

Although Web sites learn this information, they may or may not use it in any way other than to improve their services. They may also sell information about their general audience demographics to advertisers, who want this information to better target ads. In general, this isn't particularly invasive, but some cases may warrant particular attention. For example:

➠ If the Web site you just visited was a medical site containing information about an illness you have, the next Web site you visit knows you were looking at that information.

➡ If you were just on your bank's Web site, the site you
go to next knows where you bank.

If the site you go to is one you trust, this really represents no issue. If,
however, you go to a questionable site, this level of information collection may make you somewhat less comfortable. At this point, it begins
to be important that

➡ You go to only reputable sites that respect your privacy.

➡ If you log in to your bank or insurance company's
site, for instance, close your browser after you log out
of that site so that your browsing history from that
session is no longer available.

How Search Engines Use Your Information

In theory, personal information is stripped out of anything search
engines share with other companies, but in reality, this isn't always
the case.

Search engines collect information about what you search for because
they want to

➡ Improve the quality of their search results.

➡ Target advertising to you.

➡ Resell that information to other companies.

Use a search engine you trust; the major services such as Yahoo!,
Google, Ask (shown in **Figure 2-5**), and AOL are generally safe. Note
whether you get increased spam or pop-ups after using a search engine.
If it's related to what you were searching for, find another search
engine.

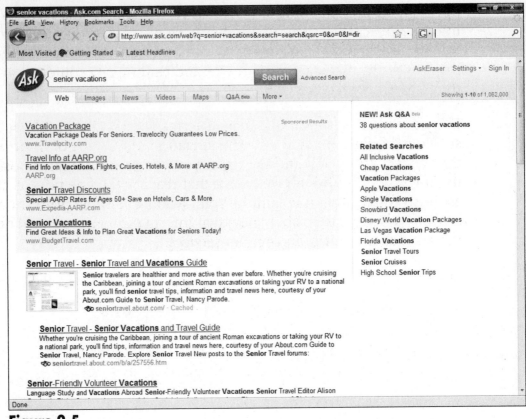

Figure 2-5

 Your searches tell a great deal about you, and search engines have come under heavy pressure — particularly in Europe — to limit the length of time they store information about all the search queries you've made. This pressure on search engines is a result of a demand for increasing your privacy and reducing the invasiveness of the information stored — and sold — about you.

Understand Terms and Conditions

Remember that an important aspect of making choices about sharing information is your trust in the company you're interacting with. Its terms and conditions can help you decide how much you trust it. For example, you're probably far more comfortable sharing your financial information on a banking site because its terms state that it holds the information in the strictest confidence. However, you may be uncomfortable with posting information or images on a social networking site that has terms that state that it owns and can use any content you place there in any way it likes.

Every service you use should state its terms and conditions of use. The statement should include a clear itemization of the type of information they collect about you and the rights you grant them if you choose to use the service. Although we realize that reading the fine print is about as much fun as watching laundry spin, reading this fine print for any site where you want to share personal information is important because there are significant differences in services.

Look at these two examples:

➡ Read the terms and conditions that the social networking site Bebo (`www.bebo.com`) uses for content ownership. (See **Figure 2-6**.) It clearly states that it has no ownership rights to your material, may not sell your material, and that you retain full control of your material.

➡ Now look at the terms that another social networking site, Facebook (`www.facebook.com`), imposes. (See **Figure 2-7**.) It claims full rights to your material, to sell, reuse, and distribute it. It also claims this right even if you remove your content because the site can retain and use archived copies.

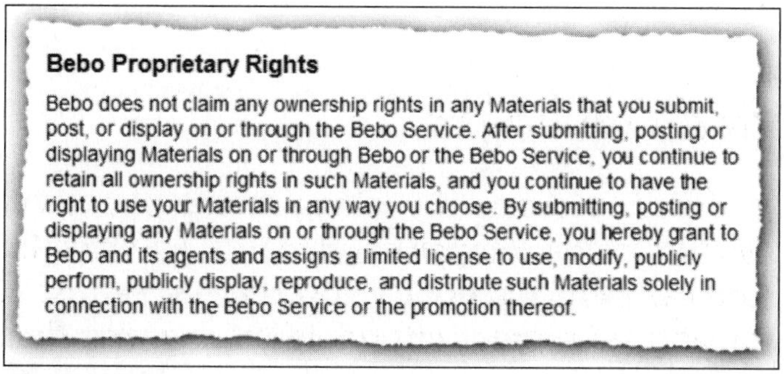

Bebo Proprietary Rights

Bebo does not claim any ownership rights in any Materials that you submit, post, or display on or through the Bebo Service. After submitting, posting or displaying Materials on or through Bebo or the Bebo Service, you continue to retain all ownership rights in such Materials, and you continue to have the right to use your Materials in any way you choose. By submitting, posting or displaying any Materials on or through the Bebo Service, you hereby grant to Bebo and its agents and assigns a limited license to use, modify, publicly perform, publicly display, reproduce, and distribute such Materials solely in connection with the Bebo Service or the promotion thereof.

Figure 2-6

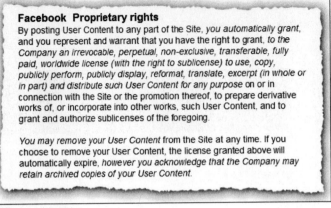

Facebook Proprietary rights
By posting User Content to any part of the Site, *you automatically grant,* and you represent and warrant that you have the right to grant, *to the Company an irrevocable, perpetual, non-exclusive, transferable, fully paid, worldwide license (with the right to sublicense) to use, copy, publicly perform, publicly display, reformat, translate, excerpt (in whole or in part) and distribute such User Content for any purpose* on or in connection with the Site or the promotion thereof, to prepare derivative works of, or incorporate into other works, such User Content, and to grant and authorize sublicenses of the foregoing.

You may remove your User Content from the Site at any time. If you choose to remove your User Content, the license granted above will automatically expire, *however you acknowledge that the Company may retain archived copies of your User Content.*

Figure 2-7

Quizzes and Surveys

Take a look at quizzes and surveys to understand how their creators use your information.

→ Quizzes are created for revenue. Ask yourself who profits from you answering the questions and who else gets to see your answers. We have yet to see a quiz that provides you with a clear set of terms and conditions informing you of the rights the company has to use your answers, and how they intend to use that information.

→ Seniors who use social networking sites that cater to silver surfers are often targeted with quizzes and surveys (see **Figure 2-8**) that often have very invasive questions about their health, wealth, and personal lives.

→ Any information posted in these quizzes is highly likely to be sold and used by many companies.

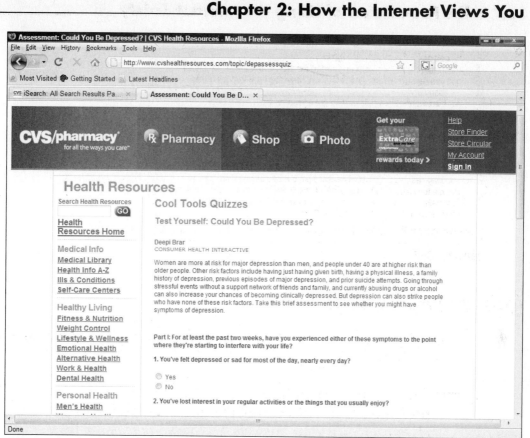

Figure 2-8

➡ If the quiz has no questions of a personal nature, how and where the quiz provider shares that information may not matter to you. But answer a health quiz and you may find that your insurance claims, even your ability to get insurance, are affected.

➡ Consider who else you may put at risk through your answers. If you answer a medical survey that asks for information about illnesses that run in your family, might this information be used to decline coverage or increase premiums for grandchildren?

➡ Quizzes can also generate targeted spam offers based on your answers. If you answer a diabetes quiz that asks about your least attractive feature, and you answer *your skin*, what do you want to bet that skin lotion and anti-wrinkle cream spam mail begins to appear in your inbox?

 You must be especially careful about spam regarding medications and miracle cures. Never buy medical supplies or medications from online drug stores that you don't already have a personal relationship with in the brick-and-mortar world.

Protect Yourself

Now that you understand the value of your information to others, you can keep yourself relatively safe by following this advice:

➡ **Interact with only sites you trust.** These might be sites that people you know recommend or businesses you trust offline. You can also use a feature in your Internet browser or a security product, such as McAfee Site Advisor (read more about these in Chapter 4), to identify and avoid sites that are known to download *malware* (malicious software) onto your computer.

➡ **Don't expose private information to the general public.** If you're sharing personal information such as your name, location, or daily schedule, keep settings in social networking and other accounts private. (See **Figure 2-9.**) If you're writing for the broader public, take care to avoid exposing private information at all.

➠ Don't click links in ads or e-mails, enter contests, fill out surveys, open attachments to e-mails that are suspicious, or respond to e-mail scams. See Chapter 5 for more about e-mailing safely.

➠ Be aware of private information about you that others — including friends, organizations that you volunteer or work with, and the government — may post online.

Keep your information private when possible

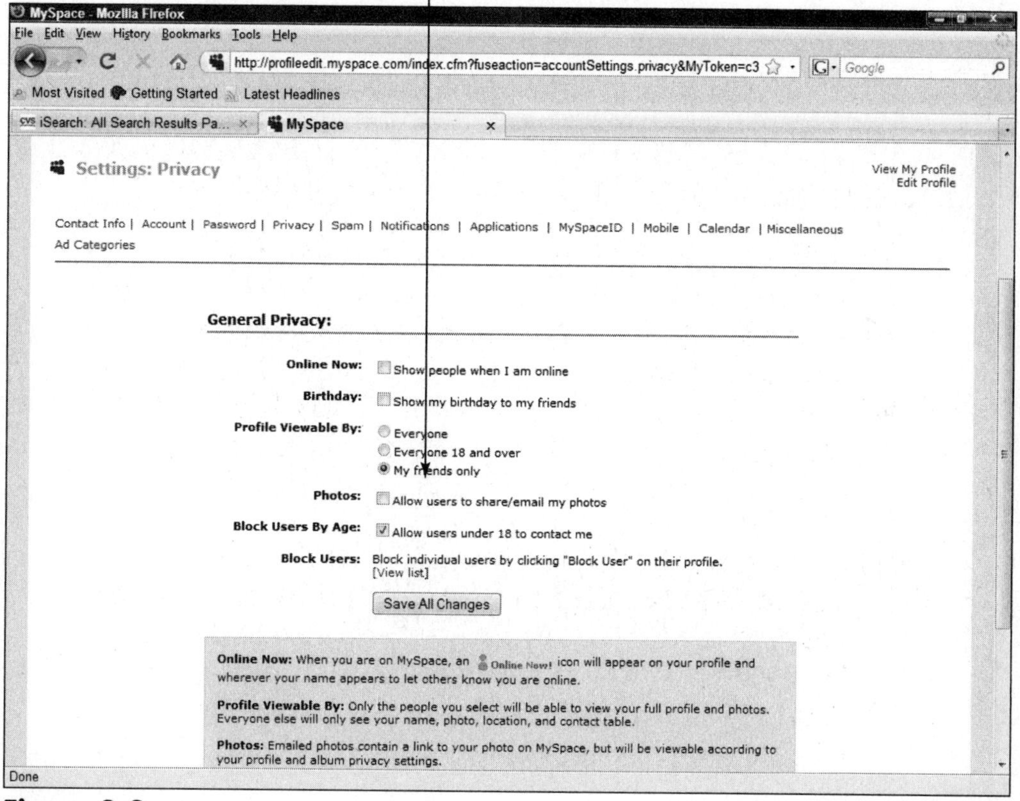

Figure 2-9

Raise Your Safety Bar Today

We don't want you to have to read through this whole book before you begin using online safety practices. You can take some simple steps today that will help you avoid online risks, and then you can build on that knowledge and acquire a deeper understanding of online risk as you go through the rest of the chapters in this book.

People fail to account for many risks not because they're dumb but because rules continue to change. Forty years ago, nobody locked their mailbox or shredded their mail because we didn't have to. Today, people routinely take such precautions.

The need to stay safe online is likewise a newer phenomenon, and you can start today to adapt your behavior to improve the safety of you and your loved ones.

Avoid Online Chain Letters

An online chain letter may be amusing, or it may carry hidden risks. Many chain letters urge you to take some action online that makes you the target of a scam, and forwarding the messages to your friends puts them at risk as well. By forwarding chain e-mail, you may help spammers collect new e-mail addresses to target people and sell a variety of products and services to them. If you do choose to forward an e-mail to a group, do so responsibly.

1. Check a site like Snopes.com or TruthOrFiction.com to see if it is a known scam. If it is, delete it. If it isn't a known scam you still have to be cautious. With the message open in your e-mail program, start by clicking and dragging your mouse over the message text to select it.

2. In your e-mail application, choose Edit⇨Copy to copy the content. (The keystroke shortcut for copying is to press Ctrl+C.) (See **Figure 3-1**.)

3. Open a new e-mail, click in the message field, and choose Edit⇨Paste to paste the message contents into the form. (Ctrl+V)

4. Place your e-mail address in the **To:** field and, if you are sending to more than one person and the people do not already know each other's e-mail addresses, place recipients' e-mail addresses in the **Bcc:** field.

Bcc means blind carbon copy. The message is sent to any e-mail addresses you put in that field, but none of the e-mail's recipients see each other's e-mail addresses. Some e-mail programs display the field on messages, in others you have to click a button or link labeled something like Show Cc and Bcc or Add Cc and Bcc.

5. Enter a subject and click **Send.**

 To check out the latest scams, visit www.snopes.com and click the Fraud and Scams link. You can use the search feature on this site to look for scams using the title of the e-mail or keywords found in it such as *bank account* or *Nigeria.*

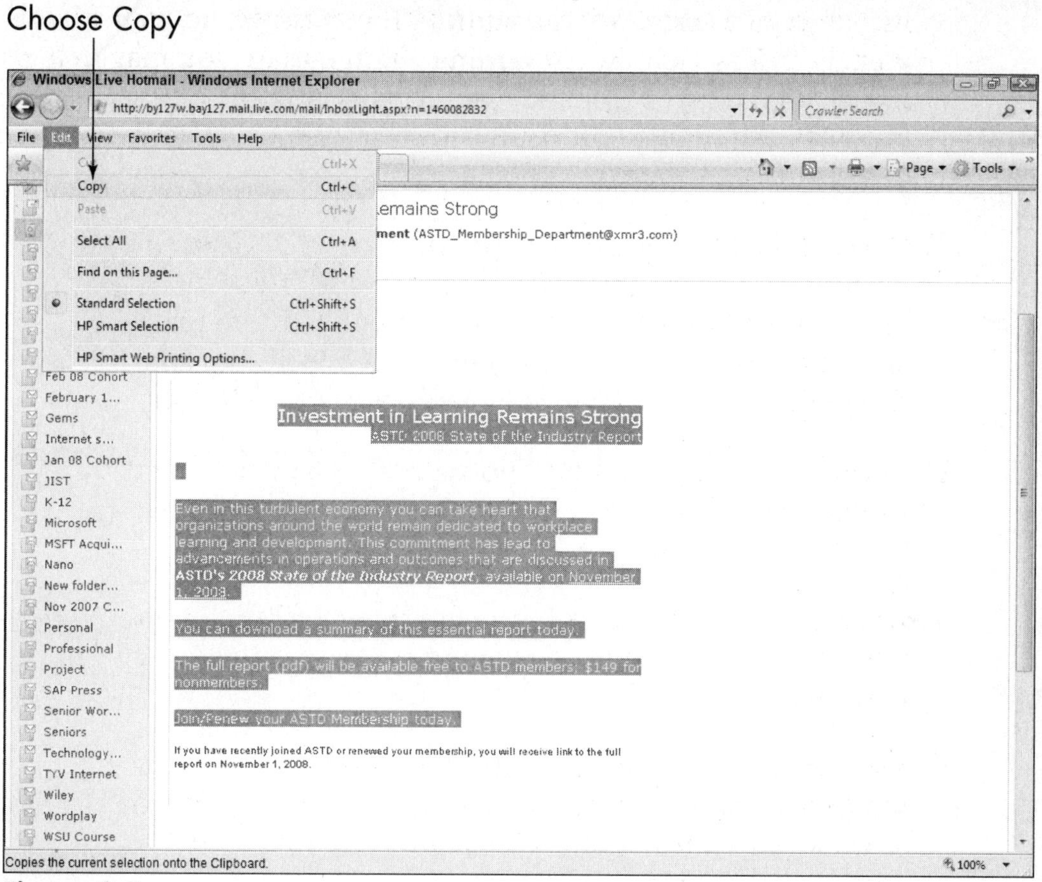

Choose Copy

Figure 3-1

Don't Play Russian Roulette with Links

Never trust a link from someone you don't know. If you click it, it may take you to a phony site that may look like your bank or credit card company, for example, but isn't. One thing a criminal can't fake is the actual Web site address of a company or bank — but they can make it look very close to legitimate. For example, eBey.com or eBay.com.il can look very close to eBay.com. Instead of clicking a link in an e-mail, protect yourself by verifying the link. Here's how you can do that:

1. Enter the company name in a search engine, such as *Google* or *Ask.com.*

2. Click the link for the site in the search results (see **Figure 3-2**) to go there. Be sure that the site you're going to is the correct site, as some criminals create phony sites with similar-sounding names. If your browser or another program provides validation for sites, as with McAfee Site Advisor, check the rating for the site before going to it to be safer.

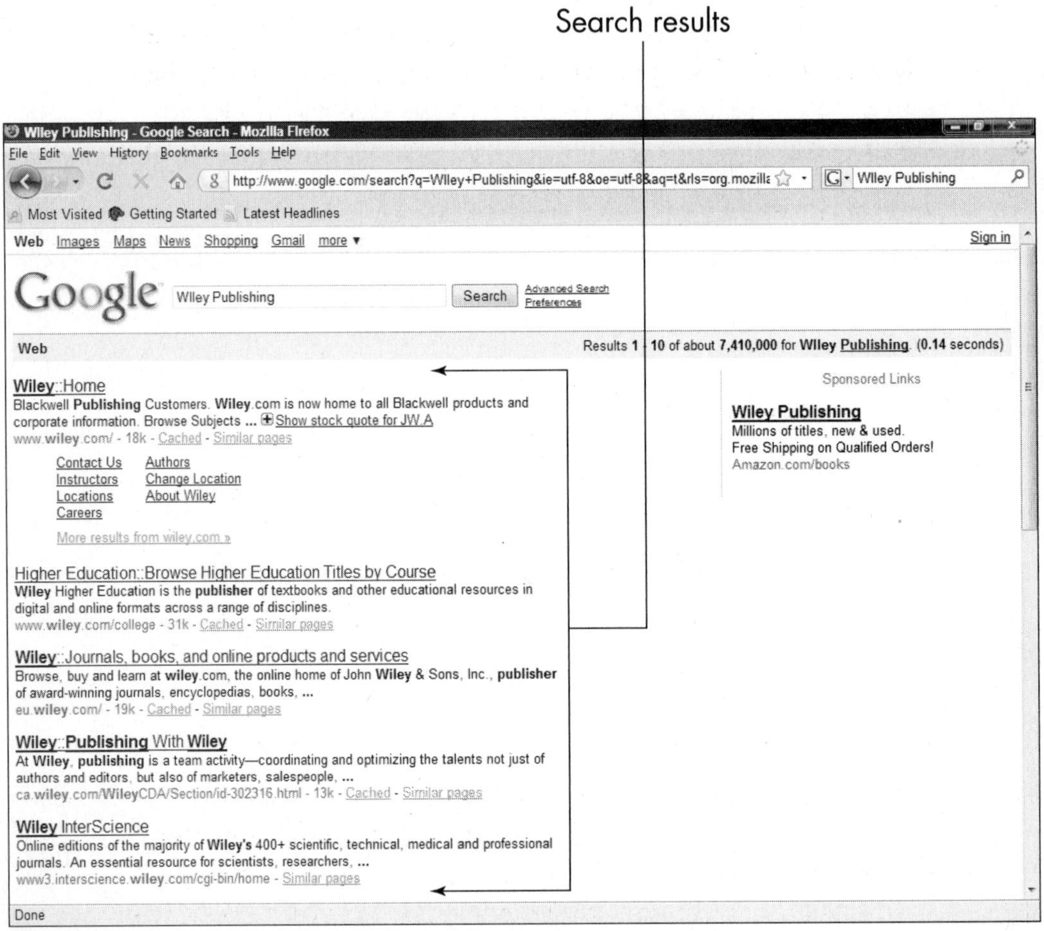

Search results

Figure 3-2

3. Use links on the search results to locate contact information for the company.

4. Either call the customer support number provided, or submit a question via the site support to ask the company about the message you received.

5. If you determine the site is legitimate and think you'll want to return to it, bookmark it. Before you leave the site, save it as a favorite in your browser so that one click brings you there anytime. in Internet Explorer, click the **Add to Favorites** button and choose **Add to Favorites** from the drop-down menu. Discover more about using the Favorites feature in Chapter 4.

6. Enter a name for the site if you don't like the one that's there and click **Add**. (See **Figure** 3-3.)

Figure 3-3

 Scams with risky links aren't only found on your computer; they can be on other Internet-connected devices such as your cell phone. Be careful if you check e-mail from any device that you don't follow a link without thinking or respond to a questionable text message.

Create Safer E-Mail Aliases

Your real name displays by default on e-mails you send from many of the major e-mail services, so whoever you e-mail can see your full name and your e-mail address. Because a last name and an online people directory (like WhitePages.com) may be all it takes to locate your family, look up your phone number, and have a sense of your income bracket based on the location of your home, you may want to avoid having your full name display in your e-mails. The good news is that you can change this setting.

1. In Windows Live (if you don't have a Windows Live Mail account, see the following tip), click the **Options** button on the right side of the screen (next to the Help icon with a question mark on it) and choose More Options; then continue with the steps that follow.

 Other e-mail services have their own procedures for changing the display of your name in sent messages. If your email service displays your name, and you don't find a setting like the one in Windows Live Mail to change, e-mail your provider or search its Help site for the proper procedure. If the provider doesn't allow you to make this change, ask it to do so, or consider changing services.

2. Click the **View and Edit Your Personal Information** link.

3. Click the **Settings** link on the left side of the screen.

4. Click the **Profiles** link under Account Information.

5. Click **Edit Your Account Profile** link (see **Figure 3-4**).

Click the Edit Your Account Profile link

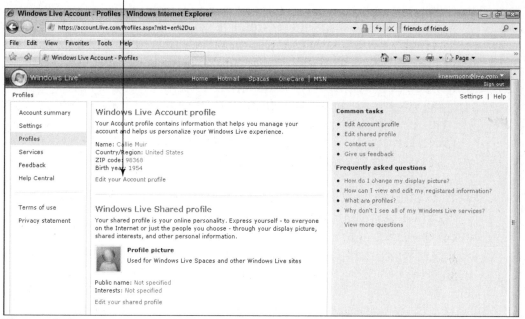

Figure 3-4

6. On the Web page shown in **Figure 3-5**, either delete your first and/or last name or replace them with other information that doesn't identify you personally (such as Knitting Queen). You can use any alphanumeric characters (A–Z; 0–9) and any of the special characters on your keyboard *except for* :, <, >, ;, (,), ", $, and !.

7. Scroll to the bottom of the page and click **Save**.

Now when you send an e-mail, only your e-mail alias shows (or only your e-mail address if you deleted your name and didn't create an alias).

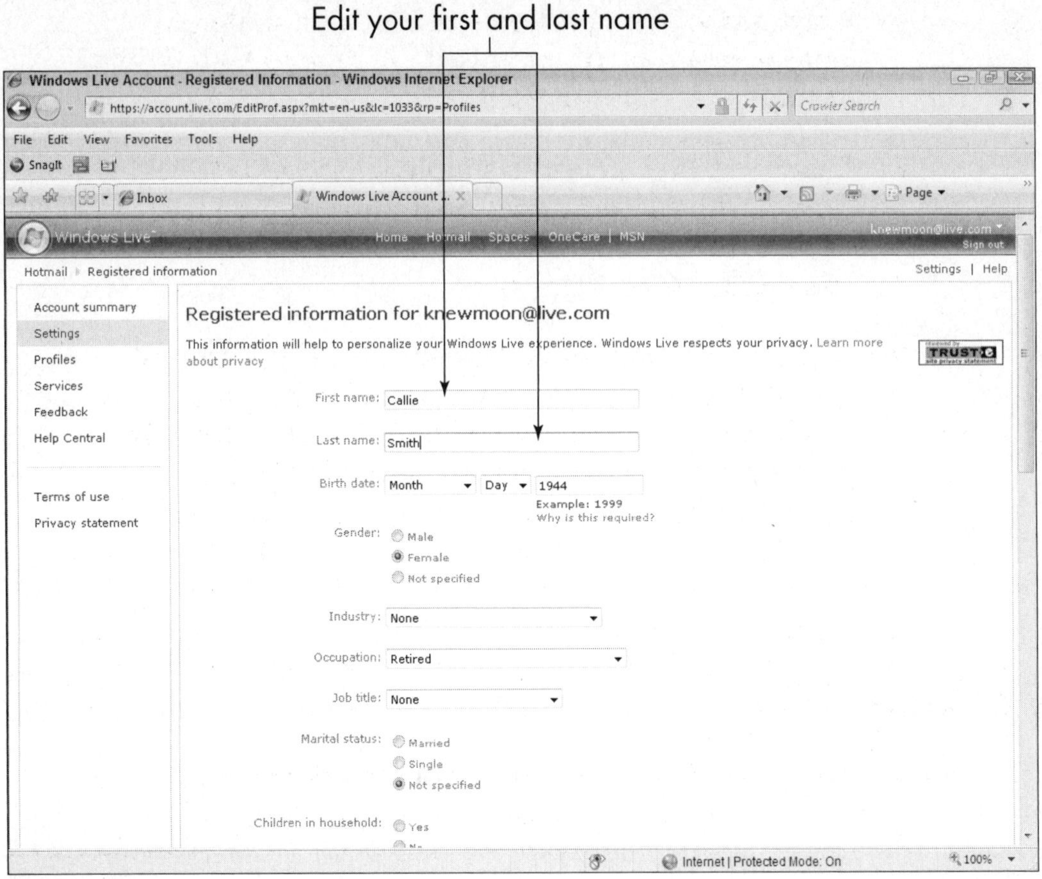

Edit your first and last name

Figure 3-5

Use Passwords Wisely

The prospect of creating a strong password, changing a password, or using multiple passwords makes many people anxious because they believe it requires memorizing multiple complex passwords, such as Wts4e_79PBa13^_qnS. The result is that people find the task so daunting that they continue to use one password. This just isn't safe, particularly if the password is a simple one.

Safe passwords don't have to be hard to create; they just have to be hard to guess. Here are a few ground rules:

➠ Use unique passwords on sensitive sites so that, if one password is compromised, all of your Web information isn't compromised.

➠ Passwords that are short, simple words or include numbers that relate to personal information (such as birth date or address) are easy to guess. Don't use them.

➠ If you made hard-to-remember passwords, you probably did so because your business or a Web site forced you to. In this case, you're likely to have a list of the passwords next to your computer — even though you know this also compromises your safety. It's okay to keep the list, just put it in a safe place that's not near your computer.

Recognize Weak Passwords

Use Table 3-1 to help make sure your passwords aren't weak.

Table 3-1	Weak Passwords
Password	**Weakness**
Password	The word *password* is the most commonly used password, and it's pathetically weak — as are *default* and *blank*. These are simple words and easily guessed or broken with a dictionary assault on the password.
Smith1968	Although this uses nine characters and includes letters and numbers, names that are associated with you or your family, or other identifying information such as birth year, are easily hacked.
F1avoR	Although it mixes upper- and lowercase letters and numbers, it's too short. And substituting the number 1 for the letter l is easy to guess.

It's *easy* and can actually be *fun* to create strong passwords — you just have to know how — and the payoff in increased safety is huge.

Create Strong Passwords

Table 3-2 outlines five principles for creating strong passwords.

Table 3-2	Principles for Strong Passwords
Principle	**How to Do It**
Length	Use at least 10 characters if the site allows it, otherwise make it as long as possible.
Strength	Mix it up with upper- and lowercase letters, characters, and numbers.
Obscure	Use nothing that's associated with you, your family, your company, and so on.
Protect	Don't place paper reminders near your computer. If you are viewing a password-protected Web site, and others are nearby, lock the computer before stepping away.
Change	The more sensitive the information, the more frequently you should change your password.

Look at Table 3-3 for examples of password patterns that are safe but also easy to remember.

Table 3-3	Examples of Strong Passwords
Logic	**Password**
Use a familiar phrase typed with a variation of capitalization and numbers instead of words (text message shorthand).	`L8r_L8rNot2day` = Later, later, not today
	`2BorNot2B_ThatIsThe?` = To be or not to be, that is the question.

Logic	Password
Incorporate shortcut codes or acronyms.	`CSThnknAU2day` = Can't Stop Thinking About You today
	`2Hot2Hndle` = Too hot to handle
Create a password from an easy to remember phrase that describes what you're doing, with key letters replaced by numbers or symbols.	`1mlook1ngatyahoo` = I'm looking at Yahoo (We replaced the Is with 1s.)
	`MyWork@HomeNeverEnds`
Spell a word backwards with at least one letter representing a character or number.	`$lidoffaD` = Daffodils (The $ replaces the s.)
	`y1frettuB` = Butterfly (The 1 replaces the l.)
Use patterns from your keyboard. (See **Figure 3-6.**) Make your keyboard a palette and make any shape you want.	`QWERTY7654321` = This is the 6 letters from left to right in the top row of your key board, plus the numbers from right to left across the top going backwards.
	`1QAZSDRFBHU8` is really just making a W on your keyboard. (Refer to **Figure 3-6.**)

Figure 3-6

Beware of Simple Password Hints

Often, a site gives you a choice of password "hints" when setting up a membership or an account. Don't use security questions with answers that someone can discover with a search engine. If hackers can answer your security question, they can access your password and expose you to theft on the site involved — and any other sites using that password if you didn't make it unique. **Figure 3-7** shows a list of password hints, some of which are safer (name of first pet) and some of which aren't (Mother's birthplace).Follow these guidelines in providing password hints:

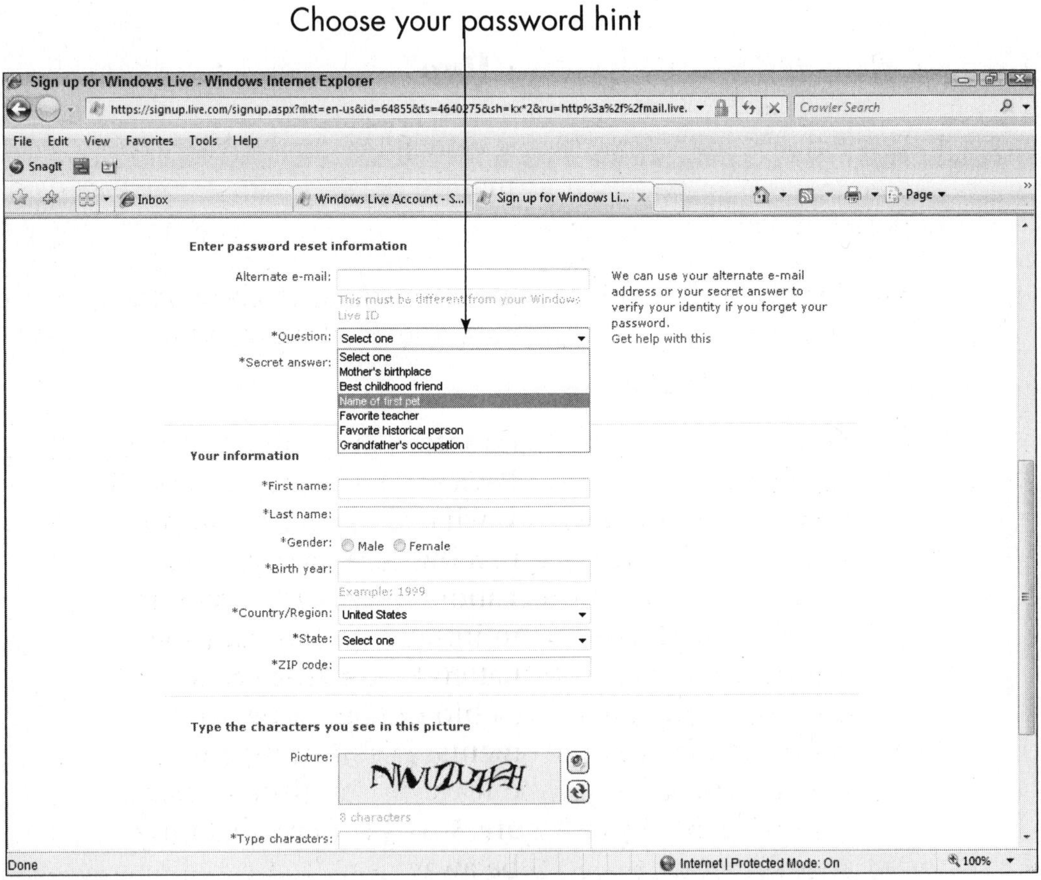

Choose your password hint

Figure 3-7

➡ Never pick a hint with an easily discoverable answer. Your street name, place of birth, mother's maiden name, and even your car model may be easy to find, whereas your favorite author may not.

➡ When all the choices are easily discoverable, ignore the question and use a word that means something to you; for example, sunshine. The site isn't validating this information for accuracy; if you forget your password they just want you to provide *the same answer* that you used to establish the account. Enter whatever you want, but make sure you remember it!

Figure Out Who's Exposing You

Remember that you aren't the only one sharing information. Use a browser to search for information about you and consider these possible sources:

➡ Family and friends may post information about you in blogs, on genealogy sites, and in photo-sharing sites, for example.

➡ Does your employer share information about you on the company Web site? Review what's posted to see if you are comfortable with what is in your employee bio. If you are working in a big company, you may also want to be cautious about how much is visible to other employees on an intranet (a company internal Internet). When you attend a conference, has your company provided a bio of you for use in online conference documents? If your company encourages employees to leave out-of-office messages on their e-mail (see **Figure 3-8**), be aware that these may reveal when you'll be away from home and make you a target for burglary.

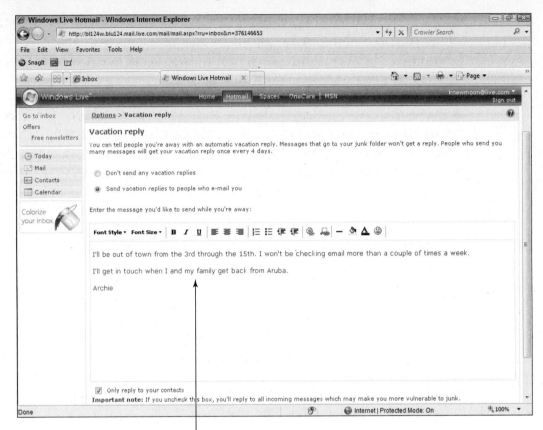

Avoid revealing too much information

Figure 3-8

➠ Many seniors head back to school in later years. Be sure your school does not expose student information on their Web sites if the general public can access those sites. If they post photos and identify students by last name this put you at risk. Posting schedules of after-school activities along with information about which activities a student participates in makes you physically locatable.

Be Careful What You Share Online

Before sharing information online, consider what you are sharing (how sensitive the information is) and who you want to share the information with. If the information is general in nature or restricted to a site that isn't available to the general public, there should be little risk in sharing it. However, if the information identifies you, your possessions, or someone else in some way, you want to limit access to that information.

Here are some categories of information you may want to consider as you determine what you're comfortable sharing — or having others share about you publicly. This list doesn't presume to be a definitive inventory of identifying information, but it can get you thinking about what you share and where you share it.

⟶ **Identifying information:** birth year, birth date, zodiac sign, social security number, city, state, hobbies, emotional state.

⟶ **Addresses:** This includes home and work addresses, as well as any other location you visit regularly, Consider what information goes in birth, wedding, graduation, and death announcements.

⟶ **Phone numbers:** This includes home, mobile phone, work number, and friends' numbers.

⟶ **Personal numbers:** Bank accounts, credit cards, debit cards, PINs, phone calling card, SSN, passport, driver's license number, birth date, wedding date, insurance policy numbers, loan numbers, VIN numbers, license plate, and more.

⟶ **Information rich photos:** A perfectly innocent photo can reveal more than you think. You might put yourself, family members, or friends at risk by posting photos that show where you live or work, for example. Learn more in Chapter 6.

 Don't place information about others online without first obtaining their express permission. And ask your friends and family to do the same for you.

Avoid Risky Default Settings

Many social sites claim in their usage terms the right to use any of the information you provide in any way they choose. See **Figure** 3-9 which shows the terms for Facebook for an example.

By posting User Content to any part of the Site, *you automatically grant*, and you represent and warrant that you have the right to grant, *to the Company an irrevocable, perpetual, non-exclusive, transferable, fully paid, worldwide license (with the right to sublicense) to use, copy, publicly perform, publicly display, reformat, translate, excerpt (in whole or in part) and distribute such User Content for any purpose* on or in connection with the Site or the promotion thereof, to prepare derivative works of, or incorporate into other works, such User Content, and to grant and authorize sublicenses of the foregoing.

You may remove your User Content from the Site at any time. If you choose to remove your User Content, the license granted above will automatically expire, *however you acknowledge that the Company may retain archived copies of your User Content*.

Figure 3-9

If they own your content and profile and decide to reuse or resell your information (for example to sell your personal information to an advertiser or use your granddaughter's picture for advertising), there isn't much you can do about it.

In addition, even if you select the Private setting on a social-networking site or discussion forum, your profile settings are typically public. When you sign up for a service and provide the required information, selecting the private mode, may not prevent your photo, name, URL, city, state, and date you last logged in from showing. Check your public profile after you sign up to see what's exposed. If you're not comfortable with the exposure, remove some information, or close your account. This information can be used to help ID thieves, cyberbullies, scammers who pretend to share your interests and other criminals.

In **Figure 3-10,** a 53-year-old set her social-networking site to private. But on this "private" page, we learn much more than she imagined:

➠ Her first name is Jessica, her last name is Massing. (Look at the URL (Web address), which ends in j_massing.)

➠ We know what she looks like and her ethnic background. How she dresses says a lot about her socio-economic status.

➠ We also know what city and state she lives in. Finding her phone number and address is just a search away. Finding articles about her in her local newspaper or on her company Web site is just a matter of another search.

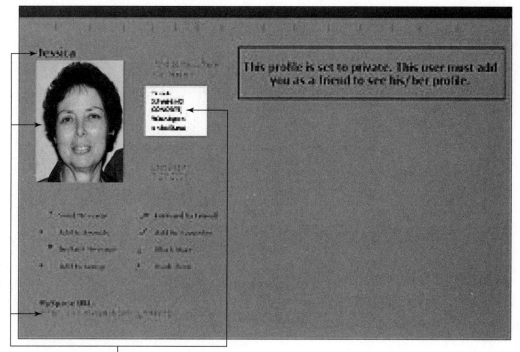

Information revealed on a ì private" site

Figure 3-10

To make this so-called private page truly private, she should do the following:

➥ Change her profile picture to something less identifiable.

➥ Take her city (at least) out of her profile.

➥ Use a nickname instead of her real name.

➥ Make her URL anonymous.

➥ Hide her age.

Spot Bad Sites a Mile Away

You're much safer online if you deal only with sites you trust. Look for a couple of things, including the following, to help you identify trusted Web sites.

➥ **Check before you click.** Use a tool that lets you know before you click a Web site if it is likely to download malware or spam. These tools display a rating to indicate whether they are known to be a safe site or if they are likely to give problems such as downloading malware, putting you on a spam list, or making you a target of fraud. Both Internet Explorer and Firefox browsers offer free tools to help warn users about questionable Web sites Additionally, some security suites like premium versions of McAfee include strong Web site reputation tools. (See **Figure 3-11.**)

➥ **Is the site listed with the BBB? or rated by other Web site rating services?** If it is topic specific, (such as a medical site) does it have association approval?

➠ **Before entering your information on any site, look for the site's privacy policy.** It should answer your questions about how it treats personal information, how it uses your information, whether it gives third parties access to your information, how accurate the information on its Web site is, what level of security it implements, and so on. If you can't easily find the site's privacy policy, *go elsewhere!* (See **Figure 3-12.**)

 See Chapter 12 for more about identifying trusted sites when shopping online and Chapter 14 for advice about using healthcare related sites.

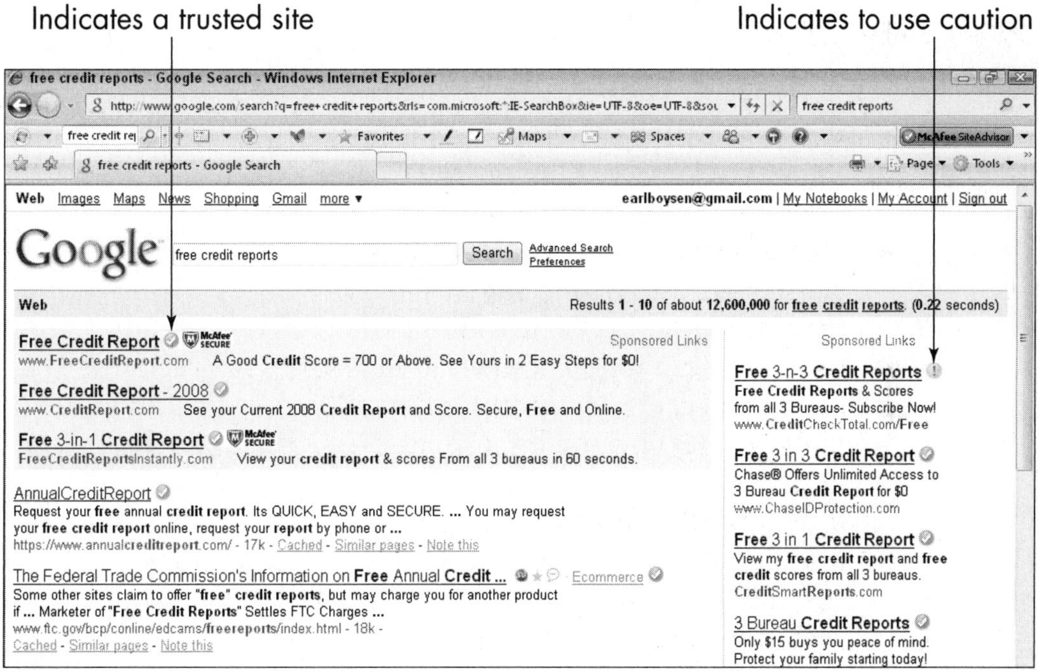

Indicates a trusted site   Indicates to use caution

Figure 3-11

A site's privacy policy

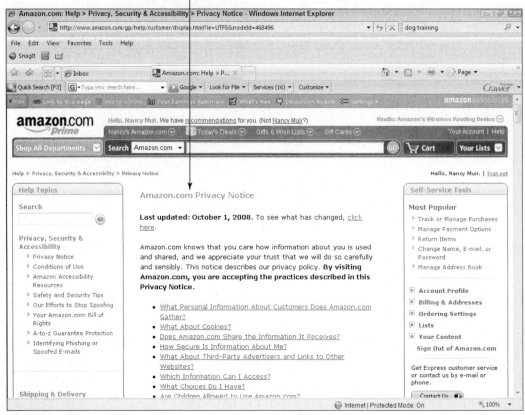

Figure 3-12

Understand the Risks in Contests and Sweepstakes

If you spend any time online, you've seen ads claiming things like "You are already a winner; click here." (See **Figure 3-13**.) Or "Click to enter our sweepstakes and win fabulous prizes." You probably also receive spam informing you that you've "Won the lottery."

These offers have only one purpose — to make money for the sender or advertiser. At best, they make you jump through all kinds of hoops to get the "free" prize. It's much more likely, however, that you will get nothing, but have given a lot – your personal information, preferences, and so on. That information may be resold to reputable, or to less than reputable, companies, organizations, and individuals.

Spam attempting to collect personal information

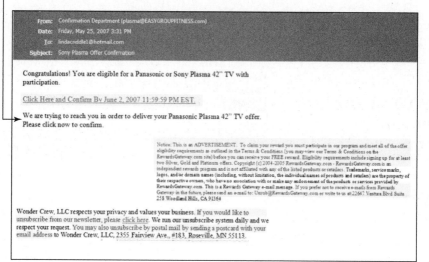

Figure 3-13

Typically, these prize awards require all sorts of information from you for "authorization" and for "transferring the funds to your bank" — which is scammer language for "We're going to steal your identity and empty your bank account." They may also try convincing you to send money to cover "handling costs" that for some reason have to be paid before they can send you what you "won."

Never provide information about yourself or others to any site that you do not know and trust. Look for clear terms and conditions and a privacy policy that protects you. An amazing number of people forget these common sense rules, and provide tons of information to spurious sites that don't even offer a privacy policy. They pay dearly for it. Fortunately, you've been around the block a couple of times and know that you just don't get something for nothing.

Even going to the Web sites these sweepstakes and contests direct you to is taking a risk; the Web sites are highly likely to download malware (malicious software) onto your computer if you don't have anti-virus or anti-spyware software in place. (See Chapter 15 for information on obtaining and using anti-virus and anti-spyware programs.)

This isn't to say that you can't find some legitimate sweepstakes and lotteries — you can. And you can identify these legitimate companies through the Better Business Bureau. (See **Figure** 3-14.) Never trust the claims that unknown companies or entities make about themselves or others. Legitimate sweepstakes, lottery, and prize-giveaway companies don't contact you via unsolicited e-mail nor do they advertise in flashing animation displayed on unrelated Web sites. These indicators are clear red flags.

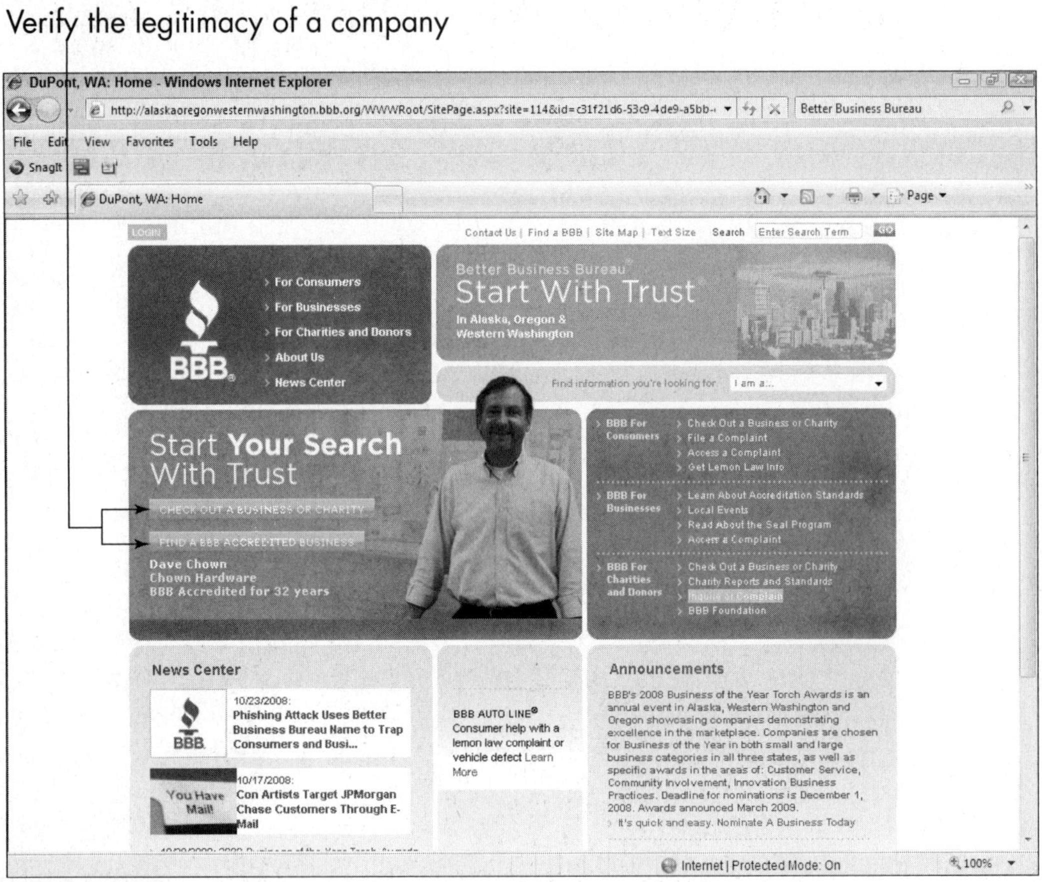

Verify the legitimacy of a company

Figure 3-14

Part II

Using the Internet While Dodging the Risk

The 5th Wave   By Rich Tennant

"Right here…, crimeorg.com. It says the well run small criminal concern should have no more than nine goons, six henchmen, and four stooges. Right now, I think we're goon heavy."

Navigating the Internet Safely

The Internet represents nearly the sum of all information humans have learned and collected. Think of any topic, and you're likely to discover a wealth of information about it — for example, for the search term *World War II buttons* you can get more than 17 million search results. The term *dust mites* returns more than two million results, and *how to yodel* shows 225,000 results. Pretty amazing.

How safe you are while surfing through all this information depends a lot on you. As you click links to various Web sites, check out special offers and ads, play games, and more, it's important that you understand how your choices and actions, the sites you visit, and the links you click protect you or put you at risk for scams, malicious software, or landing on offensive sites.

You can help keep your online browsing experience safe by using browser security settings and learning to identify safer sites. Additionally, you are accountable for your activities online; you need to understand the laws and ethics for use of online information, materials, and communications so that you can avoid committing plagiarism or other crimes, or simply being rude.

Note that we use Internet Explorer version 7 for tasks in this chapter, but other browsers and versions have similar functionality.

Choose the Best Browser for You

To navigate the Internet, you use a software program called a *browser*. There are several browsers available, free of charge. The most popular are Microsoft's Internet Explorer (see **Figure 4-1**), Mozilla's Firefox (see **Figure 4-2**), and Apple's Safari (which can run on both Mac and Windows).

 The browsers mentioned here all have reasonable security features, so your choice probably comes down to your personal preference for the appearance of the browser and ease of use of features. Remember: Offering security settings is only half the battle. You have to apply those settings to make your browsing experience safer. We tell you how to adjust those settings in the "Customize Browser Security Settings" section, later in the chapter.

Browsing the Internet with Internet Explorer

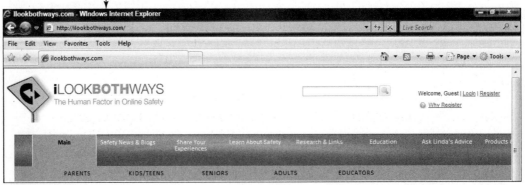

Figure 4-1

Browsing the Internet with Firefox

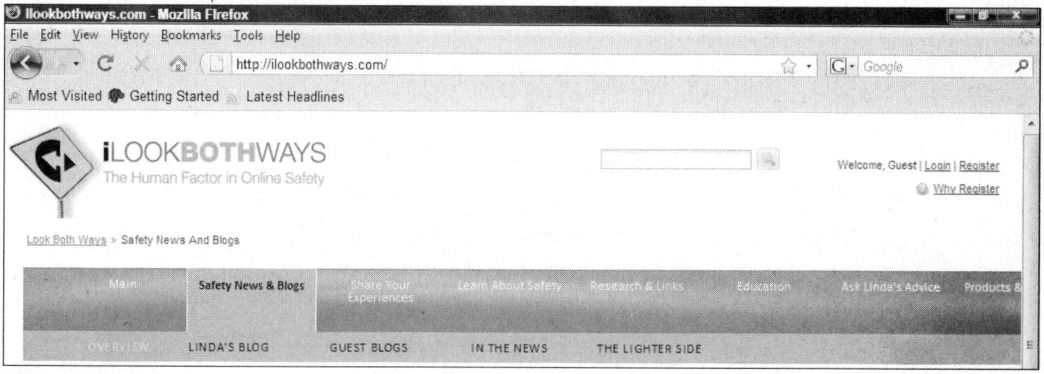

Figure 4-2

Browsers are free, so read reviews and comparisons about the various options and consider trying a few out. Look for the following features as you do:

➡ **Set up:** All browsers are fairly easy to install and set up, but not all make it easy to import your settings or contacts from an old browser to a new one. If this matters, evaluate the options.

➡ **Speed:** Browsers also perform differently in terms of how fast they download and display content and how well they display text and graphics on various Web sites. Does one browser do a better job for you than another?

➡ **Navigation tools:** A browser lets you move from one page on the Web to another, move back a page, go to a page by entering its online address (called a URL), and jump back to your *home page* (the page you want to open by default whenever you start your browser; note that many browsers allow you to set more than one home page to appear on tabs in the browser window).

➡ **Favorites, Bookmarks, and History features:** If there are sites you like to visit often, a Favorites or Bookmarks feature allows you to save those sites in a list and quickly go to them again. The History feature lets you see sites you've visited in recent days or weeks and go there again without having to look up the site names or URLs. Favorites are perfect for those times that you accidentally close a site and can't remember how you got there.

 Storing favorite sites is a really good feature to use for saving the proper URLs for sites that could be used in phishing schemes. For example, save your financial sites as favorites and open them via your favorites list instead of clicking a URL in an e-mail that may lead you to a phony site.

➡ **Security and safety settings:** All browsers let you choose the security level you want, and these settings are critical to a safe online experience. Some browsers offer more security options than others. Security features include tools that let you adjust these types of settings:

- How your browser handles small bits of downloaded code used to let Web sites recognize you whenever you visit (called *cookies*)

- How you're alerted if a Web site you attempt to visit has an out-of-date security certificate or a questionable reputation

- Whether you want your browser to save passwords for certain sites

- Whether you want to block pop-up windows from appearing

➡ **Personalization:** Browsers offer different levels of customization for the browser appearance, such as color schemes, themes that include graphic symbols, style and size of font choices, backgrounds, and so on. Many users never personalize their browsers; others swear by it.

➡ **Tools:** Download managers make downloading files easier. Viewing tools make it easy to zoom in and out or show the browser in full screen (making toolbars disappear and filling your screen with the browser). Tabs allow you to have several sites open at one time and use tabs to move among them. Thumbnails provide visual access to your most visited sites.

Identify Secure and Trusted Web Sites

You're much safer online if you go to only those sites with good reputations. These may be sites of companies you already know and trust, or sites that your browser or a third-party program indicates is trustworthy.

There are several tools to help you identify trusted Web sites:

➡ **Check before you click.** All the major browsers we mention in the preceding section provide a feature that advises you on the trustworthiness of Web sites. Products such as McAfee SiteAdvisor (see **Figure 4-3**) do this as well. These are fabulous tools that let you know, before you click a search result, if the Web site is likely to be dangerous and might download malware or spam. Such tools place a rating next to sites returned in a search to indicate how safe they are to visit. We strongly urge you to use this functionality: It will save you a great deal of grief.

➠ **Look for the site's privacy policy.** Even when a site has been tested to ensure that it won't dump malicious software on your computer, you still need to evaluate if the site is ethical. A site's privacy policy should answer your questions about how it treats and uses personal information and whether third parties will have access to your information, and it should provide assurances about the accuracy of the information on its Web site, its level of security, and so on. If you can't easily find the site's privacy policy, *go elsewhere!*

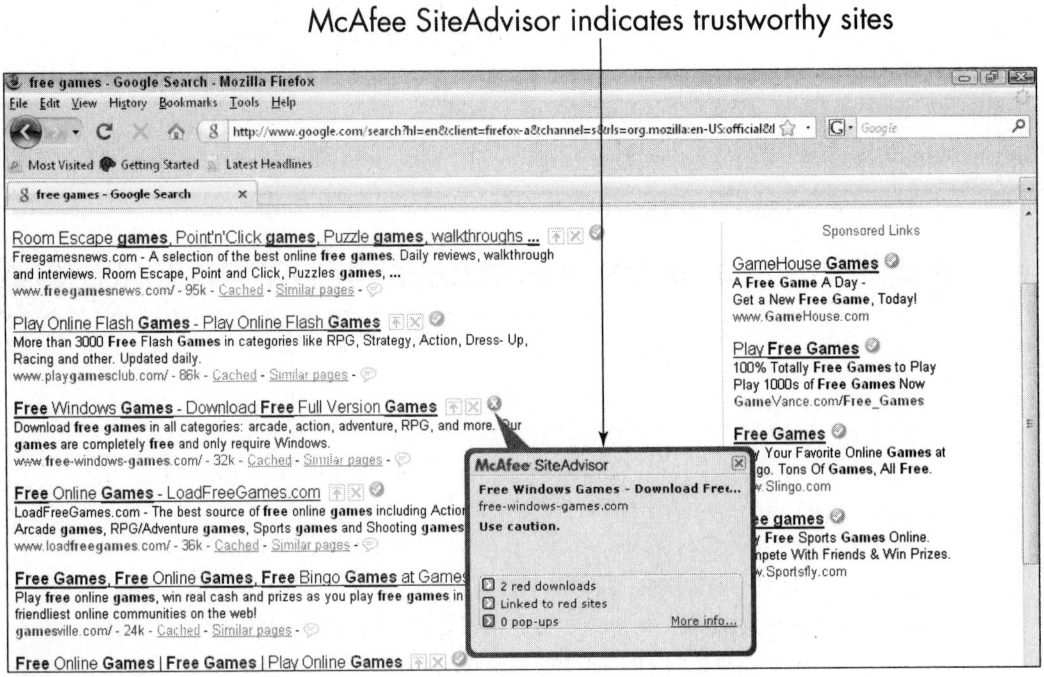

McAfee SiteAdvisor indicates trustworthy sites

Figure 4-3

Explore Browser Navigation

After you've connected to the Internet, you're ready to set foot into the virtual world. The first thing you should know is how to navigate the Web by using a browser. Internet Explorer (also called, simply, IE) from

Microsoft is probably built into your Windows operating system, so it's a good place to start. (Safari comes with Mac operating systems.)

1. Open Internet Explorer by clicking **its icon** on the Quick Launch bar located on the Windows Vista taskbar (it looks like a little blue "e").

2. If you want to adjust text size for better readability, near the top-right side of the browser choose Page⇨Text Size and select a larger size setting. You can also hold down the **Ctrl** key on your keyboard and move the scroll wheel on your mouse up or down to enlarge or shrink text.

3. Enter a Web site address in the Address bar, as shown in **Figure** 4-4, and then press **Enter.** If you don't know any URLs, type **ilookbothways.com** into the address bar to visit our Web site.

Enter a Web address here

Figure 4-4

4. On the resulting Web site, you'll notice different areas of content on the page, including a horizontal navigation bar with text or graphics you can click to visit various pages on the site. The rest of the page includes content in the form of text and graphics. Usually, the browser window doesn't display a whole page. To display the rest of the page, click the arrow on the bottom right side of the window (on the scrollbar), or press the Page Down key on your keyboard.

5. Hover your mouse over any of the text, graphics, photos, and buttons on the page. If the mouse pointer changes from an arrow to a hand with a finger poised to press a button, you know that you can click that element for more information. Click whatever interests you.

6. The **Back** button on your browser takes you back, page by page, through where you've been. If you go back one or more pages, you can use the **Forward** button to navigate toward your most recently viewed page.

7. Click the **down-pointing arrow** at the far right of the Address bar to display a list of sites that you visited recently, as shown in **Figure** 4-5. Click a site in this list to go there.

Click this button to see recently viewed sites

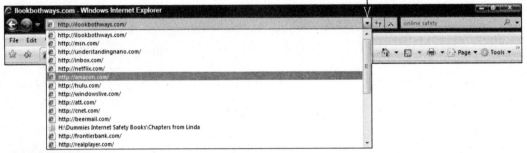

Figure 4-5

 The **Refresh** button (the up and down green arrows to the right of the Address bar) and the Stop button (the red X) are useful for navigating sites. Click **Refresh** to redisplay the current page. This is especially useful if a page updates information frequently, such as on a stock market site, or if a page doesn't load correctly; it might load correctly when refreshed. If you make a mistake entering the address or if the page is taking longer than you'd like to load, click **Stop** to halt the process.

 A pop-up is a small window that might open from time to time as you browse, and pop-ups usually contain annoying advertisements. You can use the Pop-Up Blocker to stop pop-up ads from appearing. Choose Tools⇨Pop-Up Blocker⇨Turn On Pop-Up Blocker to activate this feature. You can also use the Pop-Up

Blocker Settings command on this same menu to specify sites on which you do want to allow pop-ups. For details, see Chapter 15, which explains how you can adjust privacy settings.

 Many people feel anonymous when browsing online, but that isn't entirely correct. The level of information any site learns about you when you browse (even if you don't log in) may be considerably more than you realize. See Chapter 2 for more about how sites gather your personal information and how they use it.

Use Tabs in Browsers

Internet Explorer (IE), Firefox, and Safari, offer a feature called *tabbed browsing*. In addition to opening multiple home pages on tabs, you can open new tabs as you browse the Web. (See **Figure 4-6**.) You can then click tabs to jump to other sites that you've displayed on those tabs without having to navigate backwards or forwards in a single window to sites you've previously visited.

Using tabs when browsing the Internet

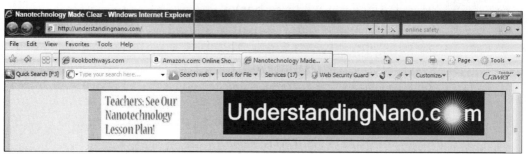

Figure 4-6

Here's how to use tabbed browsing for maximum efficiency in Internet Explorer:

1. Click the **New Tab** button to open a new, blank tab. The new tab now appears above the body of the tab area to the right of any other open tabs.

2. Type an address in the **Address** bar and press **Enter;** the site appears in your newly displayed tab.

3. Click another tab to jump to another site and keep the first site displayed in your browser.

4. Click the **New Tab** button again to add another tab for browsing.

5. Click the **Close** button (the X on the right side of the tab) on any active tab to close it.

 You can open a linked page in a new tab quickly by right-clicking the link and choosing **Open in New Tab**. A new tab opens with the page displayed.

Set Up a Home Page

If you find yourself going to one Web page often (for example, your e-mail page or the local weather), you can create one or more home pages. Whenever you open your browser, home pages display on tabs automatically.

1. To try this, open IE and choose Tools➪Internet Options.

2. In the resulting Internet Options dialog box, click the **General** tab. In the **Home Page** box, type a Web site address to use as your home page, as shown in **Figure 4-7.**

Note: You can enter multiple home pages that appear on different tabs every time you open IE. Just type a Web address, press **Enter**, and type the next Web address on the next line.

Alternatively, click one of the following preset option buttons:

• **Use Current:** Sets whichever page is currently displayed in the browser window as your home page.

- **Use Default:** This setting makes the MSN Web page your home page.

- **Use Blank:** If you're a minimalist, this setting is for you. No Web page displays; you just see a blank area.

3. Click **OK** to save your settings and close the dialog box.

4. Back in Internet Explorer, click the **Home** icon (it looks like a little house) on the top-left side of the browser window to go to your home page.

 To remove a home page that you've set up, click the **arrow** next to the Home icon and choose **Remove**. In the submenu that appears, choose a particular home page or choose **Remove All**.

Enter addresses for Home pages here

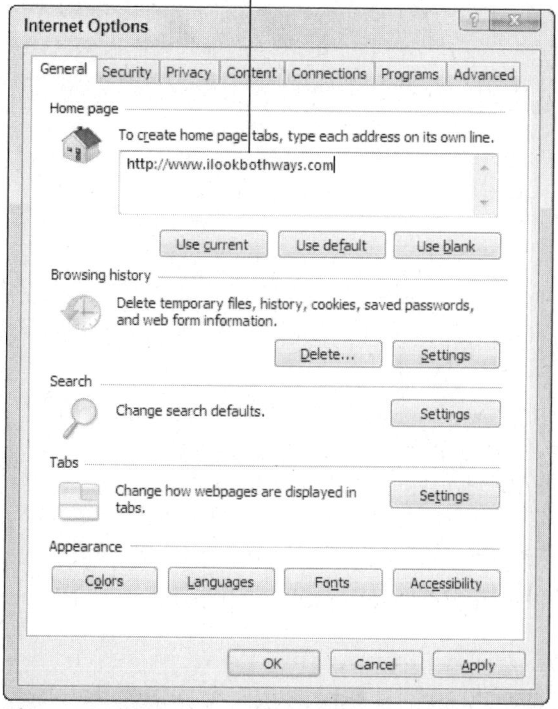

Figure 4-7

Add a Web Site to Favorites

1. Open Internet Explorer, type the address of a Web site that you want to add to your Favorites list, and then press **Enter.** (In the Firefox browser, favorites are called *bookmarks,* but they operate in the same way.)

2. Click the **Add to Favorites** button and then choose **Add to Favorites.**

3. In the resulting Add a Favorite dialog box, as shown in **Figure 4-8,** you can modify the name of the Favorite listing to something easily recognizable, or leave it as is.

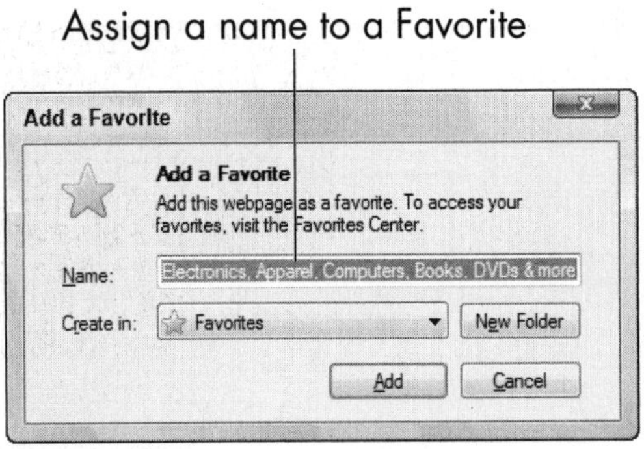

Assign a name to a Favorite

Figure 4-8

When you want to return to a site you've saved as a favorite, click the **Favorites Center** button and then click the site you want to visit in the list that's displayed. (See **Figure 4-9.**)

 Regularly cleaning out your Favorites list is a good idea — after all, do you really need the sites that you used to plan last year's vacation? With the Favorites Center displayed, right-click any item and then choose **Delete** to remove a URL from your favorites listing.

 You can keep the Favorites Center as a side pane in Internet Explorer 7 by displaying it and then clicking the **Pin the Favorites Center** button (the left-facing green arrow located to the right of the History button).

Click the Favorite Center button

Then select a Favorite site

Figure 4-9

Organize Favorites

As you add favorites, they can become jumbled, and it's helpful to tidy them up into folders or otherwise organize them.

1. With Internet Explorer open, click the **Add to Favorites** button and then choose **Organize Favorites**.

2. In the resulting Organize Favorites dialog box (see **Figure 4-10**), click a favorite, and then click the **New Folder** button to create folders to store your favorites in by topic, or the **Move, Rename,** or **Delete** button to manage your favorites.

3. When you finish organizing your Favorites, click **Close.**

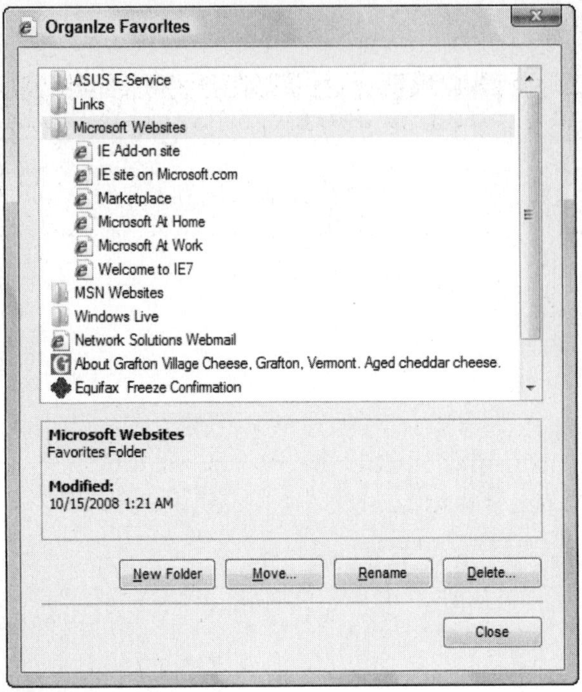

Figure 4-10

View Your Browsing History

Sometimes you need to find a site you visited but didn't save as a favorite. To do that, you can review your browsing history.

1. Click the **Favorites Center** button and then click **History** to display the History pane.

2. Click the **down arrow** on the History button (see **Figure 4-11**) and select a sort method:

- **By Date:** Sort favorites by date visited.

- **By Site:** Sort alphabetically by site name.

- **By Most Visited:** Sort with the sites visited most on top and those visited least at the bottom of the list.

- **By Order Visited Today:** Sort by the order in which you visited sites today.

Click this arrow to sort History

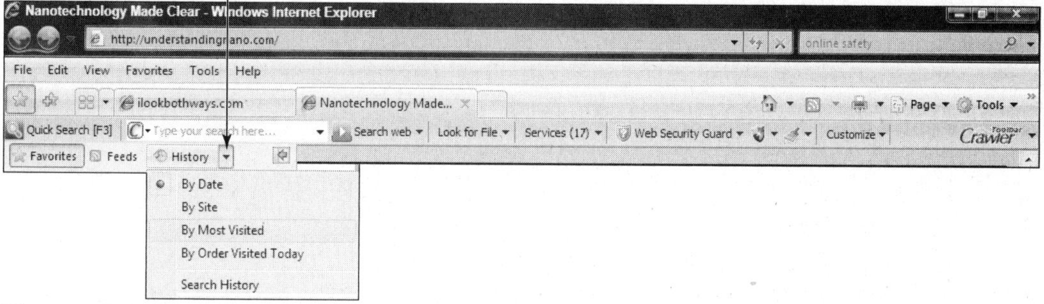

Figure 4-11

3. In the History pane, click the link to the site you want to visit (see **Figure 4-12**). It takes you to the site, and the History pane closes.

The History pane

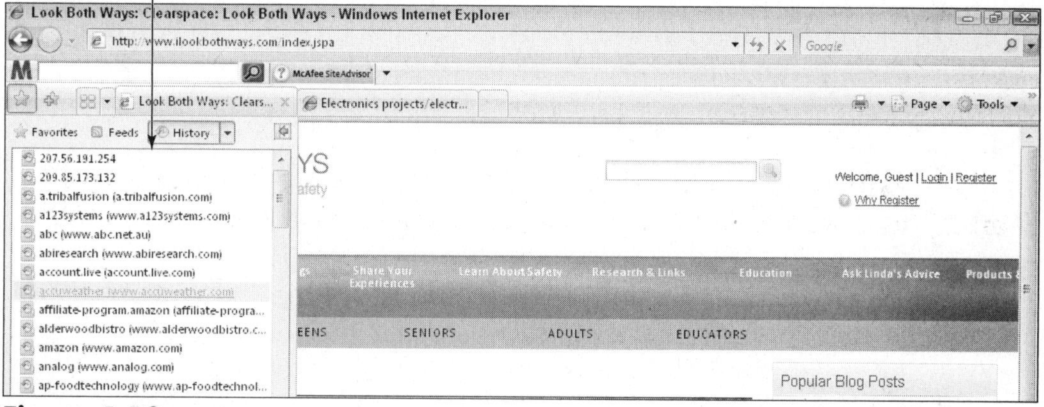

Figure 4-12

 You can also choose the **arrow** located to the right of the Address bar to display sites you've visited most recently.

 You can search your Favorites as well. With the Favorites Center open, click the **arrow** on the History button and choose **Search History** to display a search box you can use to search for sites you've visited.

You can empty your History file so that no one can see the sites you've visited. (Kids do this a lot to hide searches from their parents or grandparents, but their monitoring software will flag this.) Perhaps you don't want your spouse or partner to know that you've been researching presents for an upcoming birthday, or maybe you're using a public computer and don't want to leave a trail. Whatever your motivation, to erase your history, choose Tools⇨Internet Options. On the General tab of the Internet Options dialog box, click the Delete button under Browsing History.

Search the Internet

Simple-to-use programs called *search engines* make it easy to find information on the Internet — probably more information than you ever wanted!

1. To use Internet Explorer's search feature, open IE and click in the **Search** text box in the top-right corner on the toolbar. The default search engine is Windows Live Search.

2. Type a search term in the text box and then click **Search** (the little magnifying glass shaped button to the right of the search field). A *search term* is simply a word or phrase that relates to the results you seek. For example, if you want information about arthritis, enter the word *arthritis* or the phrase *joint pain.* Keep these guidelines in mind:

- Be as specific as possible. For example, to look for information on train travel in Canada, don't just enter *Canada*; instead, enter something like *train trips, Canada.*

- You can separate several terms with commas, such as *dogs, retrievers* to search for results with either or both words. (This depends on the search engine; Google looks for only those results with both words; some others won't.)

- You can use a plus sign to require that all terms are included in the results (such as *dogs+retrievers* so that the results include both *dogs* and *retrievers*).

- You can use phrases such as *the Civil War*. However, many search engines disregard words like *the* and *of*. Also, capitalization usually makes no difference, as search engines typically aren't case sensitive.

- The order of the terms can be important. If you want to search for a job, for example, but only freelance jobs, consider entering *freelance jobs* rather than *jobs, freelance* to put the emphasis on the type of job you want.

3. In the resulting list of links (see **Figure 4-13**), click a link to go that Web page.

 Note that browsers often return sponsored links at the top or right side of the search results page. These are sites that pay to have their information included. You can click them, but remember that they're paid advertisers, and there's a greater risk of downloading dangerous software to your computer if you click a sponsored link.

4. If you don't see the link that you need, click and drag the scrollbar on the right side of your browser to view more results.

 Before searching, find out about the data retention (what information of yours they can keep) and data resell (what information they resell) policies of the search engine you're using. If the policies don't match your comfort level for safety and privacy, consider a different search service.

The search result links

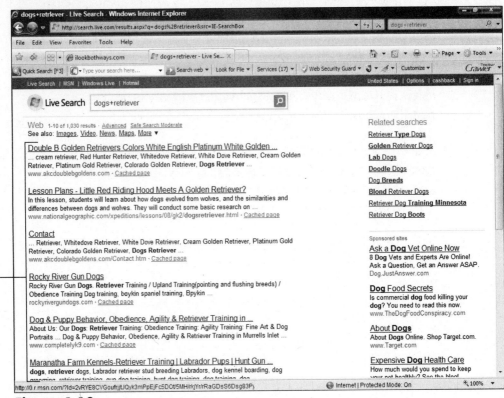

Figure 4-13

Search Within a Web Page

In addition to locating information anywhere on the World Wide Web, after you display a Web page you can search within it for particular words or phrases. This saves you having to scroll through the page and read every word to find what you need.

1. With IE open and the Web page that you want to search displayed, click the **arrow** next to the **Search** text box in the top-right corner and choose **Find on This Page**.

2. In the resulting Find dialog box, as shown in **Figure 4-14**, type the word that you want to search for in the **Find** text box. Use the following options to narrow your results:

- **Match Whole Word Only:** Select this option if you want to find only the whole word. (For example, use this option if you enter *elect* and want to find only *elect* and not *electron* or *electronics*.)

- **Match Case:** Select this option if you want to match the case. (For example, use this option if you enter *Catholic* and want to find only the always-capitalized religion and not the adjective *catholic*.)

3. Click the **Next** button. The first instance of the word is highlighted on the page. (See **Figure 4-15.**) If you want to find the next instance, click the **Next** button again. Click the **Previous** button to move back to the last match.

4. When you're done searching, click the **Close** button in the Find dialog box.

 Many Web sites, such as www.amazon.com, have Search This Site features that allow you to search not only the displayed Web page but all Web pages on a Web site. Look for a Search This Site text box, and make sure that it searches the site — and not the entire Internet.

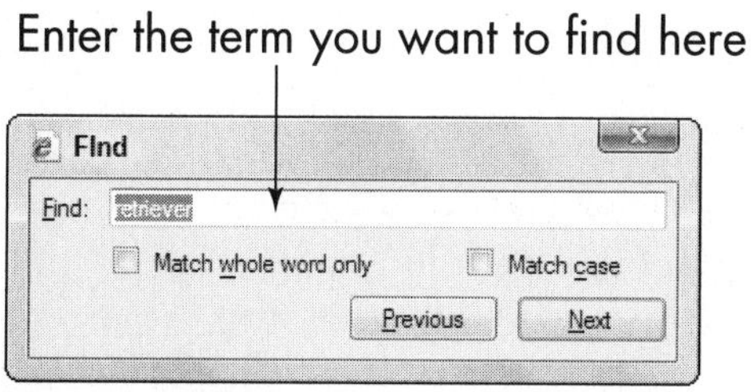

Enter the term you want to find here

Find

Find: retriever

Match whole word only   Match case

Previous   Next

Figure 4-14

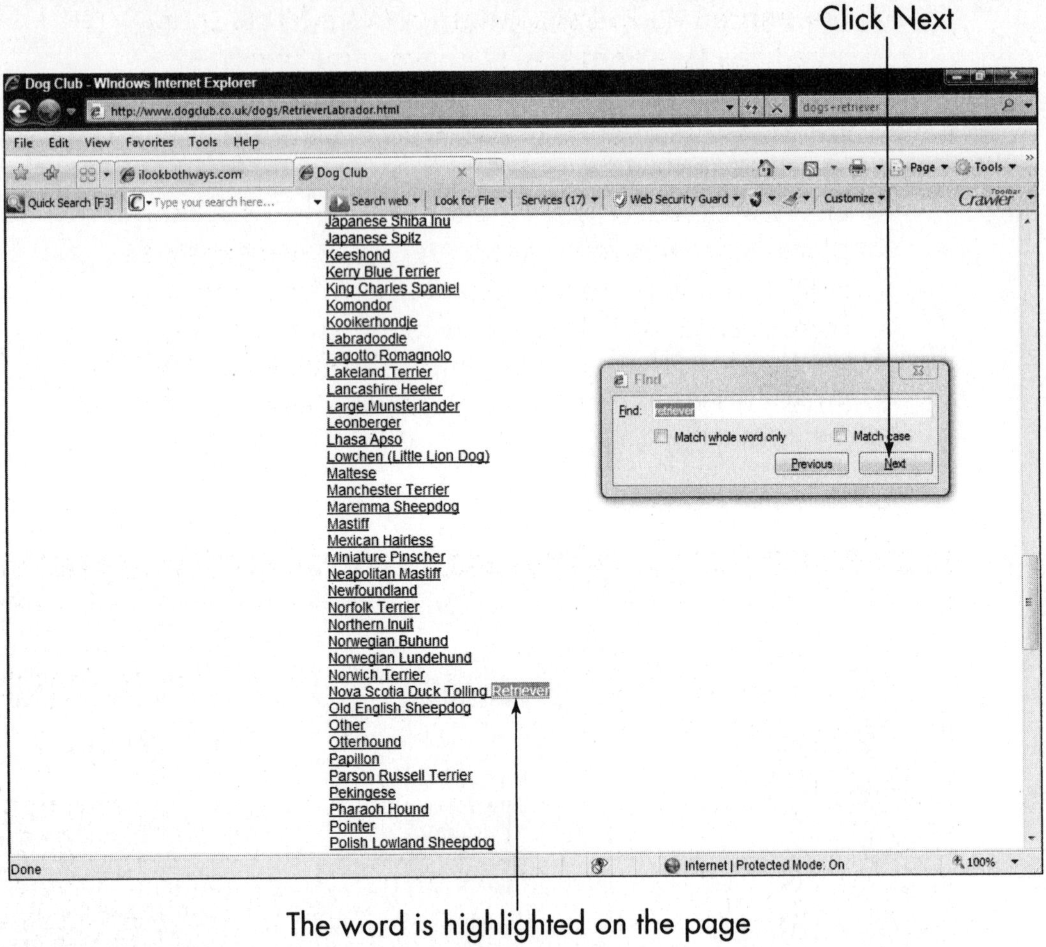

Click Next

The word is highlighted on the page

Figure 4-15

Use Caution with Internet Ads

There are several ways in which advertising on search engines or Web sites can place you at risk.

➡ **Banner ads:** Some sites still offer blatantly disreputable banner advertising. (See **Figure 4-16.**) Clicking these may put you at risk by downloading spyware, adware, or other malware, or asking for private information that will be resold to spammers, telemarketers, snail-mail marketers, and the like.

➡ **Sponsored ad links:** Most users believe that sponsored ads (see **Figure 4-17**) have somehow been vouchsafed for by the hosting company — whether by a search engine company or a Web site owner. This is incorrect. Sponsored ads are really paid placement ads. The company pays the search engine to get top placement. According to McAfee, clicking sponsored advertising is more likely to deliver malware to your computer than clicking other links. Always check a site's safety ranking from a product such as McAfee SiteAdvisor before clicking any search result.

Be cautious of banner add offers

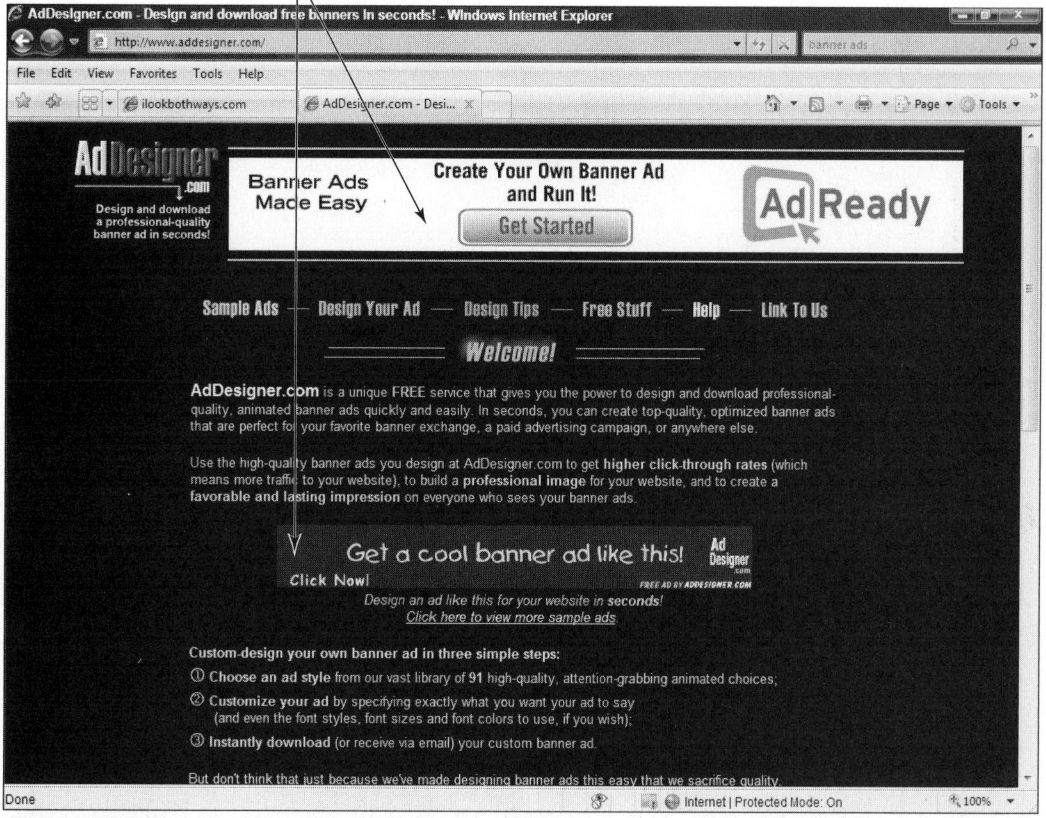

Figure 4-16

➡ **Search terms:** Choosing certain search words or phrases can also place you at risk. For searches that included the word *free,* 14 percent of the results led to disreputable or fraudulent sites, according to a McAfee study. The problems people encounter include hidden fees; misleading billing practices; charges for software that would be free from other sources; changes to your Windows registry settings; the delivery of spyware, adware, and so on; and misuse of your e-mail information to send hundreds of spam e-mails to unsuspecting users who think the e-mail is coming from you.

Sponsored ads can be more dangerous

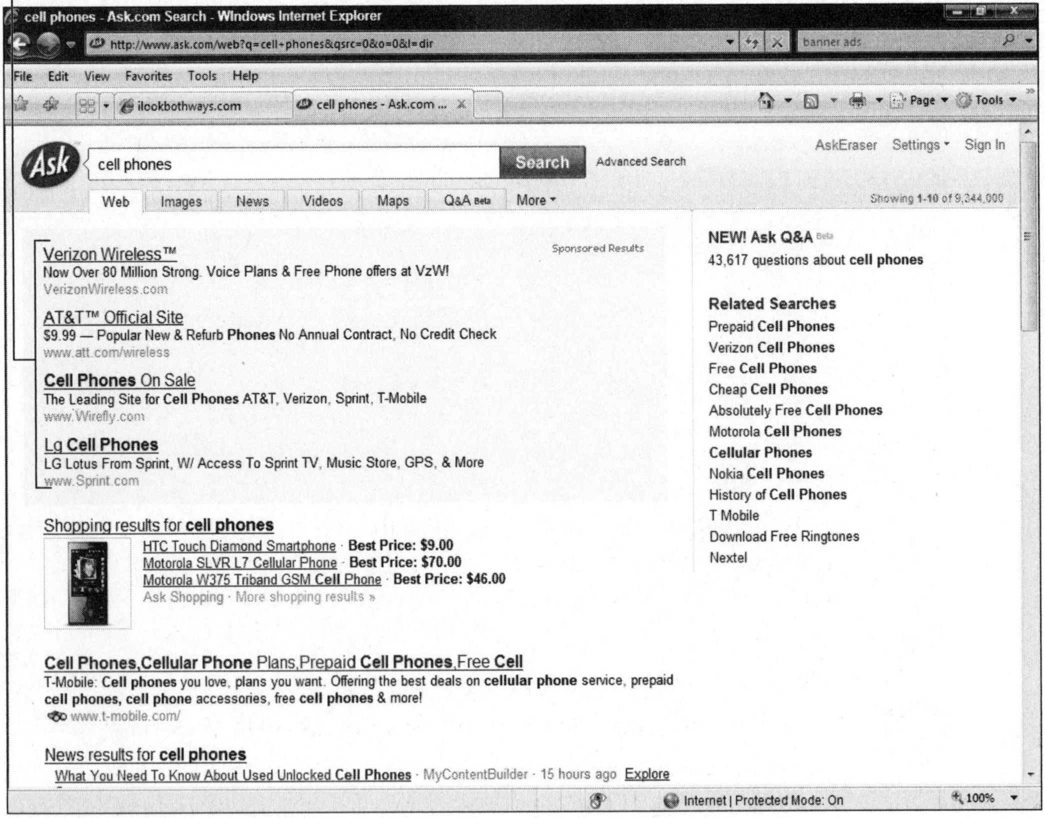

Figure 4-17

Avoid Download Theft and Plagiarism

You know that copying material to claim it as your original work is plagiarism, which is illegal. The problem is that the Internet makes it easy to plagiarize; you don't even have to retype the information; just copy and paste it. A great deal of information online is available for anyone to download and use — although you still can't claim it as your own work. However, a great deal of content is proprietary — you can read it and recommend it to others, but you may not make a copy without obtaining permission from the content owner. Many people who would never dream of breaking the law inadvertently do so by copying or downloading material that has copyright protection in place. Here are some tips to help you understand online copyrights:

➡ Read the site terms of use to see whether content on a Web site is copyrighted. Web site owners may have established rights to the materials or services they offer for download.

➡ File-sharing programs that allow users to illegally download music and videos are commonly used, in spite of some much-publicized arrests. Many people don't seem to realize that downloading a copyrighted video or song that you haven't paid for is the same as stealing from the video or music store in your town. Always check to see if permissions or restrictions apply to any content you intend to download.

➡ Assess the type of site you're viewing. Is it an educational site, government site, commercial site, or a personal site? Government information is free to use, but commercial or personal content isn't.

 Taking someone else's content, whether it's text, photos, or art, is a common problem with content posted on social networking sites. While it may not be illegal to do so, it's certainly unethical to take someone else's material without obtaining their express permission to do so.

Many sites allow visitors to upload files that others (privately or publicly) can then download. On such sites, it's safest to download from only those users you know and trust.

 Community file-sharing programs that allow music and movie downloads are notorious for infecting machines with spyware, viruses, and other forms of malware. Be very cautious if you download programs from these sites!

Download Safely

As you browse the Web, you might find files you want to download, such as music or movie files that you either buy from an online store or obtain from a site that legally offers them free of charge.

1. Open a Web site that offers files you want to download. Typically, Web sites display a Download button or link that initiates a file download.

2. Click the appropriate link to proceed. Windows Vista might display a dialog box asking your permission to proceed with the download; click **Yes.**

3. In the resulting File Download dialog box, as shown in **Figure 4-18**, choose either option:

- **Click Open to download to a temporary folder.** You can run an installation program for software, for example. However, beware: If you run a program directly from the Internet, you might introduce dangerous viruses to your system. You should buy and follow the software manufacturer's instructions to install and set up an antivirus program, such as McAfee or Norton Antivirus, to scan files before downloading them.

- **Click Save to save the file to your hard drive.** In the Save As dialog box, select the folder on your computer or removable storage media (a CD-ROM, for example) where you want to save the file. And remember where you save it. If you're downloading software, you need to locate the downloaded file and click it to run the installation.

 If a particular file will take a long time to download, you might have to babysit it for several minutes. If your computer goes into standby, it might pause the download. Check in periodically to keep things moving along.

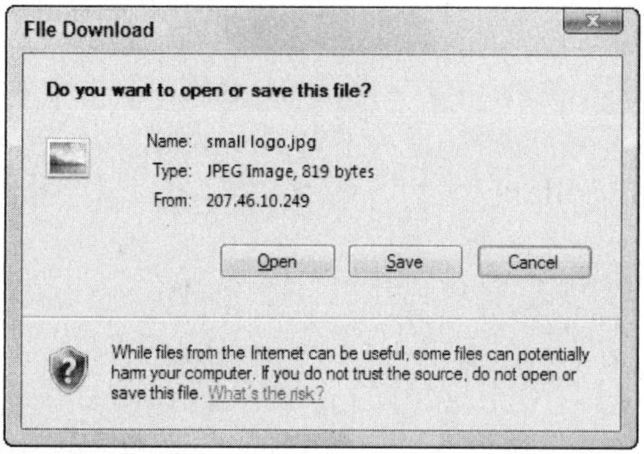

Figure 4-18

Customize Browser Security Settings

1. With IE open, choose Tools⇨Internet Options and click the **Privacy** tab, as shown in **Figure 4-19**.

2. Click the **Settings** slider and drag it up or down to select different levels of security settings. The information to the right of the slider changes depending on your setting.

3. Read the choices and select a setting that suits you.

 The default setting, Medium, is probably a good bet for most people who have a basic sense of how to avoid risks online.

If you set a higher or lower level of security and want to restore the default setting at any point, click the **Default** button on the Privacy tab in the Internet Options dialog box or move the slider back to Medium.

4. Click **OK** to save your new settings.

 Notice that on the Privacy tab, you can also adjust your pop-up blocker settings. Pop-ups can be in the form of annoying advertisements, or they can be pop-up windows that allow you to perform an action on a site, such as calculating estimated payments on a mortgage site. You can use pop-up blocker settings on the Privacy tab to specify which pop-up windows to allow or block. Just click the **Settings** button, enter a Web site name, and then click **Add** to allow pop-ups.

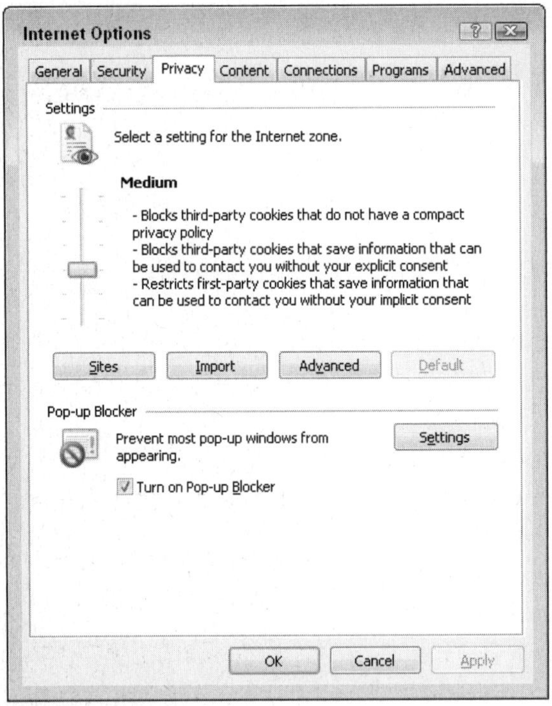

Figure 4-19

Risk-Free E-Mail

To a great extent today e-mail messages have replaced letters, providing an almost instantaneous way to stay in touch, conduct business, and exchange documents.

However, e-mail carries certain risks that you should be aware of. These typically fall into three categories:

➡ An e-mail may contain links or files that, if opened, can place malicious code onto your computer — or cell phone.

➡ *Spam* is generally e-mail advertising for some product that arrives unsolicited from somebody you don't know.

➡ Spam becomes a scam when criminals use the e-mail to commit fraud. It may be a financial scam (called *phishing*) where they make the e-mail look like an official notice of some kind to lure you into revealing financial information that they can use to steal your money or iden-tity. Or it may be to get you to click on a link to place malicious code on your computer to steal all your information. These scams come in several varieties, but they share certain characteristics that we explore in this chapter.

Luckily you can use safe e-mailing practices, filters, and your smarts to avoid spam and malware, and spot common scam characteristics so you can avoid becoming a victim. In this chapter, you discover how to e-mail . . . and do so safely.

E-Mail Safety Basics

Adopt the following e-mail practices to keep you safer every time you e-mail:

⟹ **Don't share.** Never share sensitive personal information such as passwords, social security numbers, and credit card numbers in e-mail. Even if you e-mail this information to a known person or business, it can be intercepted along the way.

 Pay attention if you use an automatic e-mail signature such as the one shown in **Figure 5-1**. This is a handy feature that automatically provides whatever signature information you choose to share. Many people include their full name, address, and phone numbers in their signatures. But if it's inserted in all your e-mail responses, you might be sharing more information with people you don't know than you intend to, especially if your friends forward your e-mail to others.

⟹ **Consider who you want to e-mail.** Just because someone sends you an e-mail doesn't mean you need to read it or respond to it. You can set up your spam filters to be fairly restrictive and then check your junk mail folder periodically to see if something important accidentally got blocked. (If you aren't sure how to do this, consult the Help documentation for the e-mail program you use.)

Automatic e-mail signature

Figure 5-1

➠ **Think twice before you open attachments or click links in e-mail.** If you don't know the sender, delete the e-mail; if you do know the sender but weren't expecting an attachment, double-check that she actually sent the e-mail. If your friend didn't send you the attachment, delete the message. If her computer is infected with malicious code, it may automatically send you e-mails (without her knowledge) with links or attachments in an attempt to infect your computer as well.

➠ **Talk to your friends about their online security.** If they don't protect their computers from viruses, spyware and other malicious code, they put you at risk every time they send something to you.

➡ **Report offensive, inappropriate, and illegal material sent via e-mail to your ISP (Internet service provider).** If the content is illegal, you should also report it to your local law enforcement agency.

➡ **Be cautious about meeting online contacts in person.** You may know certain people only through e-mail or contact on a Web site. Just remember that everything someone tells you about himself and his motivation for meeting you may be completely true — or completely false. If you decide to meet someone, don't go alone, make sure others know where you're going, meet in a very busy, public place, and keep your cell phone handy.

➡ **Consider what you're saying and sharing in e-mail and how you'd feel if the information was shared with someone other than the recipient.** Anything you say in e-mail can be forwarded to others or monitored by employers or other family members.

 Avoid typing sensitive information into public computers such as those found in libraries or Internet cafes. Sensitive information includes your name, phone numbers, account numbers, passwords, and home or e-mail addresses. These computers may be infected with spyware that records your information and sends it to a criminal. Never select the feature that automatically logs you on to e-mail when you start the computer, and don't select a Remember My Password option when using a public computer. If you do so by mistake, use the Forget My Password option in the login screen for that account to reverse the action.

Create an E-Mail Account

You can create an e-mail account through a variety of service providers. These steps take you through creating a Windows Live Hotmail account, provided by Microsoft. However, the steps are similar for AOL, Yahoo!, Google Gmail, and so on.

1. Connect to the Internet and open your browser.

2. Enter the URL www.windowslive.com in your browser address bar.

3. On the resulting page, click the **Sign Up** link.

4. Enter the information requested in the **Sign Up** form that appears (see **Figure 5-2**), enter your preferred e-mail address in the **Windows Live ID** box. (See the next section for advice on creating a safe e-mail alias).

5. Click the **Check Availability** button to find out if the name you entered is available. If it isn't, enter another name and check again until you find one that works, or select one of the alternates the service offers you.

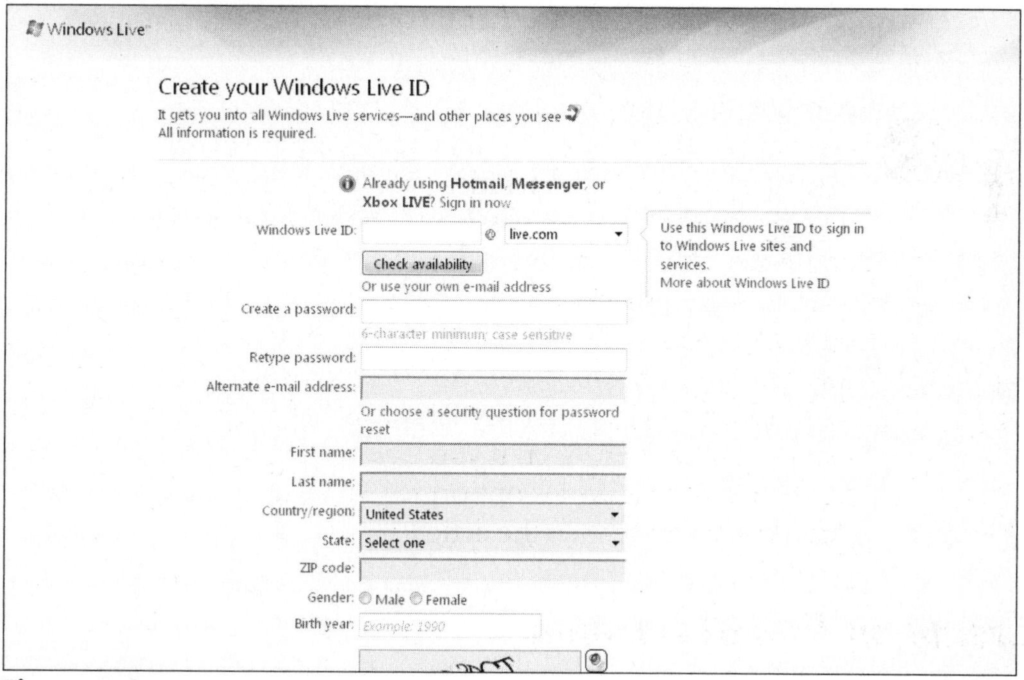

Create your Windows Live ID
It gets you into all Windows Live services—and other places you see
All information is required.

Already using **Hotmail**, **Messenger**, or **Xbox LIVE**? Sign in now

Windows Live ID: [ ] @ [live.com ▼]
[Check availability]
Or use your own e-mail address

Use this Windows Live ID to sign in to Windows Live sites and services.
More about Windows Live ID

Create a password: [ ]
6-character minimum; case sensitive

Retype password: [ ]

Alternate e-mail address: [ ]
Or choose a security question for password reset

First name: [ ]

Last name: [ ]

Country/region: [United States ▼]

State: [Select one ▼]

ZIP code: [ ]

Gender: ○ Male ○ Female

Birth year: [Example: 1990]

Figure 5-2

6. Enter additional requested information, but only the *required* information (marked with an asterisk), including

- **Password:** Learn how to create a secure password in Chapter 3.

- **Alternate e-mail:** Windows Live uses this alternate e-mail address to e-mail your ID and password to you if you forget them. If you don't have another e-mail or would rather not have a message sent, click the Or Choose A Security Question for Password Reset link and proceed with the activity in the next bullet.

- **Password hint:** Select a password hint question from the drop-down list. *Never* choose a question that you can answer using publicly-available information such as your place of birth, a school you attended, or your mother's maiden name. If none of the questions allow you to give an answer that others couldn't discover, use a fake answer — but remember it! The service doesn't know if your answer is correct, it verifies only that you can give the answer that you provided again if you forget your password.

- **The *minimum* amount of personal information required:** You may be required to include your name, gender, year of birth, country, state, and postal code.

7. Type the characters that you see in the **Picture** box. (See **Figure 5-3.**)

This feature, which asks you to enter the series of rather strange-looking numbers and/or letters that appear in a box, may seem annoying, but it's here to protect you. Services use this feature to stop malicious programs from creating thousands of fake e-mail accounts. It requires a human to read the letters or numbers displayed, which no computer program can do, to successfully complete the form.

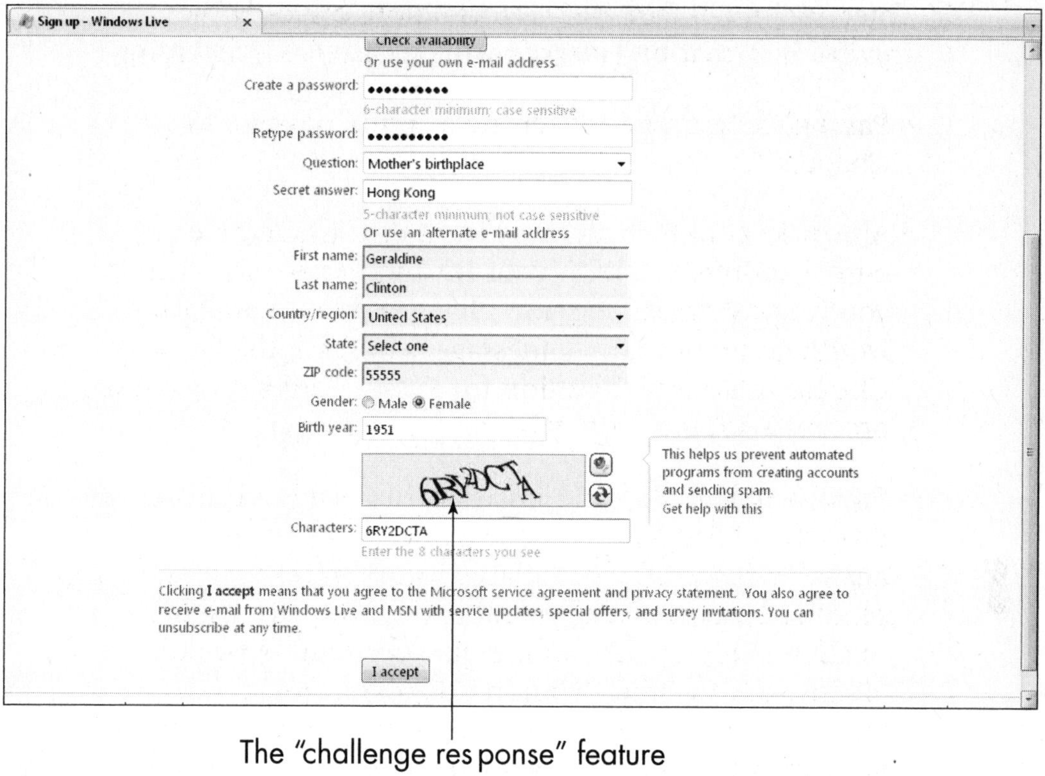

The "challenge response" feature

Figure 5-3

8. Read the **Microsoft Service Agreement and Privacy Statement**.

Every company creates its own rules for how they treat your information (like whether they'll resell it to others) and the requirements they place on users. Though reading the fine print may be the last thing you want to do, failing to read it may cause you grief down the road. If you don't like the service's terms, choose a different e-mail company.

9. Click the **I Accept** button to submit the form.

10. On the page that appears (see **Figure 5-4**), click the **Go to Inbox** link. (Note that some e-mail services require that you download software to use them.)

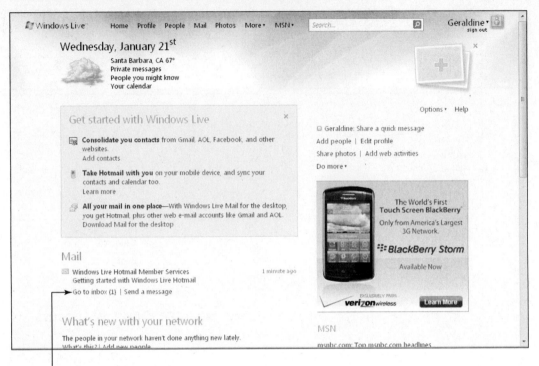

Click the Go To Inbox link

Figure 5-4

11. On the resulting Windows Live Hotmail page, (see **Figure** 5-5) you see a set of e-mail folders listed on the left. You use these to find and open new messages and store copies of messages you receive.

 It's a good idea to have additional e-mail accounts you can use to sign up for newsletters and services that require an e-mail account or communicate with groups where you may not know some of the members personally. Using multiple e-mail accounts helps you compartmentalize your privacy and safety. If one account is breached, the others are still safe.

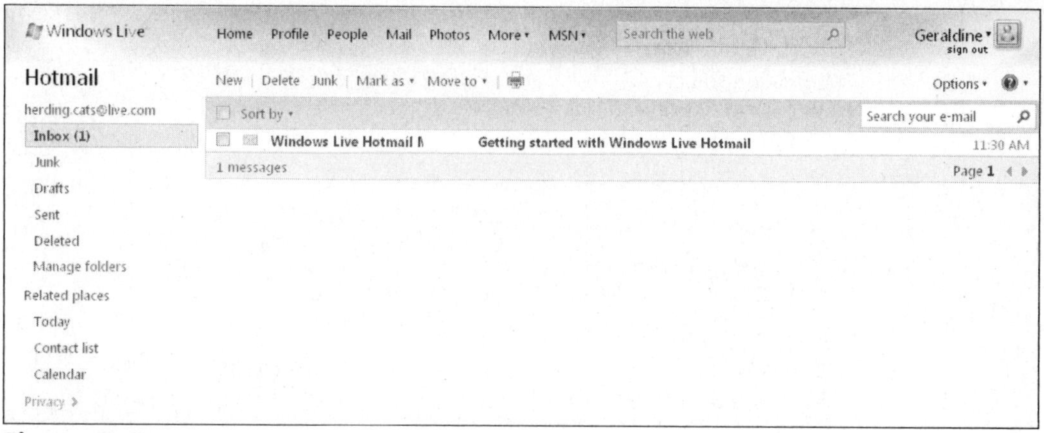

Figure 5-5

Create Safe E-Mail Aliases

Your choice of an e-mail alias can provide as little or as much information about you as you choose to share. An e-mail alias like Jack Stanfield@hotmail.com exposes your full name. This may be exactly what you want, or you may not want to give away any personal information. Just remember that whatever information you provide in your e-mail address, many kinds of criminals — whether their intent is to cause financial, emotional, or physical harm — can see it, in addition to those you trust.

Consider the exposure in this e-mail aliases: SusieDoe_64_small_town@google.com.au reveals enough for someone to find Susie — her name, age, and small town in Australia. And flirtatious names like sexyOver50 may cause unwanted attention and expose you to greater risk.

If you want the safest personal e-mail alias or nickname (versus your work e-mail, over which you may have little control), don't provide identifiable information, such as:

➡ **Names:** First, middle, or last names. Be sure to read the next section to change settings if your e-mail provider displays your full name next to your alias by default, or avoiding the use of your name won't do you any good.

➠ **Location information:** City, town, country, or region, such as Northwest. Don't give away your employer in your personal e-mail alias.

➠ **Sexual or physical suggestion:** Certain words such as *hot* or *sexy* let others know how you want to be perceived, while words like *snuggly* or *lonely* suggest an interest in intimacy that criminals can take advantage of.

➠ **Work descriptor:** Teacher, engineer, dentist, retired, or a description of your place of employment.

➠ **Emotional vulnerability:** Words such as sad, grieving, lost, suicide, and lonely place you at risk; there's always a criminal waiting to be your "best friend."

➠ **Risk behaviors:** Names that speak, even in fun, of drug use (`littletokr`), criminal activity (`carjacker`), or violence (`shootingspree`) may attract the wrong kind of person.

➠ **Ethnic identifiers:** May increase the risk of hate crimes, or they may help identify you — for example, `Asiandoll`, `N8tive` (native), or `mxed` (mixed).

➠ **Hobbies or sports:** An unusual sport such as polo or barrel racing, sports that imply a specific socio-economic bracket, or sports that are done in only a few locations (skeet shooting or bull fighting, for example) are more identifying than baseball or soccer. Criminals can use such interests to make a personal connection with a victim.

 Employers may have defined domains (`@company.com`) and assigned protocols for your name — even using your full name. It's important in these cases that you limit the additional pieces of personal information that you associate with that account. For example, you may provide your work phone number in your signature, but avoid including a personal cell phone number or your personal e-mail account.

Hide Your Name in E-Mails

Some e-mail services automatically include your full name as well as your e-mail alias to everyone you send e-mail to. If this isn't what you want, you'll need to find out if this is happening. Send yourself an e-mail and look at who it's from. If your name appears there, take steps to remove this information.

Think about it. Your last name and an online directory search may be all it takes to locate your family, find your phone number, learn the value of your home, and more.

Check your e-mail provider's help topics to get steps for this procedure. (For Windows Live Hotmail and Yahoo!, the steps are on our Web site at `ilookbothways.com`.) To hide your real name in Windows Live Hotmail, follow these steps:

1. At the top-right side of the page, click **Options**.

2. Click **More Options** at the bottom of the list. *Note:* If you're using the classic version of Windows Live Hotmail, you're automatically redirected to the Options page after clicking the Options button.

3. In the resulting Options windows (see **Figure 5-6**) under the Manage Your Account section, click the **View and Edit Your Personal Information** link.

4. Click **Profile Details** on the left side of the resulting dialog box

5. Click the **Edit** link on the left side of the Details screen.

Click this link

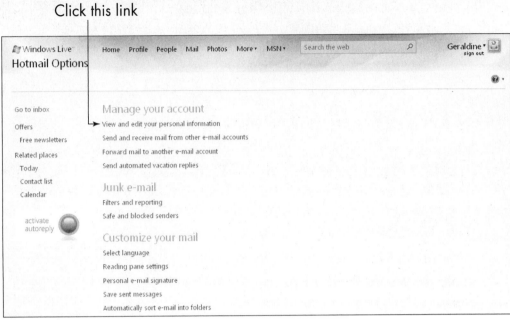

Figure 5-6

6. In the resulting window (see **Figure 5-7**) unselect the checkbox labeled **Allow Everyone to See My Last Name.**

 Unless you specifically want to be identified in your e-mail alias, pick a name that doesn't expose your identity — or leave it blank. You can use any alphanumeric character (A–Z; 0–9) and any of the special characters on your keyboard, except for :, <, >, ;, (,), ", $, and !.

7. Click **Save** at the bottom of the page to save your changes.

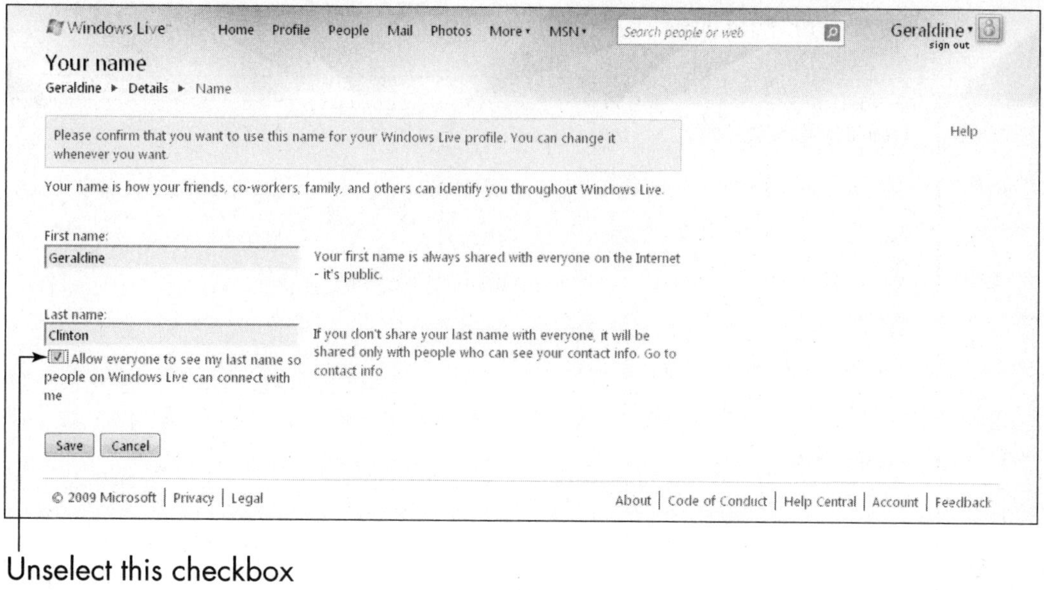

Unselect this checkbox

Figure 5-7

Send an E-Mail

Sending an e-mail through any e-mail service involves entering the recipient's e-mail address information, a subject, and the body of your message into the e-mail form and then sending it on its way.

1. To send an e-mail in Windows Live Hotmail, type the Web address of the application (www.windowslive.com)in your browser and log in.

2. Click the **Inbox** link on the left and then click the **New** button. (See **Figure 5-8.**)

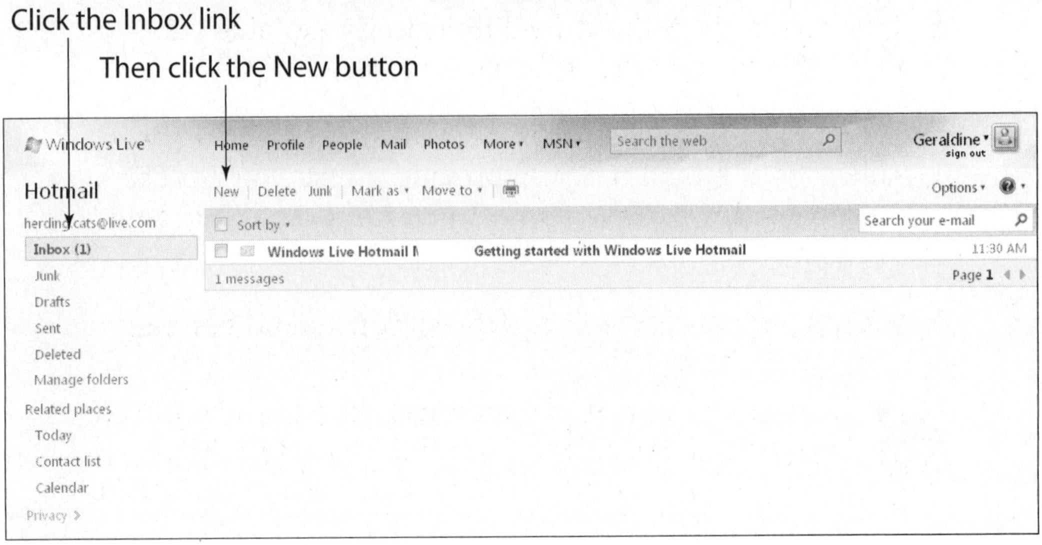

Click the Inbox link

Then click the New button

Figure 5-8

3. In the e-mail form that appears (see **Figure 5-9**), type an
e-mail address in the **To:** field (an e-mail address takes the
form of name@service.com, or name@service.net)
and press the **Tab** key. (Note that you can use the Bcc:
field for private addressing options. We talk about using
the Bcc field to hide addressees' e-mail addresses in
Chapter 3.)

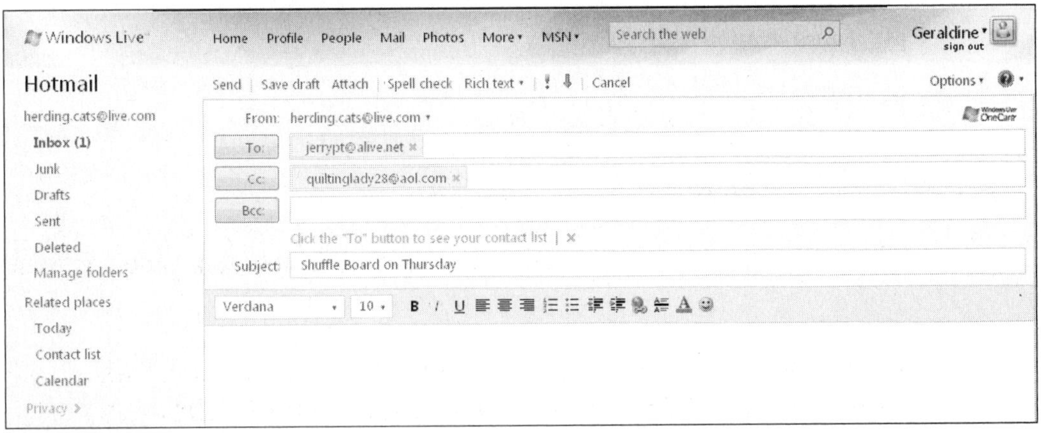

Figure 5-9

4. Type text in the **Subject** field that clearly explains the topic of your message and press the **Tab** key.

5. Type whatever text you wish in the main body of the message. If your e-mail program provides them, you can use text formatting tools to apply different fonts, colors, bold, or other effects.

6. When your message is complete, click the **Send** button.

 Believe it or not, e-mail messages have been known to suddenly get sent before you finish writing them. Great minds have conjectured that this happens when you hit some odd keystroke combination unknowingly, or perhaps it's done by magic. For this reason, some people prefer to leave the To: line empty until the message is written just as you want it to be so you're not embarrassed by an unfinished or unpolished e-mail going out before you intend.

 Any time you send or forward e-mail to a group of people who don't know each other, you need to respect and protect everybody's identity by placing all the e-mail addresses in the Bcc: (or blind carbon copy) field of the message so you don't expose everybody's name to everybody else. See Chapter 3 for details on how to do this.

Add an Attachment

You can add any kind of file to an e-mail, such as a picture or document. The procedure is pretty standardized.

1. In Windows Live Hotmail, with an e-mail form open, (see the "Send an E-Mail" task earlier in this chapter) click the **Attach** button. (See **Figure 5-10**.)

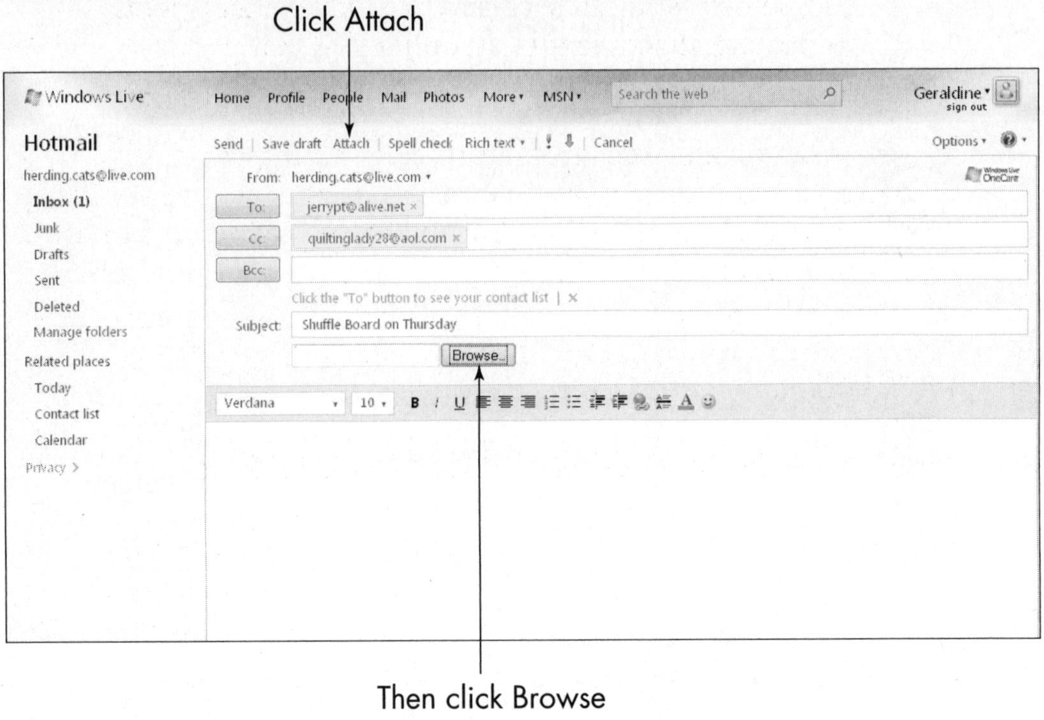

Click Attach

Then click Browse

Figure 5-10

2. In the new field that appears underneath the Subject line, click the **Browse** button (refer to **Figure 5-10**).

3. In the File Upload dialog box that appears (see **Figure 5-11**), locate the file or image you want to attach by searching through your file directory.

4. Click the file or image to select it, and then click the **Open** button.

5. Type the address(es), subject, and message body, and click **Send** to send the message along with its attachment.

Some e-mail programs have size restrictions for attachments. If that's the case and you attach a large file, it may not go through. Also remember that recipients' e-mail programs may have size restrictions that may cause them to be unable to download the attachment.

In that case, you can send several smaller attachments or post an attachment to an online file-sharing site such as Office Live.

 Don't include sensitive information such as a credit card account numbers in e-mail messages or attachments, as e-mail isn't secure and can be intercepted or forwarded.

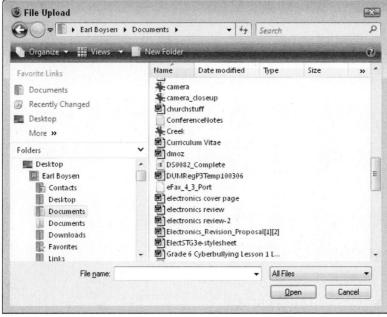

Figure 5-11

Open an Attachment

You may receive e-mails with attachments. Be very cautious about opening these if you don't know the sender — or if you don't expect an attachment from someone you do know.

1. To download an attachment, first click the e-mail message in your Inbox to open it. (An e-mail with attachments typically sports a paper clip icon to the left of the subject, as shown in **Figure 5-12.**)

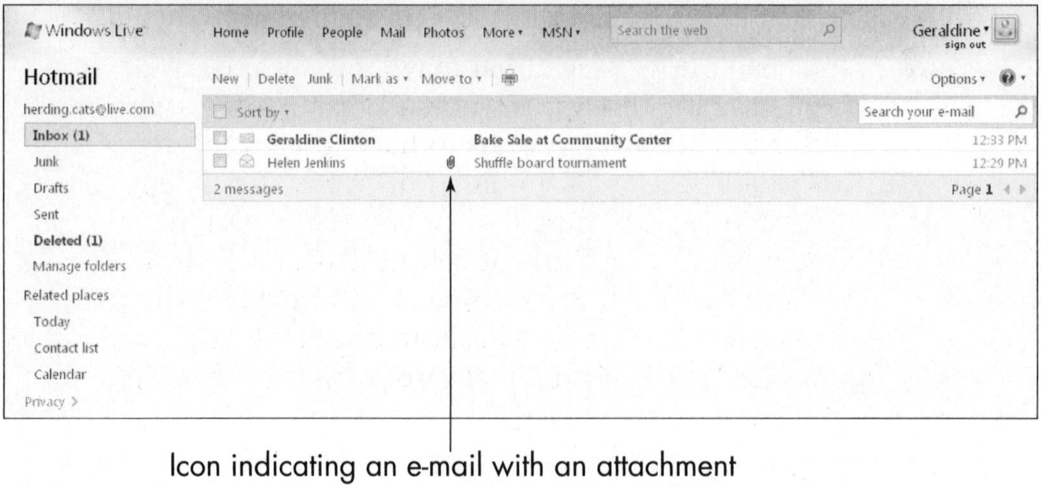

Icon indicating an e-mail with an attachment

Figure 5-12

2. In the open e-mail, click the attachment. The File Download dialog box appears (see **Figure 5-13**), offering you the option of saving or opening/running the attached file.

- If you want to save the file, click the **Save** button. In the Save As dialog box that appears, use the **Save In** field to locate the folder where you want to save the file. Then click the **Save** button.

- If you want to open the file, or run an executable file (such as an installation program for software that initiates the installation), click the **Open** or **Run** button. (The choice varies depending on the type of file.)

 Be aware that clicking **Run** is a very high-risk action. If you aren't 100 percent sure that what you're opening is an installation program for a legitimate piece of software, don't proceed.

3. Depending on your choice in the previous step, the file is saved, opened, or run.

Some malware programs can take your e-mail contacts and send out messages that may look like they come from you. It's for that reason that, even if a message with an attachment appears to have come from somebody you know, you shouldn't open the attachment unless you're expecting it — or you verify with the sender that the attachment is legitimate. Also, always be extra careful about opening an attached file with a file extension of .exe. This is an executable file, which is the file format that most malware takes.

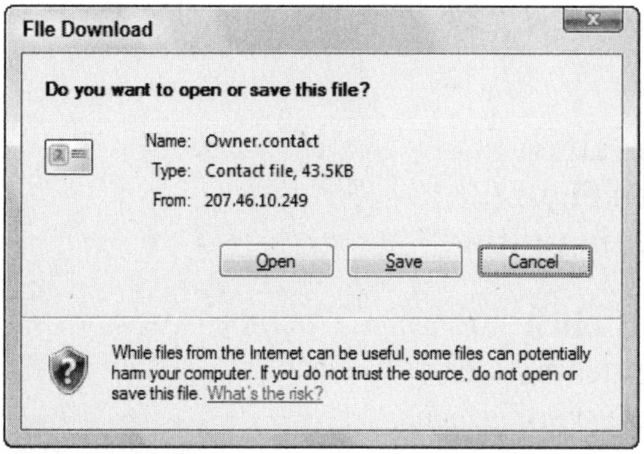

Figure 5-13

Forward E-Mails

1. If you receive an e-mail that you want to send on to someone else, with the e-mail message open, click the **Forward** button, as shown in **Figure 5-14**.

2. In the resulting new e-mail form, type an e-mail address in the **To:** field.

3. If you wish, click in the subject field to select the current subject and then type a different subject.

Click forward

Shuffle board tournament

From: **Helen Jenkins** (copperglow@msn.com)

You may not know this sender. Mark as safe | Mark as unsafe

Sent: Wed 1/21/09 12:29 PM

To: herding.cats@live.com

1 attachment(s)

rentalpos...doc (1704.0 KB)

Jerry confirmed that the tournament is scheduled for April 3-7th.

Also, I've attached a proposed flier for the storage rental unit behind the community center. Let me know what you think.

Helen

Hotmail® goes where you go. On a PC, on the Web, on your phone. See how.

Windows Live™: E-mail. Chat. Share. Get more ways to connect. See how it works.

Figure 5-14

4. Type your message.

5. *Before* you click the **Send** button, be sure you have honored the privacy of the person who sent you the e-mail. If you're sending it to someone whom the original sender doesn't know, remove the original sender's name and e-mail alias. Note that for most e-mail programs, when you forward a message, any original attachments are also forwarded. If this isn't what you want, remove the attachment before sending by clicking the **Remove** button.

When you forward a message, the original message (or string of messages) is retained. However, you can edit the message if you like. For example, if you're forwarding a message that includes several e-mails and replies, you can delete earlier message text if you don't want that information included. Be respectful of others' privacy by removing the e-mail aliases in the message that came to you.

Be cautious about forwarding e-mail messages with multiple recipients, such as chain letter e-mails. Many of these are cute, but spammers design them to collect e-mail addresses. If you really want to forward a message that came to you, start a new message and cut and paste the contents into it. Delete any e-mail aliases or names mentioned in the body of the message.

Reply to E-Mails

1. If you receive an e-mail that you want to reply to, with the e-mail message open, click the **Reply** button to reply only to the sender, or click the **Reply All** button to reply to the sender and every other original recipient of the e-mail — except Bcc: recipients.

2. In the resulting new e-mail form (see **Figure 5-15**), which is already populated with the sender's and recipients' addresses (depending on whether you choose **Reply** or **Reply All** in Step 1), enter any additional addressees in the **To:**, **Cc:**, or **Bcc:** fields.

3. The subject line references the original message subject. If you want to, you can change the text in the Subject line. Just select it and type the new subject.

 Note that for most e-mail programs, attachments that you receive aren't included in your reply. That's because the original sender and recipients already have those attachments. If you want to, you can add a new attachment to your reply before you send the message in the next step. See the section "Add an Attachment," earlier in this chapter, to find out how.

4. Type your message and click the **Send** button.

Windows Live | Home Profile People Mail Photos More ▾ MSN ▾ | Search the web | Geraldine ▾
sign out

Hotmail

herding.cats@live.com

Send | Save draft Attach | Spell check Rich text ▾ | ! ↓ | Cancel   Options ▾ ❓ ▾

Inbox (1)   From: herding.cats@live.com ▾   Show Cc & Bcc   Windows Live OneCare

Junk   To: copperglow@msn.com ✕

Drafts   Click the "To" button to see your contact list | ✕

Sent   Subject: RE: Shuffle board tournament

Deleted (1)

Manage folders   Verdana ▾ 10 ▾ **B** *I* U ...

Related places

Today   Let's go to the opening day together!
_____
Contact list

Calendar   From: copperglow@msn.com
             To: herding.cats@live.com
Privacy ➤   Subject: Shuffle board tournament
             Date: Wed, 21 Jan 2009 12:29:15 -0800

             Jerry confirmed that the tournament is scheduled for April 3–7th.

             Also, I've attached a proposed flier for the storage rental unit behind the community center. Let me know what you think.

             Helen
_____
             Hotmail® goes where you go. On a PC, on the Web, on your phone. See how.

             Windows Live™: E-mail. Chat. Share. Get more ways to connect. See how it works.

Figure 5-15

Manage Spam

Spam is e-mail sent in bulk to recipients who haven't requested it. People usually get spam from senders they don't know. Spam can be transmitted over any Internet-connected device (such as a computer, cell phone, or PDA). It's a cheap way to market products or services, but it's illegal in many countries.

Nearly 70 percent of all e-mail traffic in the world is spam. In 2007, one study showed that 90 billion spam messages are sent per day. While Internet service providers are making serious efforts to block *junk* (spam) e-mail, determined spammers are making equally serious efforts to find ways to keep filling your inbox. They constantly evolve new methods of fooling the anti-spam filters. Here is some advice about how to avoid and deal with spam:

➡ Understand your e-mail provider's anti-spamming features and use their settings to flag spam or put it in a separate junk mail folder. (See **Figure 5-16.**)

 See the next section to set up and use spam filters.

Gmail

in:spam	Search Mail	Search the Web

Show search options
Create a filter

Compose Mail

Inbox (3)
Starred
Chats
Sent Mail
Drafts
All Mail
Spam (29)
Trash

Contacts

- Chat

Search, add, or invite

● Nancy Muir
Set status here ▼

Billy Stephens
Bruce Nofsinger
David Milstein
Himmler, Arthur
Jennifer Greene
Jerry Tylman
Linda Criddle

Spam Quiche - Makes 4 servings

Spam Recipe ◄ ►

| Delete Forever | Not Spam | More Actions ▼ | Refresh | 1 - 29 of 29 |

Select: All, None, Read, Unread, Starred, Unstarred

Delete all spam messages now (messages that have been in Spam more than 30 days will be automatically deleted)

Angila Cassy	Sale Offer:- ViagraCializ Pills at LowestPrices on net! $1.31/tab, find out	9:17 am
Edith Caryn	AAA-Grade Rep1icaRolex at only $196/piece, All Famous Brands availa	5:43 am
me	Delivery Status Notification (Failure) - Click here to view as a webpage	4:44 am
Elissa Daphine	88% Cheaper than others: 10-pills ViagraL=$33, 10-pills CailisY=$38, 10-p	4:15 am
Natalia Yajaira	1 year warranty Rep1icaWatches from $190, BvlgariRo1ex, Channel, LV	2:58 am
Saran Hailey	No Degree No Job? Buy a Genuine College Degree at cheap price & de	2:40 am
me	become Big Love Boss - Having trouble viewing this email? Click here to view	2:04 am
me	RE: Message - Click here to view as a webpage	12:36 am
Cabana Orbeck	one wife iss not enough - I have One wife and two mistresses... I can keep it	12:10 am
Pablo Weber	Luxury goods at blowout prices - Christmas Luxury watches blowout sale	11:22 pm
Noel Na	Sale Offer:- ViagraCializ Pills at LowestPrices on net! $1.31/tab, find out	Nov 29
Theda Caitlin	No Degree No Job? Buy a Genuine College Degree at cheap price & de	Nov 29
Danyel Freda	Cheapest & The Best!! $1.12 forViagra, $1.92 forCializ & FREE PILLs with	Nov 29
Misti Felecia	1 year warranty Rep1icaWatches from $190, BvlgariRo1ex, Channel, LV	Nov 29
Felicidad Tonie	Cializ+Viagre=$75.95, BuyViagra Online at the "Chepeast" Price! ipiy 4h	Nov 29
Sheryll Florine	88% Cheaper than others: 10-pills ViagraL=$33, 10-pills CailisY=$38, 10-p	Nov 29
Tambra Tennille	Sale Offer:- ViagraCializ Pills at LowestPrices on net! $1.31/tab, find out	Nov 29

Figure 5-16

➠ Review the junk mail folder periodically to make sure legitimate e-mail hasn't been placed there. Then delete the spam e-mails.

➠ Stay up-to-date on spam tactics. (Visit our site at www.ilookbothways.com or sites such as www.snopes.com for the latest information.) And when in doubt about the origin or intent of an e-mail, delete it.

➠ Always have strong anti-spam, anti-virus, and anti-phishing tools installed on every computer you own, set these tools to update automatically, and use settings in your e-mail program to block spam. See Chapter 16 for more about these tools.

Use Spam Filters

Spam filters identify spam and keep it out of your inbox. Most e-mail programs have built-in filters that route spam to a Junk folder or immediately delete it.

1. To make these settings in Windows Live Hotmail, click the **Options** button in the upper-right corner and select **More Options.**

2. On the resulting Hotmail Options page (see **Figure 5-17**), click the **Filters and Reporting** link in the Junk E-Mail section.

3. On the Filters and Reporting page that appears (see **Figure 5-18**), adjust any of the following settings:

- **Choose a Junk E-Mail Filter:** This is where you select your filter level. The trick here is to find a level that won't send e-mail from legitimate sources that aren't already contacts into the Junk mail folder, while keeping your inbox relatively spam free.

 Most spam is easy for filters to identify. It can flag known bad senders or spot keywords in the subject lines, such as *Viagra* or *sex.* But no matter what filter level you choose, you should periodically check your Junk mail folder. Spam filters aren't infallible, and legitimate e-mails can end up in there by mistake.

- **Delete Junk E-Mail:** Here you choose when to delete junk mail. You can choose to just let Windows Live Hotmail delete junk e-mail immediately or place it in the junk folder and delete it after 10 days. (We recommend the latter setting so you have a chance to look for legitimate e-mails that were accidentally routed into the junk folder.)

- **Report Junk Messages:** These settings let you choose whether to report spam. If you select the setting to report junk, clicking the **Junk** button will both delete and report spam; if you choose not to employ this setting, clicking the **Junk** button simply deletes the message. By reporting spam, you can help your e-mail provider more accurately track and reduce spam for everyone.

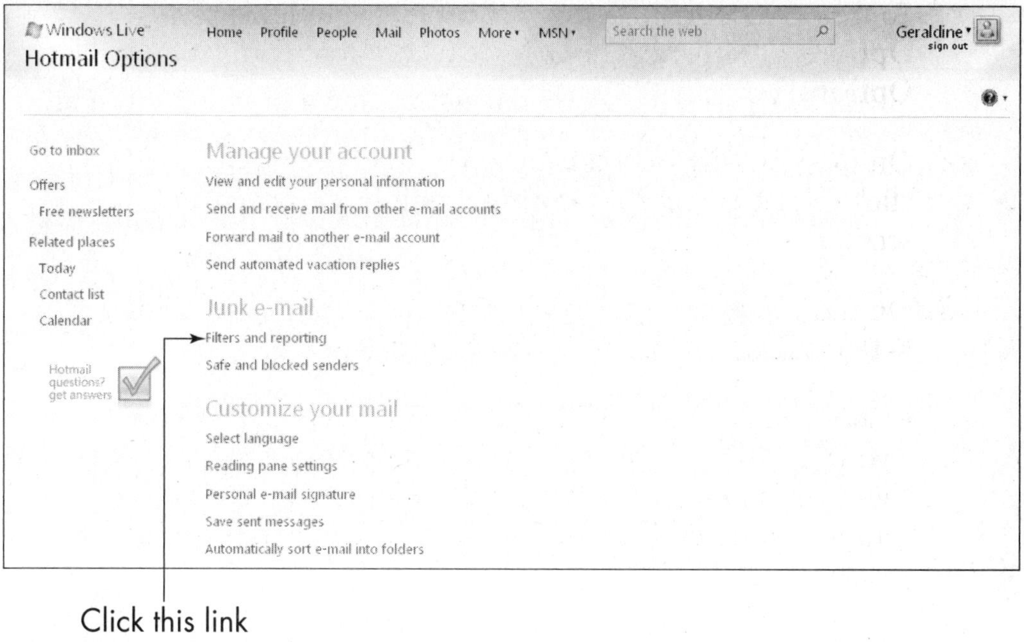

Windows Live
Hotmail Options

Home   Profile   People   Mail   Photos   More ▾   MSN ▾

Search the web

Geraldine ▾
sign out

Go to inbox

Offers
  Free newsletters

Related places

Today

Contact list

Calendar

Hotmail
questions?
get answers

Manage your account

View and edit your personal information

Send and receive mail from other e-mail accounts

Forward mail to another e-mail account

Send automated vacation replies

Junk e-mail

Filters and reporting

Safe and blocked senders

Customize your mail

Select language

Reading pane settings

Personal e-mail signature

Save sent messages

Automatically sort e-mail into folders

Click this link

Figure 5-17

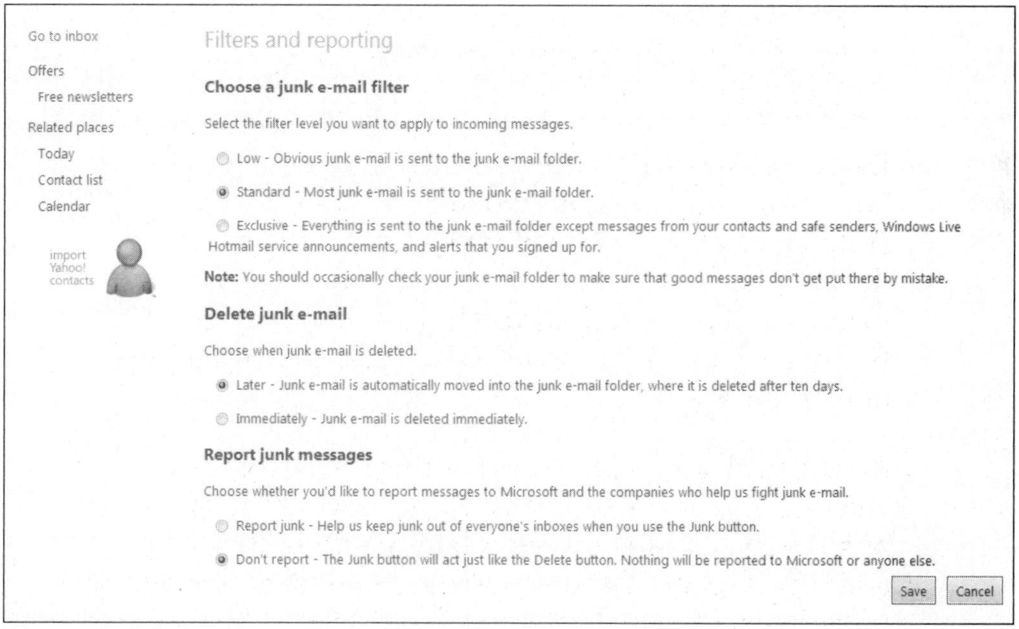

Go to inbox

Offers
  Free newsletters

Related places

Today

Contact list

Calendar

import
Yahoo!
contacts

Filters and reporting

Choose a junk e-mail filter

Select the filter level you want to apply to incoming messages.

○ Low - Obvious junk e-mail is sent to the junk e-mail folder.

◉ Standard - Most junk e-mail is sent to the junk e-mail folder.

○ Exclusive - Everything is sent to the junk e-mail folder except messages from your contacts and safe senders, Windows Live Hotmail service announcements, and alerts that you signed up for.

Note: You should occasionally check your junk e-mail folder to make sure that good messages don't get put there by mistake.

Delete junk e-mail

Choose when junk e-mail is deleted.

◉ Later - Junk e-mail is automatically moved into the junk e-mail folder, where it is deleted after ten days.

○ Immediately - Junk e-mail is deleted immediately.

Report junk messages

Choose whether you'd like to report messages to Microsoft and the companies who help us fight junk e-mail.

○ Report junk - Help us keep junk out of everyone's inboxes when you use the Junk button.

◉ Don't report - The Junk button will act just like the Delete button. Nothing will be reported to Microsoft or anyone else.

Save   Cancel

Figure 5-18

Use Verification Programs

If you've had it with spam, consider using a program (see **Figure 5-19**) that authenticates users. But keep in mind that most of these services charge a fee. These programs use a verification system to check any sender who hasn't been approved. Here's how this usually works:

➡ The program scans your contact list and automatically allows everyone listed there to contact you.

➡ When you receive an e-mail from someone who isn't in your contact list, the program holds the e-mail in limbo until two things happen. First, the service sends an e-mail to the sender and asks that person to verify that he's a real person by answering a challenge response (entering text that he sees onscreen). Second, only when the sender has successfully responded to the challenge is the e-mail delivered to your inbox. Because spam e-mail is sent by auto-mated malicious programs, there's no human to respond to the challenge. Consequently, an auto-mated sender's e-mail doesn't get through. Any e-mail that doesn't pass this test doesn't land in your inbox.

➡ People not on your list have to answer the challenge only once for each email account they use to be vali-dated for all future e-mails.

➡ Any e-mail from those who aren't verified is stored in a special folder for a week. This gives you the chance to review the messages in case you want to accept any of them.

 One such program, Spam Arrest (refer to **Figure 5-21**), allows you to try its service free for a month before you purchase a subscription. Go to www.spam arrest.com to sign up.

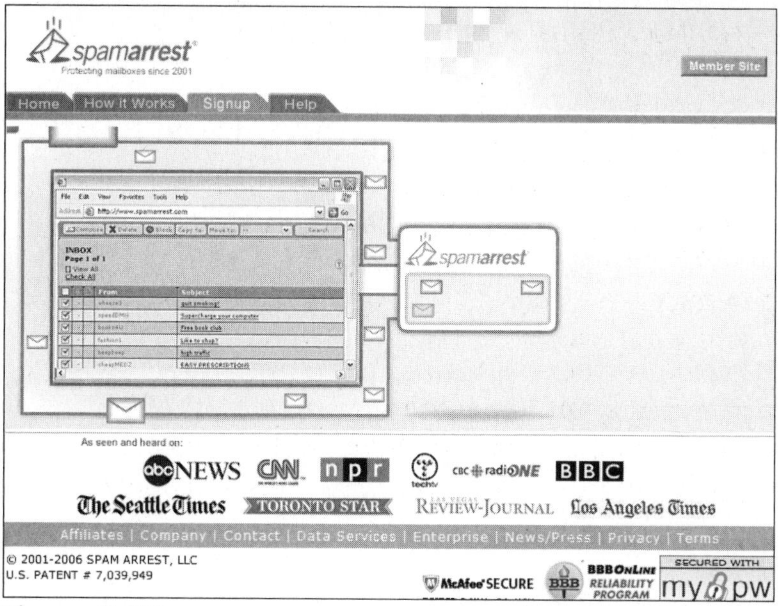

Figure 5-19

File a Spam Complaint

The United States federal CAN-SPAM Act of 2003 went into effect on January 1, 2004. The CAN-SPAM Act (Controlling the Assault of Non-Solicited Pornography and Marketing) was created by federal lawmakers as a way to reduce spam. The CAN-SPAM Act states that it "preempts all state law that regulates commercial e-mail except to the extent that state law prohibits falsity or deception."

The federal statute does the following:

➡ Requires commercial e-mail senders to provide recipients with the ability to opt out of receiving more e-mail.

➡ Requires e-mail to be identified as advertisements or commercial e-mail where applicable.

➡ Requires sexually-oriented e-mail to be labeled as such in the subject line.

→ Requires the physical address of the sender to be
included in the e-mail.

→ Creates criminal penalties for those who violate sub-
stantive provisions of the law.

To file a complaint under the CAN-SPAM Act, e-mail details to the FTC
at spam@uce.gov.

 The FTC also provides more detailed information
about spam issues and the CAN-SPAM law on the FTC
Web site, www.ftc.gov/spam.

Recognize Fraud and Scams

As in the offline world, the Internet has a criminal element. These
cybercriminals use Internet tools to commit the same crimes they've
always committed, from robbing you to misusing your good name and
financial information. Know how to spot the types of scams that occur
online and you'll go a long way towards steering clear of Internet crime.

Before you click a link that comes in a forwarded e-mail message or forward a message to others, ask yourself:

→ **Is the information legitimate?** Sites such as
www.truthorfiction.com, www.snopes.com
(see **Figure 5-20**), or http://urbanlegends.
about.com can help you discover if an e-mail is
a scam.

→ **Does a message ask you to click links in e-mail** (see
Figure 5-21) **or instant messages?** If you're unsure
whether a message is genuinely from a company or
bank that you use, call them, using the number from
a past statement or the phone book. *Remember:* Don't

call a phone number in the e-mail; it could be fake. To visit a company's or bank's Web site, type the address in yourself if you know it or use your own bookmark rather than clicking a link. If the Web site is new to you, search for the company using your browser and use that link to visit its site. Don't click on the link in an e-mail, or you may land on a site that looks right — but is just a good fake.

➡ **Does the e-mail have a photo or video to download?** If so, exercise caution. If you know the person who sent the photo or video, it's probably fine to download, but if the photo or video has been forwarded several times and you don't know the person who sent it originally, be careful. It may deliver a virus or other type of malware to your computer.

Figure 5-20

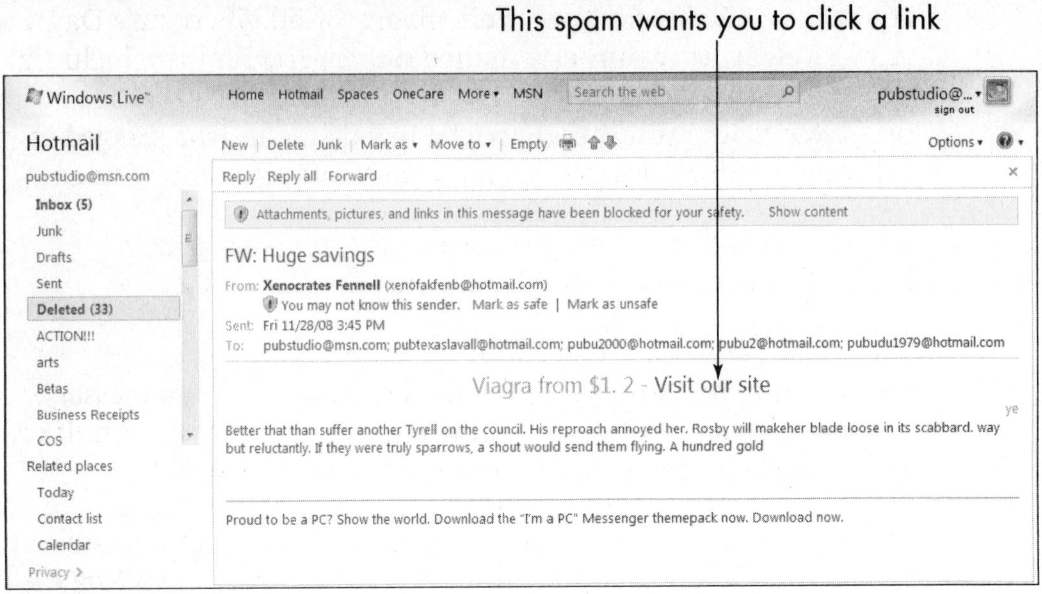

This spam wants you to click a link

Figure 5-21

In addition to these questions, also remember the following:

➥ **If you decide to forward (or send) e-mail to a group, always put their e-mail addresses on the Bcc: (or Blind Carbon Copy) line.** This keeps everyone's e-mail safe from fraud and scams.

➥ **Think *before* you click.** Doing so will save you and others from scams, fraud, hoaxes, and malware.

Avoid the Latest E-Mail Scam-of-the-Day

E-mail scams are typically low-value, high-volume crimes where the cost to a given consumer is comparatively low, but large numbers of victims mean that the money quickly adds up for the criminals behind the scam.

One of the ways consumers trip up relates to the relevancy of the scam's topic. E-mail scammers are smart about making their scams look current because people are much more likely to fall for scams related to topics already on their minds.

For example, Valentine scams circulate around Valentine's Day. Last year, a Valentine scammer e-mailed messages with titles including "In your arms," "Sending you all my love," "I love you because . . .," and so on. These have short messages and links your are encouraged to click. Clicking the links downloads malicious software onto your computer.

 The subject lines of e-mail scams morph constantly; there were at least 50 titles in circulation in 2008 alone.

Also around any holiday, be on the lookout for e-mail messages offering "great deals" on flowers, chocolates, dinners, and so on. If you aren't sure that a store is reputable, don't go there.

When you're in tax season, tax-related scams abound, including scams about being audited, getting tax rebates, or offering tax-filing assistance.

And the list goes on. There's literally a scam for every occasion.

 Routinely check our Web site (www.ilookboth ways.com) and Snopes.com to find out more about the lastest e-mail scams on the Internet.

Deal with Phishing E-Mails

Phishing scams are an attempt to trick you into divulging sensitive personal information that allows somebody to steal your identity or empty your bank account.

Don't be fooled by phishing. Be very skeptical if you receive an e-mail that looks like it is from your bank, broker, or other trusted company but asks you to verify or re-enter sensitive personal or financial information through e-mail, a Web site it directs you to, or a phone number it provides. It's quite likely a scam.

Look for these telltale signs to spot a phishing e-mail. (See **Figure 5-22**.)

1. You don't know the sender.

2. The e-mail is illiterate.

3. You're asked to provide information such as an account number, phone number, or social security number.

4. The e-mail address is odd or doesn't include the business name. Legitimate businesses have their own domain names (such as `aol.com` or `amazon.com`).

5. You are asked to click a link to respond or take an action. If you check the properties of the link in **Figure 5-22** by right-clicking it and choosing properties, you will find that the address is bismark.net, not Amazon.

6. You are told that you must click the link and provide information to get access to your account.

7. You are told not to reply to the e-mail as it is an automated e-mail and won't be answered. You are instead urged to log into your account (using the link they provide).

If you receive a phishing e-mail, take these precautions:

➡ Instead of clicking the links in the e-mail, use your favorite search engine to find the Web site for the company that sent the e-mail or locate that information on your statement.

➡ Contact the institution using a phone number from a statement or type in a company Web site address in your browser to go to its site and ask about the communication.

➡ Report the scam to your e-mail service provider.

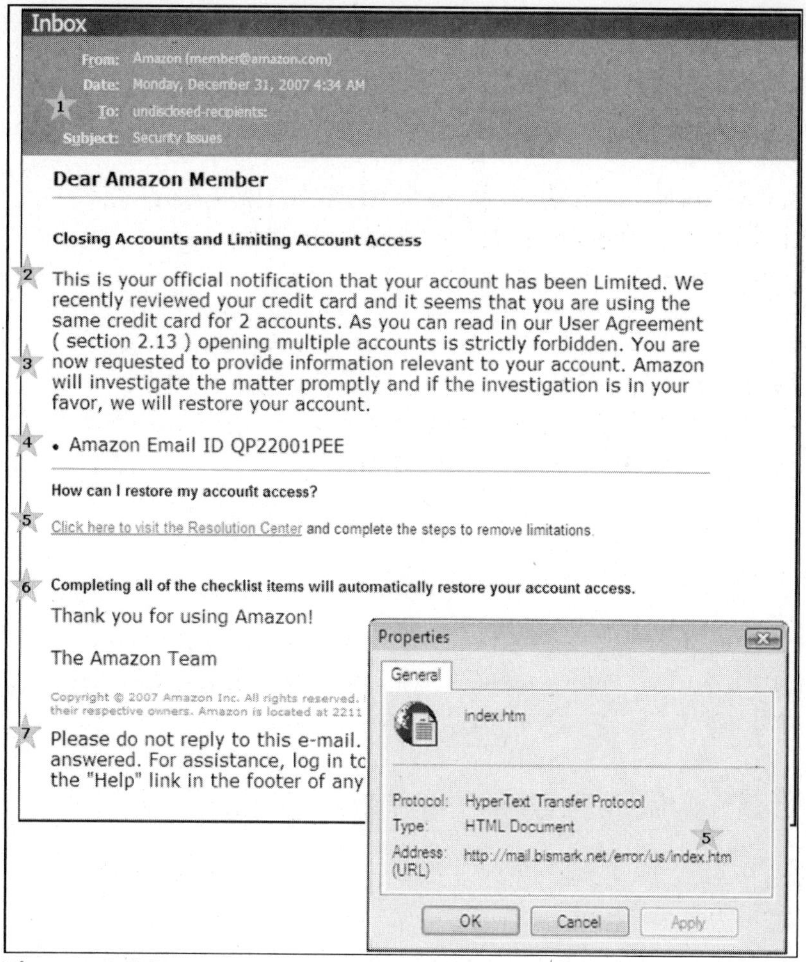
Inbox
From: Amazon (member@amazon.com)
Date: Monday, December 31, 2007 4:34 AM
To: undisclosed-recipients:
Subject: Security Issues
Dear Amazon Member
Closing Accounts and Limiting Account Access
This is your official notification that your account has been Limited. We recently reviewed your credit card and it seems that you are using the same credit card for 2 accounts. As you can read in our User Agreement (section 2.13) opening multiple accounts is strictly forbidden. You are now requested to provide information relevant to your account. Amazon will investigate the matter promptly and if the investigation is in your favor, we will restore your account.
• Amazon Email ID QP22001PEE
How can I restore my account access?
Click here to visit the Resolution Center and complete the steps to remove limitations.
Completing all of the checklist items will automatically restore your account access.
Thank you for using Amazon!
The Amazon Team
Please do not reply to this e-mail.
answered. For assistance, log in to
the "Help" link in the footer of any
Properties
General
index.htm
Protocol: HyperText Transfer Protocol
Type: HTML Document
Address: (URL) http://mail.bismark.net/error/us/index.htm
OK
Cancel
Apply
1
2
3
4
5
6
7
5

Figure 5-22

Part II: Using the Internet While Dodging the Risk

Posting Photos and Videos Safely

Photos help to record life moments big and small and capture the beauty of the world around us. The ability to nearly instantaneously share photos of a new baby, the first tooth lost, a game victory, or a tragedy can bridge the gap of distance and time to unite friends and family. With digital cameras and camera phones, we've entered a new age of sharing and documenting everyday life and events as they occur. In this chapter, we tell you how to post images in various formats and on various Web services to share them with others.

Of course, it's important that you remember that when you share images, you are sharing information about yourself with others. For that reason, you have to learn how to share photos and video online so that you can remain safe and avoid having your personal images stolen and used in inappropriate or even illegal ways.

One final aspect of sharing images online is understanding copyrights. You should know what constitutes illegal acts when forwarding or copying images you find online, and when your own rights are violated if somebody else steals your images.

How a Picture Can Put You at Risk

The most important thing about posting images online is to have an understanding of what you may expose in those images. It may be more than you'd intended. If you post images of yourself, your family, or friends online in a public place (a place that you haven't protected with private settings), you're providing a face to place with all the other information about you that may be online.

Images that you post online may provide these types of information:

➠ Information to help locate you, such as a house address, street sign, or business name (See **Figure 6-1.**)

➠ An impression of your mood or level of self-esteem from your posture or expression, which can give a predator a way to manipulate your emotions

Figure 6-1

➡ Ways to break into your house if your home is in the picture: windows, doors, possible location of a spare key, and so on

➡ Your socio-economic status, by what you wear, your home, car, and so on.

➡ People in your family or your friends, what they look like, and where they hang out

Posting photos on private sites allows you to manage who gets to see them, unless those you give access permission to download a copy and share it. Posting photos on a public Web site makes the image public, something you may well want to do. If, however, you regret posting the image and choose to take it down you are likely to find that it is very hard to remove all copies. If the photo has been copied or posted to multiple sites it is unlikely you will be able to get rid of each and every copy. For those likely to post embarrassing photos (typically teens) or photos with too much information included, this is a real concern as you may never entirely erase the damage done.

When photos and videos are posted on the Internet in a publicly accessible spot, predators and criminals can use the information contained in them to commit a variety of abuses and crimes. For example, your images can be:

➡ Manipulated to embarass you. Image-altering software is so advanced that it can be nearly impossible to tell an altered image from the real deal. Bullies alter images to humiliate, create conflicts, and deliberately expose others to risk. Sexual predators alter images for their own gratification.

➡ Sold for false passports or other forms of ID. Faces are commodities. They're bought, sold, and reused in a variety of ways we prefer not to contemplate.

➠ Sold to pornography sites. One of the fastest ways to generate 'new' pornography images is to add new faces to old material.

➠ Used in advertising without your knowledge or approval.

➠ Used to steal your identity or scam others. If a crook has a picture of you and can describe you, your home, or car, another member of your family may be more open to believing that the person knows you and may succumb to a scam.

 It isn't just photos taken with standard cameras that could cause problems. The quality of cameras embedded in cell phones is rapidly improving. The Asian cell phone market now has many phone choices with five or more megapixels, and Samsung has even developed a 10-megapixel camera phone. These phones take photos and short videos that have a high enough resolution that they become interesting to copy if posted publicly. Add this to the new services that carriers are providing to make it easy to post photos directly to the Web, and the result is many people are posting images without really reviewing them from a safety perspective — usually the comment we get afterwards is that "it seemed like a good idea at the time."

Particularly concerning are the highly sexual images that teens in particular are taking of themselves or others with their cameras and then sending to someone — typically a boy- or girlfriend, all too often these get shared much further than ever intended and a great deal of embarrassment occurs. Worse than the embarrassment however is that these images are child pornography — even when the teen is the picture taker — and sending as well as receiving these is a felony offense. These pictures (and short videos) have monetary value to predators and can make victims truly identifiable — and locatable.

Taking pictures of unsuspecting people with camera phones has become such a problem in parts of the world that some countries have enacted various levels of regulations. Saudi Arabia bans the sale of camera phones outright. South Korea requires manufacturers to make mobile devices that emit a beep whenever a picture is taken. France has strict laws about publishing digital images taken without consent.

The risk to your privacy is compounded when an image is combined with a caption or other descriptive text. You, your family, your employer, your school, a friend, a sport or after-school club, or even the local newspaper may sharing an image with text that contains too much private information.

For example, in **Figure 6-2,** note the following:

➡ The house number is displayed. (Copying the photo and enlarging it makes the number easily readable.)

➡ The photo includes the For Sale by Owner sign listing the family phone number.

➡ The text under the photo indicates that the phone number won't change. The area code would help locate the woman who posted this image, if her profile on the photo-sharing site didn't already provide her city and state.

➡ The house implies a great deal about the family's financial status.

➡ The house is empty — the family has moved. It sits alone on a hill. That's a lot of information for anyone wanting a place to party, do (or sell) drugs, steal, vandalize, or the like.

 Spotting risks in photos takes some practice. Visit our Web site, ilookbothways.com, to use interactive skills builders that help you practice spotting information exposure in images.

We've moved!!...but only two blocks away. Look for the invite to our new housewarming. P.S. Our phone number won't change.

Figure 6-2

When you understand the potential misuses of images, you can make conscious choices about what you post online. It makes sense to take precautions, use only reputable photo-sharing sites, and share with only those people whom you trust.

Share Photos Safely

With digital cameras and camera phones, we've entered a wonderful new age of sharing and documenting everyday life and events as they occur. Cell phones with cameras are with many of us all the time, and the quality of the cameras is rapidly improving. With the explosion of blogs, mobile blogs (called *moblogs)*, photo-sharing sites, personal Web sites, and image sharing in e-mails and instant messaging, sharing photos and videos has never been easier. Here's some advice for managing who sees your digital images, from photos to videos, to avoid the potential exposure of private or personal information to people outside your trusted friends and family:

➡ Use only reputable sites, and share only photos that contain *identifiable information* with people you trust.

➠ Use a photo-editing tool such as Windows Photo Gallery (see **Figure 6-3**) to cover up or crop out information that could put you at risk — for example the house number, your street sign, and so on. You may also choose to blur small sections of the image.

➠ Strip any additional information that may be stored along with your photos or video. Many cameras and cell phones have functionality that collects and stores both the time and date, and the location where the photo/video was taken. Web sites typically do not strip out this information when photos are posted, so anyone viewing a photo can right-click on it and from the pop-up menu select **Properties.** If the information was collected when the photo was taken, it will be visible. This means a photo taken in your backyard would provide anyone viewing the information with the exact latitude and longitude of your home — and online mapping services will take this information and display your home and it's address.

➠ Reduce the photo's resolution. Some Web sites allow you to copyright protect your photos, but unfortunately most do not. If the photo is one you are happy sharing publicly, but do not want people to copy and reuse and the site does not have a way for you to block copying, you may choose to post the image with reduced resolution. It can still look good on the Web, but the lower resolution makes it less likely that others will copy and reuse the photo. There are many software products available (perhaps even one that comes with your camera) that you can use to remove or hide information in photos, you may want to 'paint' over a section, blur portions of the image, adjusting the contrast or colors to make certain aspects less recognizable, or crop the image to remove information for example.

Figure 6-3

Share Videos Safely

Video sharing online through sites such as YouTube (see **Figure 6-4**) has exploded in the last couple of years with content from professional media and individuals. The content ranges from breaking news stories, to hilarious personal videos and professional comedian's material, lots of animal footage, cartoons, educational and how-to content, music videos, fashion and style videos, events and activist videos, travelogs, and of course family videos.

These sites also have hundreds of how-to videos that teach criminal skills like picking locks, pornographic material (which most sites try to remove), and videos that promote hate and violence.

Video content can be particularly compelling for criminals. Videos generally provide more visual information than a photo, plus they may allow the criminal to hear a person's voice and watch their mannerisms. There are often clues in the background of videos that provide additional personal or location information for the person who knows how to look for it.

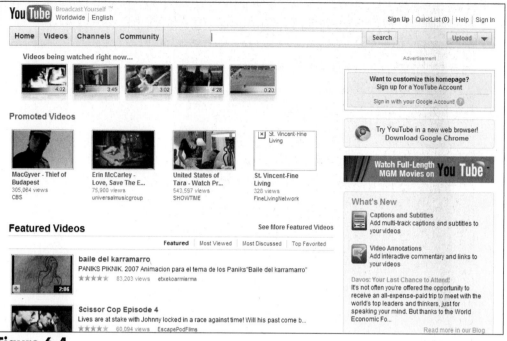

Figure 6-4

Check these tips when posting videos online:

⟹ Select a reputable service. You may want to use a dedicated video hosting company like YouTube, or you may want to post videos on your social networking site. Some ways to determine if the site is reputable are (1) have you heard of it? (2) has it received good reviews? (3) do you know anyone else using the service? (4) has there ever been a data breach on the service? (5) do they retain the right to use your material or do you control any use of your content?

⟹ Understand the site's Terms and Conditions. If it doesn't allow you to retain full control of your content, consider selecting a different site.

⟹ Before posting video content, consider all the information it contains in voice and images. If it includes personally identifiable information, consider restricting access to the video by making the site setting private so that only those you give access to can view it.

➡ Listen to what is said; words can also give away information about your identity and location.

➡ If the video shows friends or family members, you may be putting them at risk, too. You should obtain permission from everyone shown in the video before posting it.

➡ Remember that after you post information publicly, it can stay around forever and may pop up when you least expect it.

➡ If you see inappropriate content or comments on your video page, report it. The service should review the report and take appropriate action. You may choose to not even allow comments on your page if comments become a problem.

 While most Web sites have policies against pornography, violence, posting copyrighted material, and so on, they primarily rely heavily on users to report abuse (which means you have already been exposed to the abusive content) rather than filtering the content before it's uploaded. This means that you may come across a great deal of inappropriate material, so select search terms carefully.

Avoid Image Copyright Infringement

According to U.S. law, any artwork "in a fixed tangible form" automatically has copyright protection. Any use of a photo, video, or other artwork without express permission of the creator is an infringement of copyright. Unfortunately, on the Internet, copyrights are frequently disregarded and photos posted publicly are likely to be stolen or repurposed.

Consumers should be aware that anything they post online may be misused in inconsiderate, inappropriate, or even illegal ways. Do you part: Never violate a copyright or commit plagiarism with others' materials. If you don't own the image, you need to assume someone else does unless the images are on sites specifically offering the free use of images. When in doubt, contact the person who posted the image for permission.

Use Web Cams

Web cams are relatively inexpensive, and many laptops now come with Web cams embedded in their lids. (See **Figure 6-5**.) They are relatively inexpensive (many under $20).

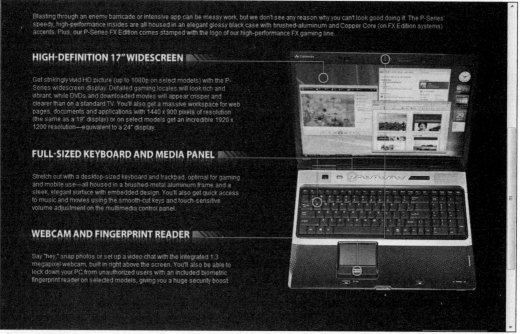

Figure 6-5

Web cams have revolutionized the way we can interact with friends and family from afar. They allow businesses to meet key people in places far away without having expensive travel. They are particularly great for grandparents who want to stay in touch with grandchildren and for parents who are divorced or traveling or away from home for extended periods and want to "see" their kids.

Like everything else, Web cams can also be used in negative ways. They have all the risk potential that sharing videos has, with lots of rich information in the background, and being able to hear and see the person in front of the lens, but they also allow for real-time interactions, not just viewing. This can make Web cams particularly concerning if they are used in conversations with strangers, or between teens in private as the conversations sometimes degrade into fairly graphic exposure.

Web cams can also be high-jacked and turned on remotely. This allows others to view and listen in without the individuals' knowing what is going on. When you aren't using your Web cam, consider turning it off, turning it to face the wall, or disconnect the Web cam if it isn't a built-in model.

 Teens in particular struggle to use good judgment when using Web cams. If you have grandchildren or other children in your care, realize that normal inhibitions seem to fall away when they aren't physically present with the person they're speaking to — and many expose themselves, figuratively and literally. In addition to having a conversation about appropriate Web cam use with children and teens, it may be wise to limit access to Web cams to specific times or in places where you have some oversight.

Save Photos and Videos in Different Formats

Photos and video files can be saved in a variety of formats. Unlike some software that saves files in its proprietary format (such as the .doc or .docx format for a Microsoft Word document or template file), most photo and video programs can save files in a variety of standardized formats, depending on your needs. Here's a quick rundown of the strengths of each.

Photos and other graphic images are often saved in one of these formats:

➥ **TIFF (tagged image file format):** If you're editing your photo, it's good to know that TIFF files retain their integrity better than formats like JPEG. However, TIFF compression isn't quite as efficient as some other formats, which can result in larger files.

➥ **GIF (graphics interchange format):** Files in this format have fewer colors, so they may work well on a Web site but aren't so great for printed photos. Their smaller sizes make them easier to exchange or share, although this format is more typically used for logos or other graphic objects rather than photos.

➥ **JPEG (Joint Photographic Experts Group):** The JPEG format often offers more options for controlling image quality. Use the lowest quality to most easily send JPEGs via e-mail or speed upload to an online site. Note that with this format, images degrade every time you save them.

Some common movie file formats include these:

➥ **MPEG (Moving Picture Experts Group):** This format was developed as an international standard for compression (squeezing memory-hog movies into a usable form). It's a common standard with good compression to save your movies in smaller-sized files.

➥ **AVI (Audio Video Interleave):** This format was developed by Microsoft, for Windows. This is probably one of the most popular formats for playing movie files, so many players support it.

➡ **MOV (the QuickTime movie format):** Originally created by Apple, the format has now become popular and can be played from computers with almost any operating system using the free QuickTime player. It's excellent at integrating text, graphics, video, animation, and 3D images in a single file.

➡ **RealVideo (from RealNetworks):** RealVideo uses streaming video, so you can watch a video while downloading it. Although it's a proprietary format that requires RealPlayer software to run (see **Figure 6**-6), it has a large group of users. (Which means that if you send someone such a file, he's likely to be able to play it.) And the free player supports various other movie formats.

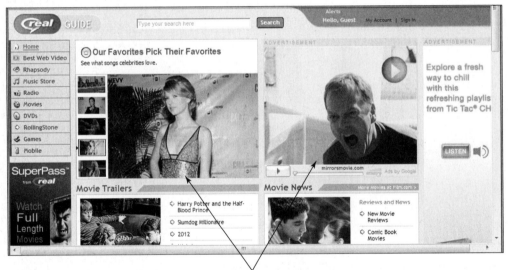

RealPlayer uses the RealVideo format

Figure 6-6

Sharing Your Information with Others

*T*he Internet offers many options for connecting with people and sharing information.

You'll find discussion boards and chat sites on a wide variety of sites, from news sites to recipe sites, sites focused around grief and health issues, and sites that host political- or consumer-oriented discussions.

There are some great senior chat rooms for making friends, and many sites allow you to create new chat rooms on topics at any time.

Another way people share information is through mini-comments on social journals (not to be confused with social networks). These sites, which limit any comment to no more than 140 characters (about three sentences), allow you to add your comments about your life in an ongoing stream of comments from many users. Creating rich, short messages has become almost an art form among devotees.

Instant messaging (IM), on the other hand, isn't a Web site but a service. Using software such as MSN Messenger, IM allows you to chat in real time with your contacts. You can access instant messaging programs via your computer or your cell phone.

As with any site where users share information (such as social networks and blogs, covered in Chapter 8, and e-mail, covered in Chapter 5), you can use these chats, discussions, social journals, and instant messaging programs safely if you know how to sidestep some abuses, including data mining for criminal intent, social engineering ploys, ID theft scams, and so forth. If you're careful to protect your privacy, you can enjoy socializing without worry.

In this chapter, we look at some ways of sharing information and we tell you how to do so safely. But first, you'll discover how information placed online accumulates. You aren't the only one to place it there.

Your Information Is Online, Even If You Aren't

Many people think that if they aren't active online, their information isn't exposed. But you aren't the only one sharing your information:

➡ **Employers:** Many employers share information about employees. Consider carefully how much information you're comfortable with sharing through an employee bio posted on your company Web site. How much should be visible to other employees on your intranet? When you attend a conference, is the attendee list shown in online conference documents? And even if you're retired, there may still be information about you on your old employer's Web site. Review the site to determine if it reveals more than you'd like it to — and ask your employer to take down or alter the information if needed.

➡ **Government agencies:** Some agencies post personal information, such as documents concerning your home purchase and property tax (see **Figure 7-1**), on publicly available Web sites. Government agencies may also post birth, marriage, and death certificates, and these documents may contain your social security number, loan number, copies of your signature, and so on. You should check government records carefully to see if private information is posted and demand that it be removed.

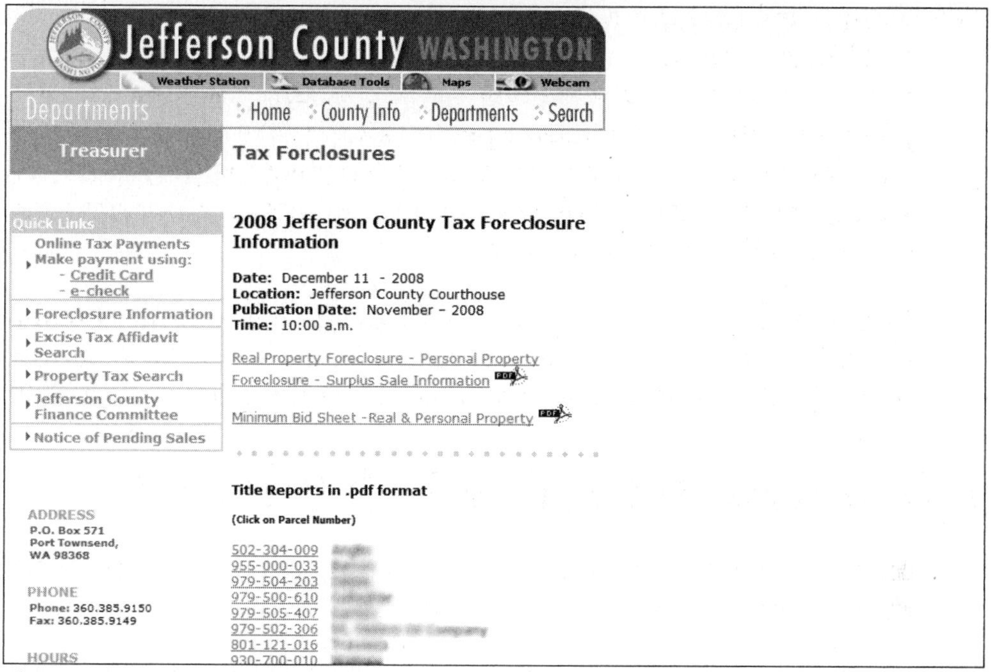

Figure 7-1

⟶ **Family members and friends:** They may write about you in their blogs or mention you on special-interest sites such as those focused on genealogy.

⟶ **Clubs and organizations:** Organizations with whom you volunteer, the church you attend, and professional associations may reveal facts such as your address, age, income bracket, and how much money you've donated.

⟶ **Newspapers:** If you've been featured in a newspaper article, you may be surprised to find the story, along with a picture of you or information about your work, activities, or family, by doing a simple online search. If you're interviewed, ask for the chance to review the information that the newspaper will include, and be sure that you're comfortable with exposing that information.

⇒ **Online directories:** Services such as www.white pages.com or www.anywho.com, shown in **Figure 7-2**, list your phone number and address, unless you specifically request that these be removed. You may be charged a small fee associated with removing your information — a so-called *privacy tax* — but you may find the cost worthwhile. Online directories often include the names of members of your family, your e-mail address, the value of your home, your neighbors' names and the values of their homes, an online mapping tool to provide a view of your home, driving directions to your home, and your age. The record may also include previous addresses, schools you've attended, and links for people to run background checks on you.

Online directories publicize personal information

Figure 7-2

Because services get new information from many sources, you'll need to check back periodically to see if your information has again been put online — if it has, contact the company or go through their removal process again.

 Try entering your home phone number in any browser's address line; chances are you'll get an online directory listing with your address and phone number (although this doesn't work for cell phone numbers).

Understand How Information Is Spread and Collected

Sharing personal information with friends and family enriches your relationships and helps you build new ones. The key is to avoid sharing information with the wrong people and shady companies because, just as in the real world, exposing your personal information online is one of your biggest risks.

Criminals come in all flavors, but the more savvy ones collect information in a very systematic way. Each piece of information is like another drop of water that, over time, collects to form a very clear picture of your life. And after criminals collect and organize the information, they never throw it away because they may be able to use it many times over.

Fortunately, information exposure is a risk you have a great deal of control over. Before sharing information, make sure that you're comfortable with how the recipient will use each type.

➡ **Address and phone number:** Abuse of this information results in you receiving increased telemarketing calls and junk mail. Although less common, this information may also increase a scammer's ability to steal your identity and make your home a more interesting target for break-ins.

➡ **Names of husband/wife, father, and mother (including mother's maiden name), siblings, children, and grandchildren:** This information is very interesting to criminals, who can use it to gain your confidence and then scam you, or use it to guess your passwords or secret question answers, which often include family members' names. This information may also expose additional family members to ID theft, fraud, and personal harm.

→ **Information about your car:** Limit access to license plate numbers; VINs (vehicle identification numbers); registration information; make, model, and title number of car; your insurance carrier's name, coverage limits, loan information, and driver's license number. The key criminal abuse of this information includes car theft (or theft of parts of the car) and insurance fraud. The type of car you drive may also indicate your financial status, and that adds one more piece of information to the pool of data criminals collect about you.

→ **Information about work history:** In the hands of criminals, your work history can be very useful for "authenticating" the fraudster and convincing people and organizations to provide them with more of your financial records or identity.

→ **Information about your credit status:** This information can be abused in so many ways that any time you're asked to provide this online, your answer should be *no*. Don't fall for the temptation to check your credit scores for free through sites that aren't guaranteed reputable. Another frequent abuse of credit information is found in free mortgage calculators that ask you to put in all kinds of personal information in order for them to determine what credit you qualify for. See Chapter 13 for more about financial safety online.

Many people leave messages on their e-mail letting people know when they'll be away from their offices. This is really helpful for colleagues, but exercise caution and limit who you provide the information to. Leaving a message that says, "Gone 11/2-11/12. I'm taking the family to Hawaii for ten days," may make you a prime target for burglary. And you'll probably never make the connection between the information you exposed and the offline crime.

You may need to show your work history, particularly on resumes you post on Internet job or business networking sites. Be selective about where you post this information, create a separate e-mail account to list on the resume, and tell what kinds of work you've done rather than give specifics about which companies and what dates. Interested, legitimate employers can then contact you privately, and you won't have given away your life history to the world. After you've landed the job, take down your resume. Think of it as risk management — when you need a job, the risk of information exposure is less than the need to get the job.

Consider the Cumulative Effect

Every detail you or others share online about your life and the extended group of people you interact with is stored *somewhere*. That information may be copied, posted in other locations, and perhaps stay online for a very, very long time. Understanding the way this information accumulates, and how permanent that information may be, is critical.

Over the years, you may have built quite a profile of yourself through items you and others have posted about you online, including the following:

➡ Resumes

➡ Blogs you've written

➡ Comments in discussion groups

➡ Information you've posted in wedding or baby registries (see **Figure 7-3**) or on grief sites

➡ Articles you've published in your professional life

➡ Government records

➡ Friends' Web sites

➡ Clubs, church groups, and other organizations

Those who want to build a picture of you can work from all that information and, potentially, offline sources of information. Before you share information online, consider how sensitive the information may be, how you'd feel if it was abused, and who (including which companies) you want to share the information with.

Gift registries can expose personal information

Figure 7-3

If the information is restricted to a site that isn't available to the general public, has a strong password, and respects your privacy, there should be little risk in sharing with friends and family. If the information is something you're comfortable sharing with the general public, feel free to do so. However, if the information identifies you, your possessions, or someone else in some way, you may want to limit access to that information or not post it at all.

Find Yourself Online

Start by getting an idea of what information about you is online. Make sure you're using a browser such as Internet Explorer or Firefox that shows you if the Web sites that appear in your search results are legitimate by including a ranking icon and information about level of risk for activities such as frequency of downloaded malware. Or make sure that you have a product such as McAfee Site Advisor installed.

1. Navigate to your favorite search engine, such as www.google.com, and enter your name in the search field.

2. Click the **Go** or **Search** button (depending on your browser) to search for your information.

3. In the results (see **Figure** 7-4), ignore any listing that obviously isn't you. If you see a listing that might concern you, and your browser/site adviser considers the link safe, click it to open the Web page. Or you can enter the site URL in your browser address field to go there.

4. Scan the contents to see what information about you is displayed and evaluate whether you're comfortable with that information online. In some cases, you may want to request that the site owner removes part or all of your information.

Look for your name in the search results

Figure 7-4

5. Click the **Back** button (the left-pointing arrow) to go back to the search results and continue to review listings about you.

You should use at least a couple of search engines (such as Yahoo!, Google, Ask.com, and so on), as they're likely to find slightly different results. In addition, use online directories, such as www.white pages.com and www.anywho.com, to search for your address information.

Visit government sites that might list information about family marriages, births, and deaths, home purchases, property tax, school records, and powers of attorney.

If you find listings you want to ask a site to remove, find and click the **Contact Us** link on the site and submit an e-mail requesting that the information be removed. Not every site will do this, but it's worth a try if the information reveals too much about you. Persistence helps.

 You may want to build a list of sites that contain information about you, and you can easily do this within your browser by bookmarking (saving) the links to those sites. In Internet Explorer, for example, use the Add to Favorites tool to save any open Web site addresses so you can find them again easily.

 You may not be able to convince government sites to remove all information from public access (by law, some information is public), but no law says that it has to be online. For many people, these records contain far more information than is legally required, and all too often the records contain information that can place you at economic and personal risk. At the very least, when you know what information about you is public, you'll be much less likely to fall for requests from people who seem legitimate just because they know some of your personal information.

Respect Other People's Information

You know what's okay to say about your friends in the physical world, but consider some differences in talking to, or about, others online.

➡ The first thing to consider is who will see your words online. In face-to-face conversations, you see who you're talking to and modify your comments to fit the situation. Over the phone, you know who's on the call and can do the same. Online, however, you may or may not know who will read what you say because recipients forward e-mails, a friend may change permissions for accessing a social networking page, and so on.

➡ If someone else's site (or your site) is locked down to just friends you both know, you can use the same considerations as you would face-to-face or over the phone.

➡ If you don't know who else may see the interaction, you have to assume that anyone can see it; respect your friends' privacy as you would expect them to respect yours. It's rude to expose information about someone — including pictures and videos — without permission.

 How do you know what information your friends and family are willing to expose? It's low tech, but the only way you'll know what they want kept private is to *ask them*; and the only way for them to know what you want private is to *tell them*.

Spot How People Expose Others

You may be surprised to discover how much you may inadvertently expose about others, especially on *social networking sites*, which host personal journals that often contain mention of people other than the author. **Figure 7-5** shows a public social networking site of a woman who made her profile anonymous. She didn't give her name, used a photo of her cat instead of herself, didn't provide her age or city, and mentioned only her state. But three comments by friends completely exposed her. Read through these postings to her blog and find the information that was exposed:

➡ Her name is Blanche O'Connelly, her birthdate is July 16th, and she turns 66 in 2009.

➡ You know where her party is going to be held, where she lives, and the name of the hospital where she volunteers. (Her state combined with the hospital name gives it away.)

➡ You know where to find her and how to identify her. (She'll be with her friend, and you know what her friend looks like.)

➡ A friend has also provided her telephone number.

➡ In addition, all of these friends have photos of Blanche on their sites — you know who Blanche is because the photo captions show her name.

That's a lot of information to expose about someone who went to great lengths to remain private. There are two problems here: Although Blanche did a lot to protect her privacy, she didn't tell her friends that her privacy was important to her, and Blanche's friends were disrespectful by posting identifiable information about her without first learning her privacy boundaries.

Chris		*7/16/09 6:14 pm* Hey, happy birthday, Blanche! Your 66th will be a Lucky year! I can't seem to find your cell phone number. Is it 555-1082? Maybe send me an e-mail with directions to your party?
Mary		*7/16/09 5:37 pm* Darn, O'Connelly, you're finally growing up ☺. The party's at Cafe Richelieu, right? Hey Karen, nice "do".
KSwift		*7/14/09 4:30 pm* *Blanche, dear, we'll be in Taos this weekend so can't make your party. Let's meet at the cafeteria at Bridger Women's Hospital on Monday during your morning coffee break. Check out my new hairdo!*

Figure 7-5

Use Discussion Boards

A *discussion board* is a place where you can post written messages, pictures, and videos on a topic. Others can reply to you, and you can reply to their postings.

Discussion boards are *asynchronous,* which means that you post a message (just as you might on a bulletin board at the grocery store) and wait for a response. Somebody might read it that hour — or ten days or several weeks after you make the posting. In other words, the response isn't instantaneous, and the message isn't usually directed to a specific individual.

You can find a discussion board about darn-near every topic under the sun, and these are tremendously helpful when you're looking for answers. They're also a great way to share your expertise — whether you chime in on how to remove an ink stain, provide history trivia about button styles on military uniforms, or announce the latest break-throughs in your given field. Postings are likely to stay up on the site for years for people to reference.

1. To try one, enter this URL in your browser address field: `www.microsoft.com/communities/newsgroups/en-us/default.aspx`.

2. On the left side of the screen, click **English** (or another language of your choice) and then click a topic area, such as **Home and Entertainment**.

3. In the topic list that appears, click another topic, such as **Games,** to see more options. Continue to click until you get to a specific discussion board, such as the one shown in **Figure 7-6**.

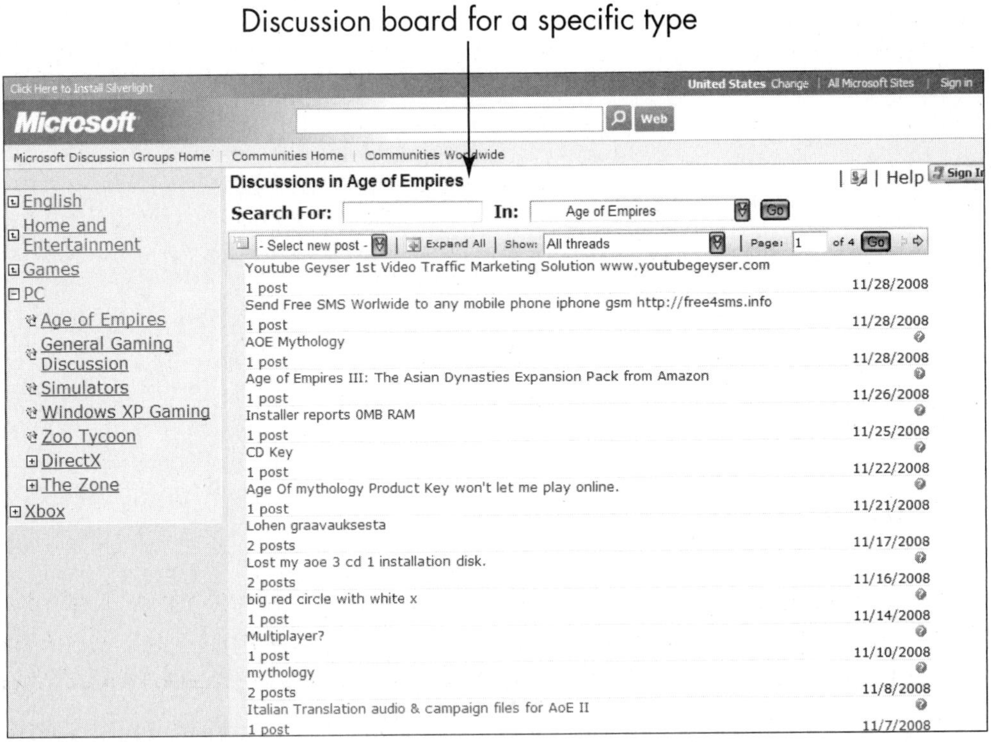

Discussion board for a specific type

Figure 7-6

4. When you click a posting that has replies, you'll see that they are organized in the middle of page in easy-to-follow *threads*, which arrange postings and replies in an outline-like structure. You can review the various participants' comments as they add their ideas to the entire conversation.

5. To reply to a posting yourself, click the **Reply** button, fill in your comments (see **Figure 7-7**), and click **Post**.

Comment on a posting here

Reply to "Problem with Age of Mythology ..."

| Post In Discussion Group | microsoft.public.ageofempires |

Subject
RE: Problem with Age of Mythology Cursors
Message
Thanks for the great information. I struggled with this myself but now I know how to fix it.

"Zagorath" wrote:

> I have age of mythology: gold edition, and it installed fine and works
> perfectly except for one minor problem with the cursors. A number of the

Your Display Name
Your display name is shown with your posts in the discussion groups. Try to make yours unique, and try not to change it so that others can more easily recognize you.

Nanc7y

Terms of Use
Please read and accept the Terms of Use to enable the Post button. You will only have to accept once.

Terms of Use

By clicking I Accept, you are agreeing to the Terms of Use.

Also, by offering comments and/or materials through this page you give Microsoft full permission to use them freely to improve our products. For suggestion submissions, we can't guarantee we will use your suggestions. Due to the volume and variety of suggestions, we can't provide compensation or attribution. We appreciate your input.

◉ I accept ◯ I do not accept

As is the practice of other software programs that interact with USENET communities, the IP Address of your computer will be included in the header of this post. More....

☐ Notify me of replies   [Post] [Close]

(Please read and accept the Terms of Use to enable the Post button...)

Cross-post to these discussion groups

(use full USENET designation)

Figure 7-7

Participate in Chat

A *chat room* is an online space where groups of people can talk back and forth via text, audio, Web camera, or a combination of media. (See **Figure 7-8**, which shows a Web site that links to hundreds of chat rooms.) In chat, you're having a conversation with one or more people in real time, and your entire conversation appears in the chat window. Here are some characteristics of chat you should know:

⟶ When the chat is over, unless you save a copy, the conversation is typically gone.

⟶ Interactions are in *real time* (synchronous), which means you can interact with others in the moment.

⟶ Several people can interact at once, although this can take getting used to as you try to follow what others are saying and jump in with your own messages.

⟶ When you find a chat you want to participate in, you simply enter the chat room, enter your message, and submit it. It shows up in the stream of comments and others may — or may not — reply to it.

 When you're talking to someone in a chat room that multiple people are visiting, you can, if you'd like invite him to enter a private chat room, which keeps the rest of the folks who wandered into the chat room out of your conversation. Also, others can invite you into *private chat rooms*. Be careful who you interact with in this way, and be sure you understand the motivations for making your conversation private. This may be entirely reasonable, or it may be that you're dealing with someone with suspect motivations.

 Before you get started, check out the Web site's Terms of Use, privacy, and monitoring and abuse reporting procedures to understand the safety protections in place before joining a conversation. Some sites are well monitored for signs of abusive content or interactions; others have no monitoring at all. If you don't like the terms, find a different site.

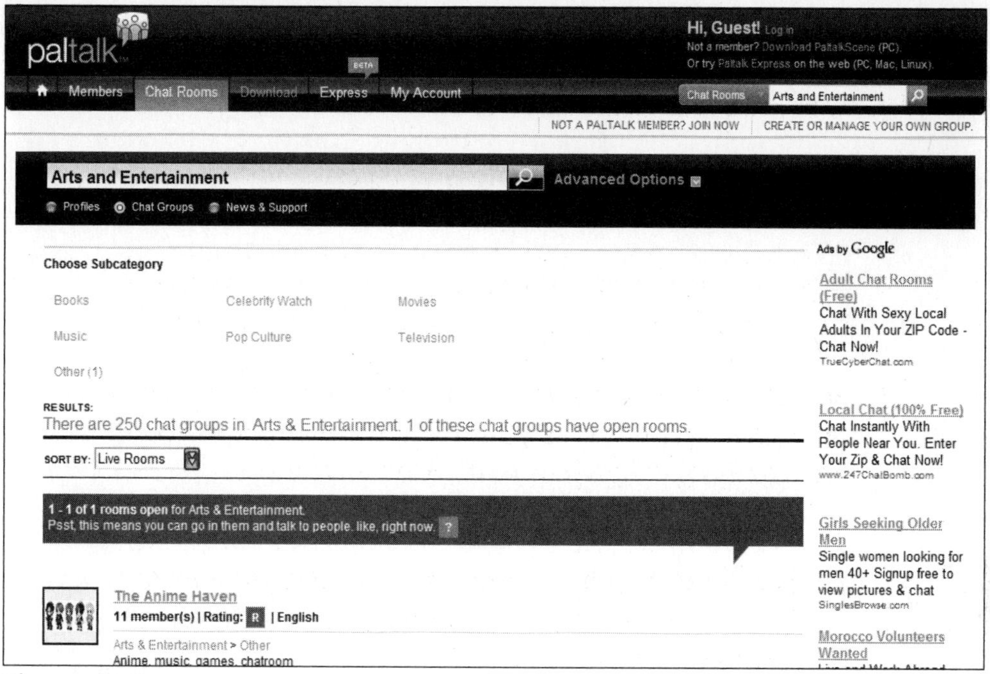

Figure 7-8

Contribute to Social Journaling Sites

Social journaling sites are like collective blogs in real time, in that they ask everybody visiting to throw in their two cents, often about a specific question such as "What are you doing right now?" The Web site might show the various comments in a moving timeline, as on Plurk.com. (See **Figure 7-9**.)

Consider these safety tips when using social journaling sites:

⟶ As with other social networking types of sites, be careful about the profile you create for yourself when you join and how much information it gives away.

⟶ Don't reveal too much personal information in your publicly viewable comments. This is harder to do than you might imagine because little bits of information add up. One time you say, "I'm headed out for my Pilates class," and the reader notices it's Tuesday at 6:15 p.m. You probably have the class every week at that time. Another comment says, "Volunteering for Emily's class at Carl Sandburg," and the time is 11:15 a.m. A reader learns that you volunteer and you know a little girl (probably related) at a specific elementary school. Between friends, this intimacy can be a wonderful exchange, but with the public, it quickly represents a level of risk you may not welcome.

➡ These sites often ask you to see if your friends are on online; they do this by searching your e-mail contacts database, which gives them access to all your family, friends and acquaintances.

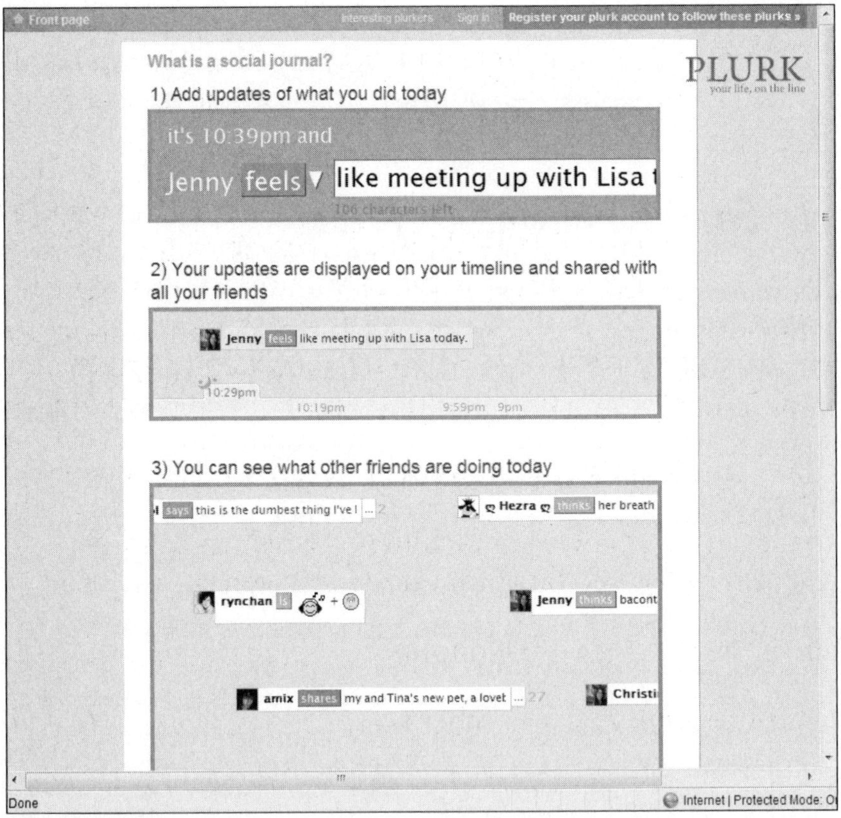

Figure 7-9

See Chapter 8 for more about social networking and blogs.

 One of the most popular companies offering this functionality are Twitter (elite users are called the *Twitterati*). Nearly a thousand entries were received for Twitter's first haiku writing contest in November 2008. On average, most people have about 10 people following their comments, and they follow about 10 other people's comments themselves.

Send and Receive Instant Messages (IMs)

Instant messaging (often called just *IMing*) used to be referred to as real-time e-mail. It used to onlybe *synchronous,* meaning that two (or more) parties could communicate in real time, without any delay. It still offers synchronous communication, but now you can also leave a message that the recipient can pick up later.

Instant messaging is a great way to stay in touch with the younger generations, who rarely use e-mail. IM is ideal for quick little messages where you just want an answer without forming a formal e-mail, as well as for touching base and saying hi. Text messaging on cell phones is largely the same phenomena: This isn't a tool you'd typically use for a long, meaningful conversation, but it's great for quick exchanges.

Depending on the IM service you use, you can do the following:

➡ Write notes to friends, grandchildren, or whoever, as long as they use the same IM service that you're using.

➡ Talk as if you were on the phone.

➡ Send photos, videos, and other files.

➠ Use little graphical images, called *emoticons* (such as smilies or winks) and *avatars,* to add fun to your IM messages.

➠ See participants via Web cameras.

➠ Get and send e-mail.

➠ Search the Web, find others using Global Positioning System (GPS) technology, listen to music, watch videos, play games, bid on auctions, find dates, and more.

➠ Track the history of conversations and even save transcripts of them to review later.

Instant messaging programs vary somewhat, and you have several to choose from, including Windows Live Messenger (available at `http://download.live.com/?sku=messenger`), Yahoo! Messenger (available at `http://messenger.yahoo.com`), and AOL Instant Messenger, also know as AIM, (available at `www.aim.com`).

To get started with a new messaging program, you need to follow the general steps in the upcoming list. But as with any software, if you aren't sure how to use its features, consult its Help documentation for specific instructions.

1. Download and install the messaging program according to the instructions on the provider's Web site.

2. Set up an account and sign in; this may simply involve entering your e-mail address and password.

 You can send IMs from a computer to a mobile phone (and vice versa) and from one mobile phone to another. If you include your mobile phone number as part of your IM profile, anyone who can see your profile can view it. This is useful information for friends *and criminals*, so it's important to consider whether you want your number exposed — especially if you have many people on your contact list who you don't personally know.

3. Click a contact to initiate your conversation. (You can import contacts from your e-mail contacts when you sign up, or you can add them yourself.)

4. Click the phone button or icon to initiate a phone call.

 IM programs let your contacts see when you're online, unless you change your settings to hide this information — something that's good to know when you're busy and don't have time to chat. You can choose availability settings such as Online, Busy, Be Right Back, Out to Lunch, or even display your status as Offline, even when you aren't. In the Windows Live Messenger IM program shown in Figure 7-10, click the arrow next to your name to access such a list.

IM is one place where people use shortcut text. Some of this will be familiar to you, such as FYI (for your information) and ASAP (as soon as possible). Other short text may be less familiar, such as LOL (laughing out loud). Visit `http://look-both-ways.com/stayingsafe/IM.htm#having_trouble` for a table of common shortcut text terms. Knowing these will make communicating with younger folks more fun.

Click this arrow to change your status

Figure 7-10

Safety Tips for Instant Messaging

Get the instant messaging bug, but just consider this safety advice first:

➡ Choose a safe screen name that doesn't give away personal information.

➡ Most programs let you upload a photo or create a cartoon character that represents you, called an *avatar*. Some people choose to use their own photo, and some use photos of pets or objects that represent them (their sailboat, for example).

Deciding to share your photo depends on whether you talk to friends only, and how you feel about having your photo publicly available. Consider what your photo tells people about you, including your age, ethnic background, identifiable objects in the background, economic status, and so on.

➡ Consider who you want to use IM with. You create buddy lists in instant messaging programs and enter the online addresses of people with whom you want to exchange instant messages. Most services allow you to block messages from anyone not on your buddy list. (See **Figure 7-11.**) Remember: A friend of a friend is often a stranger.

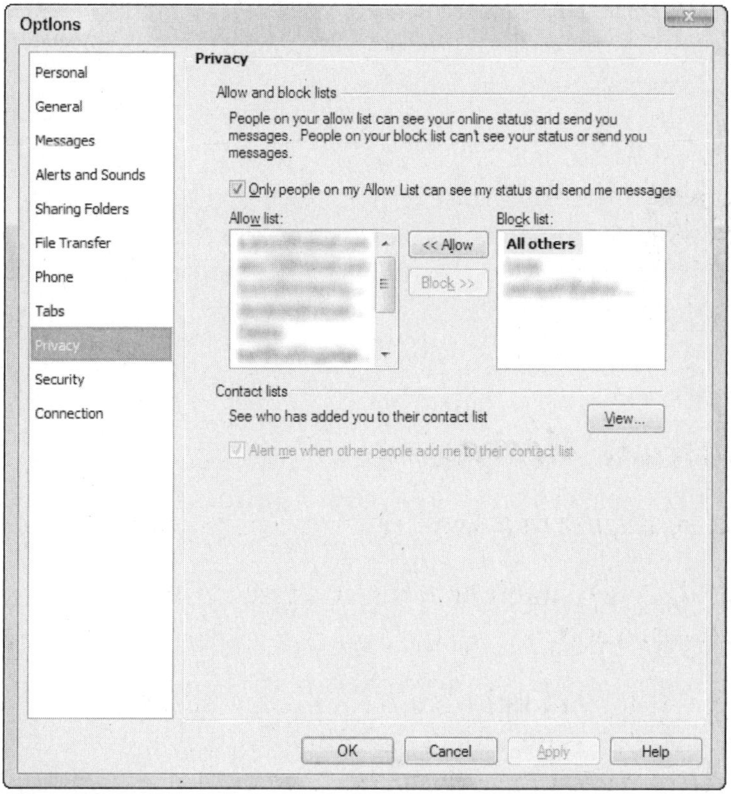

Figure 7-11

➡ Sending photos, documents, and links in IM is an easy and convenient way to share with others. Just think twice before opening attachments or clicking links in instant messages. Make sure that you know the sender, are communicating with that person at the time, or are expecting the material. Links or attachments sent out of context may indicate that the sender's IM has been infected with a virus, and opening the attachments or clicking the links will then infect you and send the virus to all of the people in *your* address book. There are many things that are great to share; computer viruses aren't.

➡ Understand that IM isn't a totally secure communication channel. Your conversation will probably never be snooped on, but for safety's sake, don't share sensitive personal information such as passwords, social security numbers, credit card information, and the like in IM messages.

➡ Be careful about the information you show in your status bar, where you can leave short messages and show your mood. Avoid showing emotions to people you don't know well. Don't expose yourself to burglary by saying that you're headed out of town on a specific date.

➡ Most services allow you to keep your online status private so that you simply appear to be offline. But of course, that means your friends don't know when you're online either.

➡ You may get an invitation to join someone else's IM buddy list, or a request to add someone to your buddy list. Before adding people to your list or joining other people's lists, be sure you know who they are. Many scammers use names that make you feel comfortable. Once added, they send *spim* (IM spam) and malicious links, or they try to gain your trust for confidence tricks — or flood you with pornography.

➡ If you use a Web camera with IM, be careful that you don't expose visual information to a stranger, such as the location of your home or office, images of your home that expose your financial status, or your possessions.

➡ If anyone sends you inappropriate material, report it. If you need to document the material to report it to the police, don't shut down the computer; instead, minimize the application or turn off *the monitor* only and seek advice on how to report the occurrence. Inform your ISP (Internet service provider) and the police, if appropriate.

➡ Be cautious about meeting up with someone you know only through IM. If you decide to meet someone, never go alone, meet in a busy public place, and make sure your loved ones know where you're going and when to expect to hear from you. Always have your cell phone handy.

➡ Think about how to use the IM features safely. For example, some IM games may contain mature material, and you might want to limit voice and video interactions with people you haven't met.

➡ One great feature that also has great risk in IM is the ability to give someone else remote access to your computer. This is great if you need help fixing something that isn't working. Just make sure that you totally trust the person you're giving access to. Remember that you need to trust two things: that she won't make the problem worse and that she won't snoop through everything you've stored on your computer. Never give anyone but the most trusted individuals this kind of access to your computer via IM.

➡ Report harassment or bullying to your IM service provider. As in real life, this is unacceptable behavior, and in some cases, it can be illegal. Every service

should have a clearly visible Report Abuse function
(see **Figure** 7-12); if it doesn't consider switching
providers. If you feel physically threatened, contact
your local law enforcement agency immediately.

 Consider what you're saying and sharing in IM and
how you'd feel if the information was made public.
IM allows you to store your conversation history,
which is super useful if you need to go back and check
something that was said. But it has its downside.
Anything you include in IM can be forwarded to others. If you're at work, keep in mind that many
employers monitor IM (and e-mail) conversations.

 If you run across illegal content — such as child
pornography — downloading or continuing to view
this for any reason is illegal. Report the incident to
law enforcement immediately.

Always report abuse, harassment, and bullying

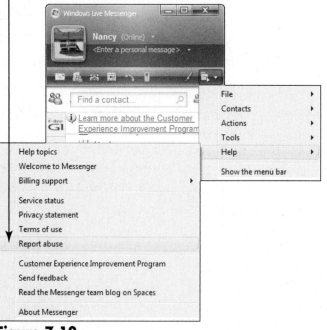

Figure 7-12

Getting the Most from Social Networks and Blogging

In this chapter . . .

*T*he Internet provides rich opportunities for making new friends, getting in touch with old friends, finding romance, and sharing interests with others . . . but there are some risks to think about.

When you meet a person offline, you have visual clues as to her age, gender, and general demeanor. Online, you have to find new ways to assess social contacts, and you have to be cautious about how much you expose about yourself before you're sure who you're dealing with.

Whether you're posting a *blog* (online journal) on a *social networking site* (which is a category of Web site where people share their thoughts, images, or videos) or using a dating site, you may encounter risks from individual predators who want to take advantage of your emotions or steal your money. You might also unwittingly provide information to companies who want to mine your data. They might use this data for marketing campaigns directed at you and/or sell your data to others.

Although teens make up a large percentage of social networkers, they aren't the largest user segment. In fact, millions of adults and seniors are also active on social networking sites. Some social networking sites exist for very specific purposes — such as creating business contacts — but most of the popular sites offer a wide variety of functionality. These sites are likely to host blogs, photo and video albums, classified ads, forums, e-mail, instant messaging, and entertainment.

Social networking sites allow people to build and maintain online networks of friends and others with common interests. They open up great new opportunities to share, communicate, and meet new people. However, social networking products and services have widely different levels of protections for consumers, and it's important that you understand the safety and privacy protection of any service you choose to use.

In this chapter, you discover some of the things you can do to stay safe as you roam social sites.

Overview of Collaborative and Social Networking Sites

Although you may think kids are the most active group using social networking, you can see from the table in **Figure 8-1** that it isn't the case. In fact, persons 35–54 years old make up the largest segment of social networkers.

There are several types of sites where people collaborate or communicate socially. The following definitions may be useful:

➡ **Wiki:** A Web site that allows anyone visiting to contribute (add, edit, or remove) content. Wikipedia, for example, is a virtual encyclopedia built by users providing information in their areas of expertise. Because of the ease of collaboration, wikis are often used when developing group projects or sharing information collaboratively.

➡ **Blog:** An online journal (*blog* is short for *web log*) that may be entirely private, open to select friends or family, or available to the general public. You can usually adjust your blog settings to restrict visitors from commenting on your blog entries, if you'd like.

➡ **Social networking site:** This type of Web site (see **Figure 8-2**) allows people to build and maintain online Web pages and create networks of people that they're somehow connected to — their friends, work associates, and/or other members with similar interests. Most social networking sites also host blogs and have social networking functions that allow people to view information about others and contact each other.

Social networking isn't a 'teen phenomenon'

August 2006
Demographic Profile of Visitors to Select Social Networking Sites -Percent Composition of Total Unique Visitors   Total U.S. – Home/Work/University Locations

	Percent (%) Composition of Unique Visitors				
	Total Internet	MySpace. com	Facebook. com	Friendster. com	Xanga. com
Unique Visitors (000)	173,407	55,778	14,782	1,043	8,066
Total Audience	100.0	100.0	100.0	100.0	100.0
Persons: 12-17	9.6	11.9	14.0	10.6	20.3
Persons: 18-24	11.3	18.1	34.0	15.6	15.5
Persons: 25-34	14.5	16.7	8.6	28.2	11.0
Persons: 35-54	38.5	40.6	33.5	34.5	35.6
Persons: 55+	18.0	11.0	7.6	8.1	7.3

Figure 8-1
Source: Score Media Matrix

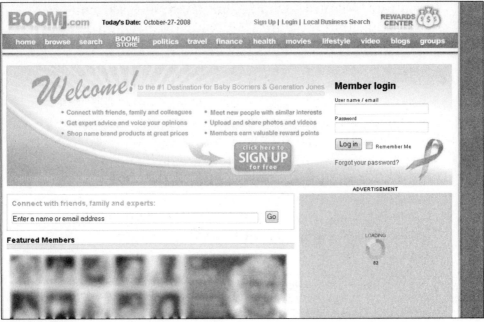

Figure 8-2

Tips for Safe Blogging

Simply put, blogs are online journals. Just as with any journal, the blog owner (or *blogger*) can hold forth on any subject he or she wants to, in words, photos, or videos. But unlike traditional journals, entries can also include videos, links to Web sites, search tools, and quizzes. Depending on your settings and the site's privacy policy, millons of people may view your blog.

Each blog entry usually contains a title, a date stamp, the blogger's name, and the blogger's comments. (See **Figure 8-3**.) It may also include a profile of the author and a photo or videos.

Here are 12 steps to take to stay safe while blogging:

➧ Make sure the blogging site you use has clear privacy and security policies and outlines how the site will respond to reports of abuse. The site should offer site monitors and tools to help protect your safety, such as a way to control who has permission to see your blog, the ability to block harassing users, and a setting that allows you to turn coments off.

➡ Read the terms and conditions of the blog site. (See **Figure 8-4**.) Even some of the most popular blog and social networking sites have clauses that give the service the right to use anything you post in any way they choose. Choose a service that respects your right to own your content and keep your privacy.

➡ Think carefully about how public you want your blog to be. If your blog isn't set to private, anyone can visit and possibly comment on what you're saying or posting. Most blog sites default to public access, and you have to change the setting to make your blog private.

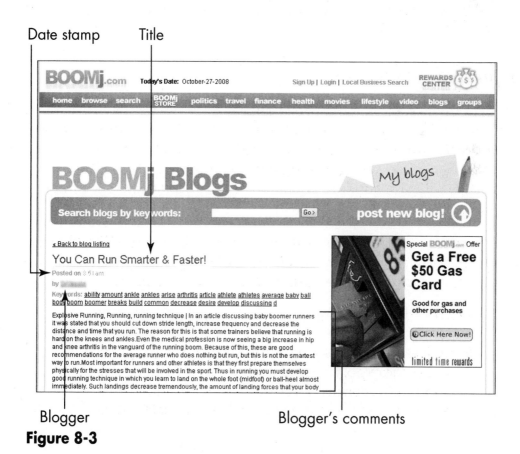

Date stamp   Title

Blogger   Blogger's comments

Figure 8-3

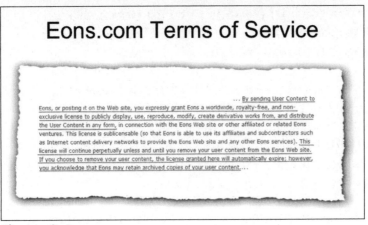

Eons.com Terms of Service

... By sending User Content to Eons, or posting it on the Web site, you expressly grant Eons a worldwide, royalty-free, and non-exclusive license to publicly display, use, reproduce, modify, create derivative works from, and distribute the User Content in any form, in connection with the Eons Web site or other affiliated or related Eons ventures. This license is sublicensable (so that Eons is able to use its affiliates and subcontractors such as Internet content delivery networks to provide the Eons Web site and any other Eons services). This license will continue perpetually unless and until you remove your user content from the Eons Web site. If you choose to remove your user content, the license granted here will automatically expire; however, you acknowledge that Eons may retain archived copies of your user content....

Figure 8-4

The more personal or identifiable the information you share, the fewer people you should share it with. If you choose to make your blog public, disclose only information that you want anyone and everyone in the world to know.

➡ Periodically review who has access to your site and make changes if necessary. Friends change over time, and once-trusted people may become less trusted.

➡ Keep identifying details to yourself and close friends.

- Think carefully before using your real name on your site (or anyone else's real name, either). Create a nickname or screen name that doesn't attract the wrong kind of attention or allow someone to find you.

- Be cautious about giving information that puts you on the map. Don't mention such details as your address, where you work, or even your town name (especially if it's a small town).

➡ On blogs that are set to be viewable by the general public, be smart about the photos you post. Consider these things:

- What's in the background? Does the photo show your house number, a street sign, a license plate, or landmark?

- Did you caption your photos with full names or other identifying details?

- What's printed on your shirt? Don't post photos that show the name of your bowling team or crafts club.

- Who's in the picture? If it shows friends or family members, you may be putting them at risk, too.

- Can someone tell your economic status from the photo? This may be an enticement for offline crime.

➠ Be careful about sharing your feelings if your blog is public. You can express feelings in your blog in various ways. The poems you select, the music you list, and the pictures you post all tell a lot about who you are and how you feel. This allows a predator who's on the hunt to find opportunities to prey on your vulnerability. Whether what you reveal is greed, sadness, anger, or even happiness, there is always a scam or exploit that can be tailored to take advantage of it.

➠ Check out what your friends write about you in their blogs. They may be giving out your address or real name or revealing which church you go to, or perhaps they have a photo of you on their site with a caption indicating who you are. Any of these actions may enable someone to find you. Check the comments friends leave on your blog to make sure they don't give away personal details.

➠ Be very cautious about meeting in person someone you know only through blogging. As with online dates, keep first meetings with blogging buddies short, and agree to meet in a public place during a busy time of day.

➡ If there's a problem on your blog or on a blog that includes information about you, report it immediately. No one has the right to threaten or upset you. If anyone (even someone you know) behaves threateningly or asks lots of personal questions, report the problem. Every service should make it easy to report abuse; if your blogging service doesn't, consider switching providers.

➡ Talk to your family about the kinds of information they're willing to make public and what they'd rather keep private. Posting information about others isn't okay — in comments, photos, and so on — unless they agree to share that information. When asking permission to share, make clear who can see your site.

➡ Before changing your settings to be more public, it's your obligation to again seek permission from all people you may expose. If they aren't comfortable with additional exposure, remove any content about them from your site.

Sign Up for a Social Networking Service

When signing up for a service, understand what is **required** information and what is optional. You should clearly understand why a Web service needs any of your personally identifiable information and how they may use that information — before providing it. Consider carefully the questions that sites ask users to complete in creating a profile.

 Accepting a social networking service's default settings may expose more information than you intend.

Walk through the signup process for Eons, a senior social networking site, to see the kinds of information they ask for. Follow these instructions to do so:

1. Type this URL into your browser address line: www.eons.com.

2. Click the **Sign Up** button.

3. In the signup form that appears (see **Figure 8-5**), enter your name, e-mail address, a password, your birthdate, gender, and zip code.

Note that the site requires your birthdate to verify that you are a senior, but you can choose to hide this information from others later if you don't want it displayed. (We recommend hiding your birthdate.)

4. Click **Sign Up**. On the screen that appears (see **Figure 8-6**), note that your actual name is the screen name that members will see. We recommend you change this by highlighting the text and typing your alias over it.

Consider nicknames and the messages they send. Names like `lookin'forlove` or `lonelyinHouston` may send a message that you're lonely and emotionally vulnerable.

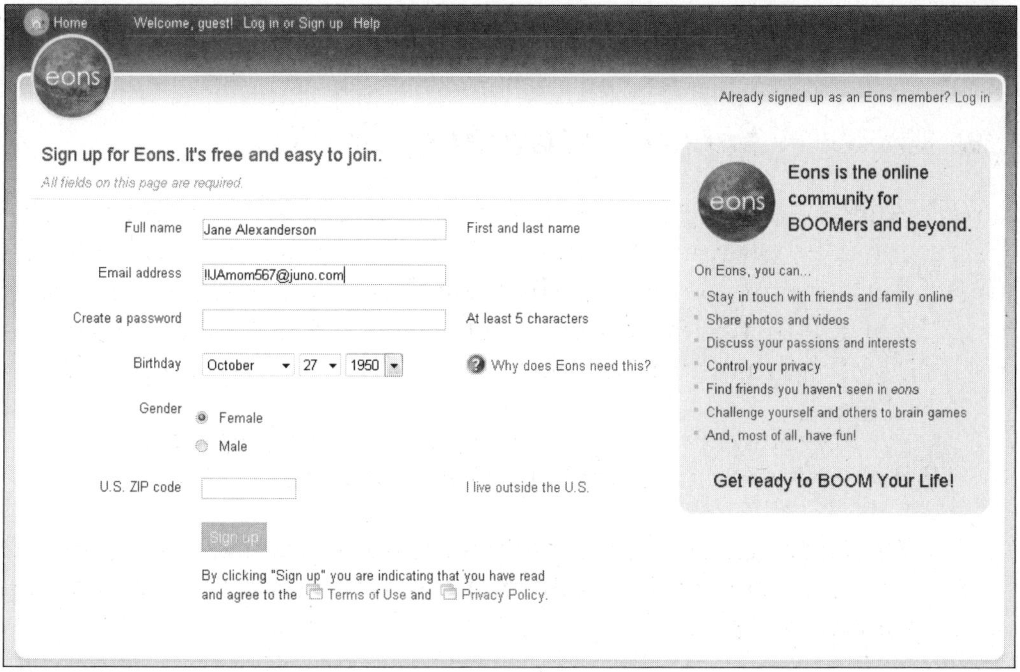

Figure 8-5

Change your screen name

See if your new screen name is available

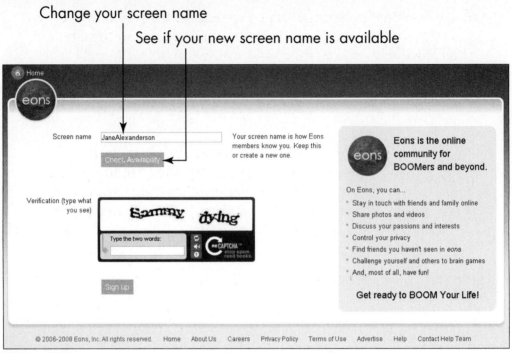

Figure 8-6

5. Click **Check Availability** to see if the alias you entered is available or already in use as a screen name. If the screen name you request is already taken, choose another screen name and try again.

6. Type the word or phrase shown in the **Verification** field and click **Sign Up**.

7. At this point, you're instructed to check your e-mail account for a message. When you receive the message, click the link in it to confirm your e-mail address.

8. Note that after you verify your e-mail address, a confirmation appears, offering a link to enhance your profile. Click that link.

9. Scroll to the bottom of the page. In the last paragraph on the page, click the **Privacy Settings** link.

10. On the Privacy Settings page (see **Figure 8-7**), note which settings default to Everyone, allowing anyone on the site to view your information, see you recent activity, comment on your blog, contact you, and so on.

11. Change any privacy settings you wish and click **Save**.

Remember that social networking sites sometimes ask for information during signup that they use to provide you with a customized experience that suits your needs. But sometimes the information isn't needed for the service they're providing you at all — they simply want it for marketing purposes, to show to other members, or to sell.

It's often very difficult to remove information from sites if you later regret the amount of information you've shared. It's best to be conservative in the information you share during the signup process; you can always add more later.

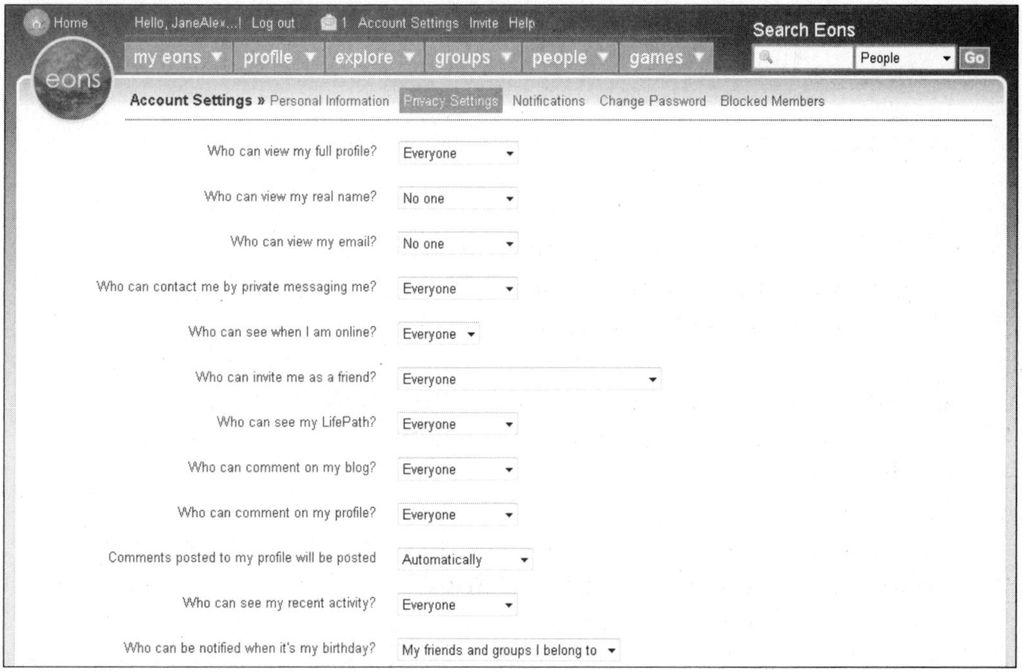

Figure 8-7

Spam and Other Malware on Blogs and Social Networks

Advertisers understand the value of blogs. Legitimate advertisers pay to have their ads posted on the sites; disreputable advertisers often create fake user profiles and blog sites for their marketing campaigns. These run the gamut of legal to entirely illegal offers. These fake blog sites are called *splogs* (*splog* is short for spam blog), and they can be an annoying and potentially harmful form of spam.

Some splog ads appear as comments that get spammed onto social networking sites. These typically include links to sites that may place malware on your computer, or they may contain content that's offensive to you. This is a good reason for you to make settings to your blog so that you can review and approve comments before they are posted, if such settings are available. See Chapter 5 for more about spam and Chapter 15 for more about malware and how to protect your computer from it.

Understand Site Privacy Settings

Permission settings determine who has access to your and your family's information. These settings typically include the following:

➡ **Public:** This setting allows every Internet user (more than two billion people) to see your information.

➡ **Friends of friends:** Allows your friends and their friends to see your information. (See **Figure 8-8** for an example of how many people this might involve.) Remember that the friend of a friend is likely to be a stranger, so this setting is often the one that exposes people the most. You may feel safe because visitors are "friends," but in reality, this setting can result in thousands of people viewing the information.

➡ **Friends only:** Selecting this setting means only the people in your friends or buddies list can see all your information.

➠ **Private:** This allows you to decide who (if anyone) can see your information. Some people may choose to keep their site entirely private and use it as their personal diary.

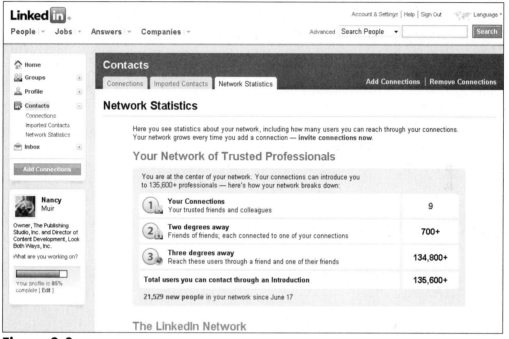

Figure 8-8

Work towards an understanding about which information each person involved with your blog or social network needs you to keep private for safety reasons and which information each is comfortable sharing, and with whom. You should have conversations with the following people:

➠ Spouses and partners.

➠ Family members and extended families.

➠ Colleagues and employers.

➠ Clubs, organizations, churches, charities, or other groups that you're affiliated with — or were affiliated with in the past.

➠ Your grandchildren. See Chapter 11 for more about working with your grandchildren to keep each other safe online.

Meet Someone Safely Offline

If you decide to meet an online acquaintance offline, follow these guidelines:

➠ Meet in a safe environment, preferably a public place during a busy time of day.

➠ Keep the first meeting short.

➠ Make sure somebody knows where you are.

➠ Take a mobile phone with you.

➠ If the person doesn't look as he or she represented, walk away.

➠ If you have any problems, report the person to the social site.

 The advice we provide here applies no matter where on the Internet you meeting someone. If you are involved in online dating or considering taking the leap, see Chapter 9 for more specific advice for using dating services.

Online Quizzes and Surveys

Quizzes and surveys you find online, including those on social networking sites, are usually entertaining and may seem like a harmless pastime. But quiz and survey companies are for-profit businesses. Because consumer information is a commodity, you should assume that anything you enter in quizzes and surveys is being sold. Some sites allow users to create their own quizzes and surveys, but in most cases, the sites are still making money from the answers.

Just by reviewing the types of surveys or quizzes you take, a criminal may learn a great deal. Answering whether you're Hot or Not or a Fashion Disaster or Diva provides not only businesses in the fashion or teen magazine industries with information, it also provides information to a potential predator about topics that interest you. Some quizzes and your answers are displayed on your social networking sites, which is something to consider carefully if your site is publicly viewable — because your answers may expose personal information to a criminal.

Quizzes and surveys on senior social networking sites are typically more financially or medically invasive. For example, the information from a medical quiz may be passed directly to pharmaceutical companies, online drugstores, or insurance companies. (See **Figure 8-9**.) After answering a quiz, you may find you receive spam targeted to your medical conditions or financial interests, or have a health insurance policy cancelled.

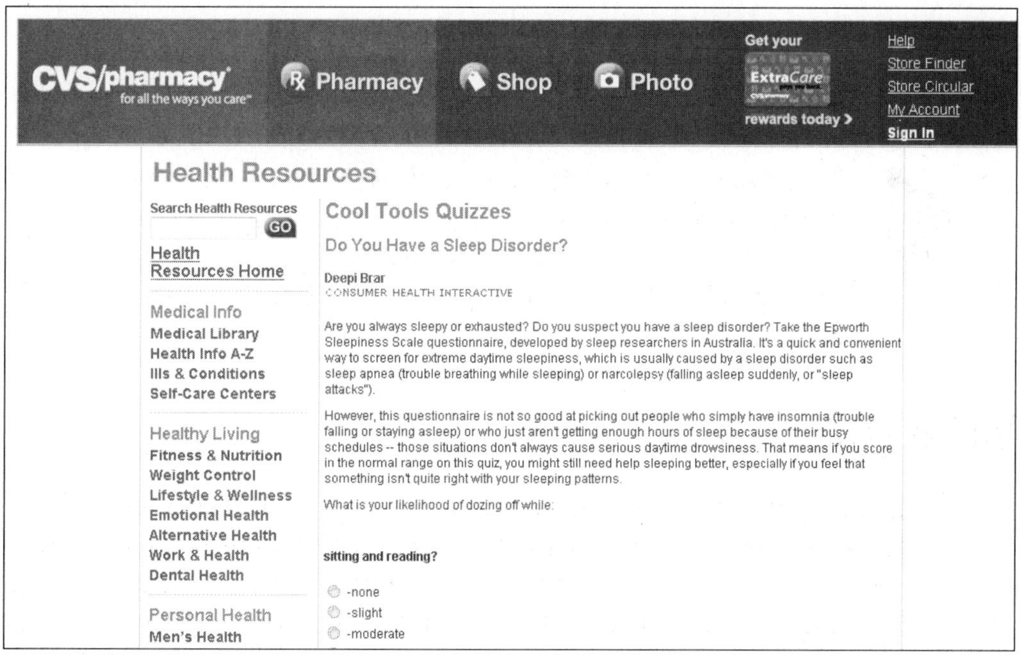

Figure 8-9

Make sure you understand the reputation, privacy policies, and terms of use of the site creating or hosting the quizzes. Before taking any quiz or survey, consider the answers to the following questions:

➡ Why did the company create this quiz?

➡ What will they do with the information?

➡ Who will see my answers?

Report Abuse

If you experience abusive behavior as a result of your participation in a Web site, it can help others if you report the abuse so that companies - and, when needed, law enforcement — understand the potential for online crime and act to improve conditions. If physical abuse occurs, first help the victim get to safety and reassure them they will get help. Then take these steps to report the crime and find help:

1. Report the abuse to your local law enforcement agency and the Web site where you first encountered the predator.

2. Contact the Rape, Abuse, and Incest National Network (RAINN, at www.rainn.org), the nation's largest anti-sexual assault organization. (See **Figure 8-10.**)

3. Consult the Department of Justice Web site (www.usdoj.gov), which lists organizations in every state that provide assistance to sexual abuse victims and their families.

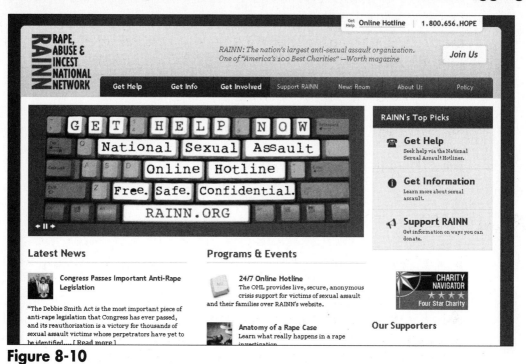

Figure 8-10

Dating Safely Online

Although you may never have thought about using the Internet to find a partner, the fact is that millions of people use online dating services — or less formal online social settings — to meet a mate. Seniors aren't to be left out of this; they use dating and social networking sites targeting seniors. These sites often host chat or other ways to connect, flirt, and discover others.

In this chapter, you find out how to use online dating services safely as you search for the love of your life (or a casual date), how to be aware when you're exposing your emotions, and how a criminal — whether he's after your money or you — might take advantage.

How Online Dating Works

Here's how you can jump into the world of online dating:

⇒ Choose a reputable dating site. (See the section, "Select a Dating Service," later in this chapter).

➡ Sign up and provide information about your likes, dislikes, preferences, and so on. This often takes the form of a self-guided interview process. See Chapter 2 for advice about creating anonymous online aliases.

➡ Create and modify your profile to both avoid exposing too much personal information and ensure that you're sending the right message about yourself to prospective dates. (Get more information about this in Chapter 8 on social networking).

➡ Use search features on the site (see **Figure 9-1**) to find people who interest you and send them messages or invitations to view your profile.

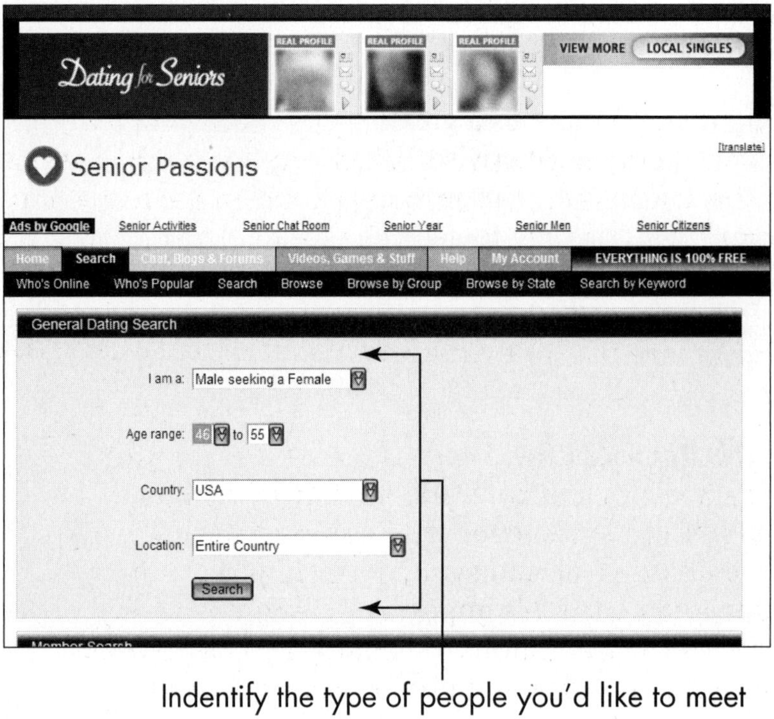

Indentify the type of people you'd like to meet

Figure 9-1

➡ You'll get messages from other members of the site, to which you can respond (or not). Use the site's chat and e-mail features to interact with potential dates. You may also be able to read comments about the person from others who've dated him or her, if the site has that feature.

➡ When you're comfortable with the person and feel there might be a spark, decide if you want to meet the person offline. See the next section for detailed advice about meeting an online acquaintance offline for the first time.

Guidelines for Safer Online Dating

Millions of people of all ages have tried Internet dating services, such as the one shown in **Figure 9-2**, as a way to meet new friends and possibly find a lifelong partner. It's a great way to get acquainted with people you never would've met otherwise. When you do it with caution, online dating may be safer, even, than meeting people in the real world because you have more time to get to know the person before meeting him or her in person.

Dating online requires that you take steps to protect yourself, including these:

➡ **Learn the lingo.** Online daters use some phrases with specific meanings that go beyond the literal translations. For example someone who wants a "discreet" relationship may be asking you to join him or her in an extramarital affair. It's important to understand any subtext in the conversations, especially if you're new to online dating. You may want to just read entries for a while to get used to what's really being said.

→ **Be cautious about marital status.** About 30 percent of males on dating sites are, in fact, married and just looking for something on the side. A certain number of women may be doing the same. Be sure to ask pointed questions.

→ **Maintain anonymity to protect your identity.** Don't include your full name, phone number, where you work, or detailed location information in your profile or during early communications with potential dates. Stop communicating with anyone who presses you for this type of information.

→ **Be smart about choosing profile pictures.** Make sure your photos reflect what you want to say about yourself. Provocative pictures may attract the wrong people. Make sure that your images do not contain identifying information such as nearby landmarks or a shirt with your town's name embroidered on it.

Figure 9-2

➠ **Check to see if a potential date has a good reputation among other daters on the service.**

➠ **Be realistic.** Read the profiles of others with skepticism. As you correspond or talk on the phone, ask questions, seek direct answers, and note any inconsistencies. Look for warning signs such as a display of anger, an attempt to control you, disrespectful comments, or any physically threatening or otherwise unwelcome behavior. *Rule of thumb:* If they're weird online, they'll be weirder in person.

➠ **Trust your instincts when interacting with a potential date.** If something doesn't feel right, cut off contact. If a person becomes abusive, report it and block that person (using your account settings) from contacting you again.

➠ **When you decide to meet, create a safe environment.** Keep first dates short, and agree to meet in a public place during a busy time of day. Use your own transportation. Make sure somebody knows where you're going. If your date doesn't look like his or her photo, walk away and report that person to the dating service.

 Formal dating sites aren't the only places that people meet online, but they typically have the best safeguards in place. If you want to interact with people you meet on other sites, you should provide your own safeguards. Create a separate e-mail account (so you can remain anonymous and abandon the e-mail address if needed). Many dating sites screen participants and provide strong reporting measures that are missing on other types of sites, so be particularly careful. Take your time getting to know someone first before connecting.

Select a Dating Service

Select your online dating service carefully.

➡ Look for an established, popular site with plenty of members and a philosophy that matches your own.

➡ Review the site's policy regarding your privacy and its procedures for screening members. Make sure you're comfortable with them.

➡ Use a service that provides an e-mail system that you use for contacting other members only (sometimes called *private messaging*). By using the site's e-mail rather than your own e-mail address, you can maintain your privacy.

➡ Some sites, such as `http://saferdates.com`, shown in **Figure 9-3,** offer stronger levels of authenticating members. Safer Dates, for example, uses fingerprint identification and screening to make you more confident that you know who you're interacting with.

➡ Visit a site such as `www.onlinedatingtips.org` for comparisons of sites. Whether you choose a senior-specific dating site such as DatingForSeniors.com or a general population site such as PerfectMatch. com, reading reviews about them ahead of time will help you make the best choice.

 If you try a site and experience an unpleasant incident involving another member, report it and make sure the service follows through to enforce its policies. If it doesn't, find another service.

Figure 9-3

Avoid Emotional Exposure

The Internet, and particularly dating sites, blogs, and social networking sites, are wonderful outlets for emotional sharing and building and maintaining friendships, but when you find yourself experiencing extremes of joy or grief, consider carefully what you share online. Just as there are offline criminals who read birth, graduation, wedding, and obituary announcements in newspapers to find vulnerable people to target, there are online criminals watching as you post information about your feelings and significant life events. Be careful when using sites that reveal your emotional condition and potential vulnerability. (See **Figure 9-4** for an example of site where members express grief over a lost or ill pet.)

The Petloss.com website TOTALLY supports our heroes who so willingly place themselves in harms way for the freedom of so many all across the globe.
"Remember Me" video

Pet Loss Grief Support Website

Click here for a text-only version of this page

Send this site to a friend!

Welcome to Petloss.com, a gentle and compassionate website for pet lovers who are grieving over the death of a pet or an ill pet. Here you will find personal support,

Figure 9-4

The joy of a wedding or the arrival of a new grandchild may inspire individuals to share information on wedding sites and baby registries that they would otherwise keep private. People may post pictures, full names, locations, dates, and a great deal more. Your daughter, for example, may join a baby registry site. If she puts your names in the Grandparents field and states that her parents are coming east for the birth on such and such a date, it may put your home at risk of a burglary. This kind of sharing may also help criminals identify and target you for ID theft or financial scams.

There are four simple guidelines for safely sharing strong emotions, from grief to joy, in any online socializing. Always do these things:

→ **Learn whether the Web site allows you to make some (or all) information private.**

→ **Review the information fields and a few sample pages to see what material is typically displayed.** To get an idea of what does and doesn't seem appropriate to share, review other people's postings and look for risks to which they may have inadvertently exposed themselves.

➠ **Make a conscious choice about whether you want the site to have** *restricted* **(only those whom you allow) or** *public* **(available to anyone) access.** Then you can decide what information you want to provide.

➠ **Let others know your safety boundaries so they can share with you on the site in a way that respects your wishes.** And take the time to learn other's restrictions so that you're respectful of their safety and privacy.

➠ **Think about using a friend as a safety check.** When you're caught up in joy or grief, safety may be the last thing on your mind. Asking a friend to monitor the site for risks — so that you can concentrate on what matters to you in the moment — is a great way to let others help.

➠ **Create a unique e-mail address if you put contact information online.** That way, if the account ends up getting too much spam, you can shut it down without compromising your main e-mail account.

Understand How Criminals Groom Victims

Criminals, unfortunately, are an unpleasant fact of life. The idea that criminals are online is concerning, but there is a large gap between the sensational way that news reports present facts and the reality. With some simple steps, you can significantly reduce your risk of falling victim to online crimes.

Criminal grooming occurs when criminals interact with potential victims to create an environment of trust that enables crime. Criminals may do this to gain your trust for a confidence trick or to get access to your financial holdings or belongings. A person may pretend to be a friend to more effectively cyberbully or smear your reputation.

In rarer cases, grooming may be aimed at physically or sexually exploiting the victim. Although the group most at risk for sexual predation is teens between the ages of 13 and 15, adults and seniors can also be targets.

As a senior, you may be at risk for criminal grooming in several ways, including the following:

➠ A financial predator may create a trusted relationship as a way to get at your money.

➠ An online dating or other connection may turn out to be physically threatening in an in-person meeting.

➠ A criminal may use information you post online to approach another family member — your child or grandchild, for example.

Criminals who attempt to groom or socially engineer their victims share some common tactics:

➠ They try to gain your trust by indicating common interests or claiming common friends or organizations. (They gather most of this information through reading information that you, or others, have posted online and through communications with you designed to elicit this information.)

➠ Criminals often act generous in ways that cost them nothing. They may be liberal with praise and virtual gifts, such as sending you e-cards or photos to win you over. If a gift is well received, they may begin offering real gifts to make you feel further indebted.

➡ Groomers look for emotional or character weaknesses — if you're lonely, they want to be your friend; if you're sad, they'll cheer you up, if you're in need of money they have a get-rich-quick scheme.

➡ If they can, criminals may attempt to drive a wedge between you and the people in your support network because if you feel estranged from others you will be easier to manipulate and they are more likely to succeed in their goal.

➡ Over time, a criminal will subtly seek information that gives clues to your social standing, your financial assets, your location, and so on. This may come in the form of asking advice, including these types of questions:

• I'm unhappy with my current bank; what bank do you use?

• I'm tired of living in the Midwest; why did you pick the town where you live?

• E-mailing is so cumbersome. Here's my phone number; let's talk sometime. (The person will see your number on caller ID when you call.)

➡ Another method criminals use is to gain your sympathy by telling you of their own hardships, with the end game of asking you for a loan, or exploiting you in some other way.

Anyone who's been around the block a couple of times knows that con artists use a thousand angles to elicit information — and that you have to be on guard against these tactics. Always ask yourself, "What is motivating this question or action?"

 If a date or other online acquaintance asks you for a loan or any financial information, no matter how sad the hard-luck story, it's virtually always a scam. Block further contact and report it.

Being Entertained Online

Today, you can get entertainment online in the form of games, gambling, music, socializing, TV shows, and blockbuster movies.

The ease of access and low price of these diversions (from free to a few dollars) is appealing. But you have to be aware of your responsibilities as an online entertainment consumer, and you need to know the potential ways that using these services can put you at risk.

In this chapter, we look at the online gaming environment, the dos and don'ts of online gambling, and how to legally download music and videos.

Play a World of Games Online

Playing games online is entertaining, allows you to connect with others, helps maintain your mental fitness, and relieves stress. Here's some basic information about playing online games to get you started.

➡ Some games are Web games — you play them on the Internet only — while other games require you to download a client (a piece of software that you need to play a game online) or even the whole game to your computer.

➡ Some games are installed on your cell phone; others require game consoles. Some games cross multiple device environments.

➡ You aren't likely to break anything. For some reason, many adults are very hesitant about playing games on dedicated gaming devices, because they seem to think they're going to break something. In reality, gaming devices are sturdy and in a legitimate game you aren't going to get you into trouble, so press all the buttons, move all the levers, and try all the features — Worst case? You lose the game.

➡ You can find a broad range of online games, from simple games you play against the service (such as Solitaire, shown in **Figure 10-1**) to two-person games such as chess and checkers that you play with a friend or against the service, to highly interactive games that you can play with thousands of people at a time in enormous fantasy worlds. (See **Figure 10-2**.)

➡ A 2008 study by NPD Group notes that 72 percent of Americans have played online games. Contrary to popular belief, the average player of casual games isn't a teen — it's the teen's mother or grandmother. 71 percent of survey respondents were 40 years or older, 76 percent of them female.

 You can find much more information about gaming and kids on our Web site, www.ilookbothways. com, if you want to help your grandchildren stay safer when gaming online.

Figure 10-1

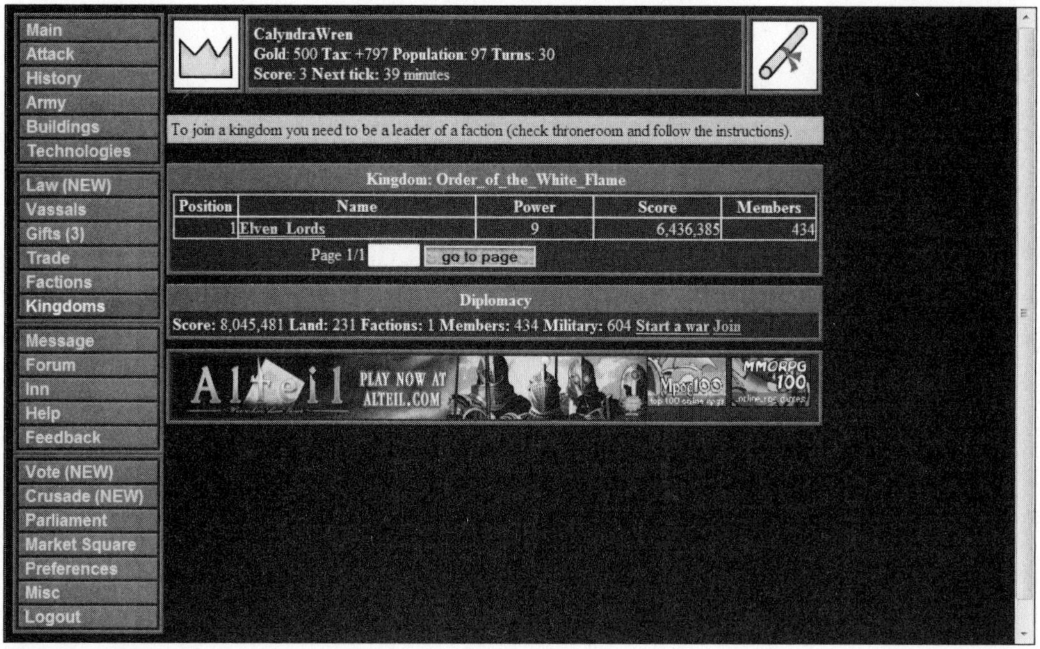

Figure 10-2

Safely Gaming Online

Before you dive into the world of online gaming, consider these basic safety issues:

➠ **Make sure you're using a reputable site or software.** MSN Games, for example, allows you to choose free online games, for-pay online games, downloadable games, and games you play within MSN Messenger.

➠ **If you want to interact with other players, but don't personally know them, set up a safe profile with nicknames, usernames, and gamer tags that don't identify you.** Consider what information about yourself you want to share — including name, photos, location, e-mail address, and so on.

➠ **Understand the game's rating.** (If it doesn't show one, it's probably for general audiences.) The Entertainment Software Rating Board provides ratings for downloadable and purchased games. Take a look at **Figure 10-3** to see the rating icons used by ESRB. The ratings help parents (and grandparents) supervise kids' online gaming; but they are equally useful in helping you identify games you find appropriate for your own use. Other countries have their own version of ESRB ratings. (For more information on ESRB's system, go to www.esrb.org.)

➠ **Review the site's Terms and Conditions to understand what types of behavior it allows.** This document should also state the site's policies and practices for monitoring behavior and responding to abuse. (See Figure 10-4 for an example of a typical Terms and Conditions statement for a gaming site.)

➠ **Be alert to inappropriate comments or suggestions on chats and messages you receive.** Let the game site know if anything makes you uncomfortable, including requests for your real name or location.

➡ Report any abuse and, if needed, block the abuser from further contact.

Now . . . have fun!

 Getting to know new people online is a great way to expand your social circle, but be cautious about trusting or meeting someone you've met only through online gaming. Keep personal information private, and if you choose to meet, keep first meetings short. Meet in a public place during a busy time of day with people present. Let people know where you're going and when to expect a call from you. Always bring a cell phone.

 Some gamers are very poor sports when they lose, and some are cyberbullies. If you experience anyone who is insulting or abusive, use the game settings to block further contact and notify the service.

Know the ratings of the games you play

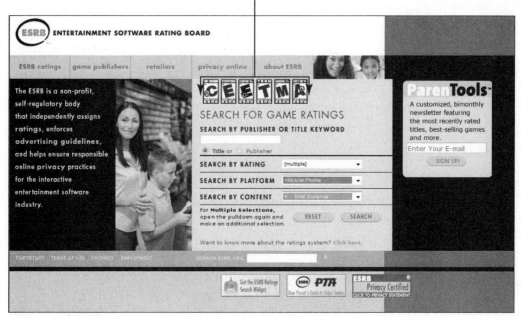

Figure 10-3

All gaming sites should list their Terms and Conditions

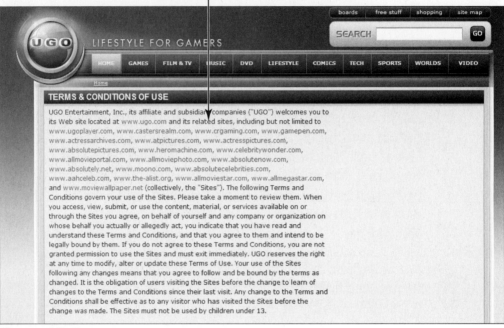

Figure 10-4

Select a Gaming Site

A great deal of what keeps you safe playing online games involves selecting a site that's respectable and safeguards its users. Safe, in this case, involves a site that won't download malware, has good policies about behavior on the site, and enforces those policies.

Consider these issues when determining whether a site is safe:

→ If you play online or download games for your computer from reputable sites such as Yahoo! Games, MSN Zones, and AOL Games (see **Figure 10-5**), you run very little risk of any harm.

→ If you aren't familiar with a site's reputation, search online for trustworthy gaming sites by searching on reviews of games.

Figure 10-5

➠ Trustworthy sites make a clear distinction between what they provide for free (without hidden clauses or malware threats) and what you pay for.

➠ If you use a less well-known site, you should check the fine print first. If a gaming site is free, ask yourself what its getting in return. Is it just the ability to place ads in front of you, or does it reserve the right to sell your information to others?

➠ If you use a search engine to find online games, do *not* assume that sponsored gaming sites in search results are safe. A *sponsored site* is one in which the company specifically pays a search engine to put it at the top of the list of results. This does not guarantee quality or safety. A McAfee study of search engine safety found that sponsored results are still two-and-a-half times more likely to return risky Web sites than non-sponsored results.

 Spam e-mails or shady Web sites that offer free games might ask you to fill out extensive profiles. They may then sell the information you provide in those profiles.

These e-mails and Web sites may also download malware and adware to your computer. Be alert and avoid clicking links in e-mail or using gaming sites unless you trust the source.

Play Console Games

Not all games are played on a computer. Many are played on other devices, called *game consoles,* like Microsoft's Xbox (see **Figure 10-6**), Nintendo's Wii, and others. These consoles typically plug into a TV to give you a large screen for interacting.

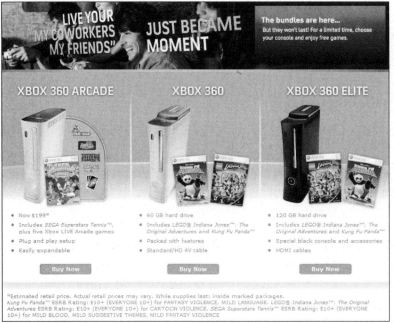

Figure 10-6

Here are the basics on console games:

⟶ Many game consoles can be enabled with Internet connectivity, but they don't have to be. Connecting online allows you to interact with other players outside your home, even around the world. This gives you a great opportunity to play against many new people, but of course, it carries with it the same types of risks you can face in other interactive online environments.

➡ Having an Internet connection allows you to download new games and game demos directly, instead of purchasing games in stores or shopping online from your computer.

It's important to remember that other players may or may not be who they claim to be, so take care not to provide personal information.

Report any obnoxious or offensive behavior to the game company.

➡ In the past, most console games were like computer games where you just sat still and played. Now, many games get you up and moving to exercise at whatever level you're comfortable with. You can play golf or tennis, bowl, ski, play baseball, practice your balance, or work out with your own virtual trainer right in your living room. And the games are a lot of fun to play. In fact, they are so engaging and entertaining that many seniors (and senior centers, retirement communities, and retirement homes) are buying game consoles as a great way to motivate activity, strengthen bones, loosen joints, and increase eye-hand coordination.

 With an emphasis on gentle motions, balance, and coordination wrapped in appealing games, you can play lots of console sports without throwing your back out or risking other injury. The games also encourage a bit of fun competition and socializing among friends, and they're a great way to bond with grandchildren of all ages.

Play Games on Handheld Devices

You've seen kids playing with handheld devices such as Game Boy, Sony PSP, and Nintendo DS, but these easy to take with you devices have lots to offer seniors as well. Most handheld devices can connect with other players, and interact with other devices in your nearby vicinity so you can play with other gamers. If used to play with people in your vicinity that you do not know, these devices carry the same types of risks you can face in other interactive online environments and the same precautions should be taken.

With great games like Tetris, any number of card games, Sudoku, and more, these devices provide lots of entertainment while you're sitting in your dentist's or doctor's waiting room, or waiting for a bus. Playing challenging games is a great way to keep your mind sharp.

Play Games on Your Mobile Phone

Your cell phone probably has at least a couple of games installed on it — have you tried them out? Mobile games that come preinstalled on mobile phones or are downloaded for a small fee are mostly *single player games.* (It's just you against the game.) Hundreds of mobile phone games are available (see **Figure 10-7**). Check on your mobile phone carrier's site to see which games your phone can support.

Figure 10-7

Many adults find that the phone's keypad is rather small for gaming and opt for handheld devices for on-the-go gaming, but with a bit of practice, you can get the hang of the tiny keys and enjoy the convenience of playing on your phone.

To be safest, stick to downloading games (or ringtones, background screens, and so on) from your carrier. This ensures that there's no *malware* (malicious software) in the games and that the games are compatible with your particular phone. If you are more savvy and want a greater selection, be sure you download from a reputable site, as mobile viruses are, unfortunately, an increasing threat.

Participate in Massively Multiplayer Online Games (MMOGs)

Massively multiplayer online games (MMOGs) place huge numbers of gamers in a single environment, hence the name. (Popular games have tens of thousands of users online at any time.) Some MMOGs (such as Second Life, see **Figure 10-8**) aren't games as much as whole virtual worlds that may have their own currencies, stores and businesses, social clubs, events, and more. MMOGs are usually subscription services (others are ad revenue driven) and offer consistent virtual universes where the game continues whether or not any specific gamer is playing.

Here are some safety guidelines for playing MMOGs:

➡ Select a game that matches your comfort level for language, violence, etc.

Although many conversations are monitored by others in the game, with the ability for users to chat online in real time, you have the risk of negative behavior. Stay in the main areas of the games, where this abuse is much less likely to occur.

➡ Just as with any online interaction, be careful about what personal information you expose to other gamers and the level of trust you place in them.

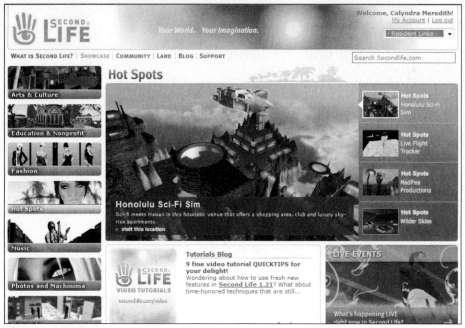

Figure 10-8

➠ Many sites offer points, tokens, extra lives, clothes for your game character, gifts, and currency you can trade or give to others. (See **Figure 10-9.**) Gift giving in any of these forms is a fun way to interact with friends and strangers. However, keep in mind that undesirable people sometimes use gift giving as a tactic to befriend and gain the trust of others for a variety of reasons.

Some users get very addicted to playing online games, particularly young players. Think about setting time limits for minors in your care, and be mindful of the amount of time you spend playing. If the gaming begins to interfere with other aspects of your life, you may need to consider scaling back.

New @ -UK- Couture
Island Boutique -... [teleport now]

NEW RELEASES!!

Come along to -UK- Couture Island
Boutique and check out the gorgeous new
releases!! Sexy, Stylish & Trendy Fashion
from the streets of London. You're...

Figure 10-9

Gamble Online

We're living in a society where legalized gambling isn't only socially
accepted, it's widely promoted and highly visible. Online gambling is illegal in the United States, but despite that we're in the midst of an Internet-
gambling boom. Young Americans and adults place millions of bets on a
regular basis in online casinos (see **Figure 10-10**) and sports sites.

Figure 10-10

Know what you're getting into if you gamble online:

➡ According to an article in the *Washington Post* (November 30, 2008, by Gilbert M. Gaul), worldwide online gambling revenue has more than tripled over five years, to an estimated $18 billion in 2008. As Internet gambling grows, so does Internet gambling fraud. This is partially due to the fact that many gambling operators are based in countries with little online regulation and even less enforcement.

➡ In contrast to the real-world casinos that have strong security, in online casinos you have little or no way to know who is viewing your hand, where exactly your money is being held, or if the dice have been shaved. Because casinos are often partnerships with locations in various countries, it's even hard to hold any one group accountable if your winnings are never paid and your stake disappears.

➡ Another significant problem with online gambling is the addictive nature of the activity. With a pace that's considerably faster than in real casinos, and where you can play multiple games at one time, losses can quickly pile up.

To help identify when gambling has become an addiction, whether online or offline, review the following list of questions from the Connecticut Council on Problem Gambling (www.ccpg.org):

➡ Is gambling the most exciting activity in your life?

➡ Do you miss work, activities, or other events due to gambling?

➡ Has anyone expressed concern about your gambling?

➡ Do you lie to your friends or family about your gambling?

➠ Do you borrow money to gamble?

➠ Have you sold personal belongings to get money to gamble?

➠ Have you stolen from your family, friends, or employer to gamble or to pay back gambling debts?

➠ After losing, do you try to win your money back by gambling?

➠ Are you preoccupied with thoughts of gambling?

➠ Have you tried to stop gambling but can't?

Access Videos and Music Online

You can find a wealth of entertainment content online, from music to your favorite TV shows and Hollywood blockbusters. Sites such as Netflix and Hulu allow you to watch content online for free, or you can purchase content for download for a small fee (as low as $1.89 or so for video and $0.99 for MP3 music downloads as of this writing) from sites such as Amazon.

Here are the steps for watching a show on Hulu, which is free, but be aware that it does insert commercials into the programming:

1. Connect to the Internet and enter www.hulu.com in your browser address field. Click the Sign Up link to create an account and log in.

2. In the resulting window (see **Figure 10-11**), click a category, such as **Movies**, and click the picture above an item that appears to play it. If you don't find something you want to watch, enter the name of a movie or TV show in the **Search** field and click the **Search** button.

3. When the item appears in the window shown in **Figure 10**-12, use the tools at the bottom of the screen to control the playback.

Figure 10-11

Figure 10-12

 It's up to you if you want to use the buttons on the left for rating the ads you view here. Obviously, the marketing company is hoping you will because they can use that information in several ways. Some companies including Hulu.com, may modify ads shown when you view programs or make your information available to their advertisers to market other products or services to you. Others may push spam at your e-mail. Read terms of service carefully and decide how much you are willing to "pay" to get free programming or other services or products online.

 Even with the very low pricing on downloading content, many are tempted to share content that they don't have the rights to give away. It may seem harmless, but it isn't like loaning a book to a friend. The idea that you may inadvertently steal content catches many seniors by surprise. Even if you share downloaded content with only a few friends, any artwork in a fixed tangible form automatically has copyright protection. Any use of music, a photo, video, or other artwork without express permission of the creator is an infringement of copyright. Loaning or giving such a file to someone else is violating copyright and constitutes an act of plagiarism.

Part II: Using the Internet While Dodging the Risk

Grandparents Rule!

Chapter 11

Whether you have grandkids (or grand nieces or nephews) that live at a distance — or you're a child's care giver — it's important that you understand what those kids and teens are doing online and how you can interact with them online and help them stay safer.

Kids may understand the technology better than you, but many of the risks online have nothing to do with technology and everything to do with human nature. Your life experience is an invaluable asset because you understand human behavior better and have many more years of experience in interacting safely in the world.

Some of the advice we provide in this chapter for helping kids stay safe is similar to advice we give you throughout this book, but here we put the emphasis on the specific risks for younger people you should be aware of, suggest ways to discuss online safety in a positive, nonconfrontational manner, and outline skills that help keep kids and teens safer. Finally, we provide advice about protecting your own privacy when kids use your computer.

In this chapter . . .

Understand How Kids Use the Internet

Your first step in helping kids is to understand what services they're using online and what devices they're using to connect to the Internet. Kids go online through many devices including cell (mobile) phones, game consoles, iPods and other media players, and, of course, computers.

And what are they doing with that access? A lot.of kids use the Internet for a variety of tasks, such as the following:

➡ Researching topics for homework

➡ Using social networking sites to hang out with friends and share their photos and thoughts

➡ Sharing videos — often made via their cell phones — on sites such as YouTube.com

➡ Sending text messages (called texting), sharing music, photos, and videos via their cell phones with friends

➡ Playing games — single-player and interactive, multi-player games

➡ Collaborating on school projects

➡ Shopping

➡ Selling items on classified sites

➡ Finding new bands and downloading music

➡ Applying for jobs and college

➡ Finding dates and flirting

➡ Seeking out advice, humor, content, styles, and how to do things

The odds are that your grandkids are getting far more benefit from the Internet than harm, but just as you pay attention to their behavior offline to keep them safe, it helps if you're aware of what they're doing online. Talk to them about their Internet activities and be observant if you notice any unusual behavior, such as spending too much time online, making or receiving cell phone calls or instant messages late at night, or developing a serious relationship with someone they've met only online.

 Bond online with your grandchildren. Learn how to use the tools your kids are using: blogs, e-mail, instant messaging, and so on. This is a great opportunity to ask for help to set up your own blog, get started with instant messaging, start searching, or show you whatever it is you don't yet know how to do.

Checklist for Online Family Safety

By the time kids turn 18 they need to have fully developed the skills to be productive, responsible Internet users ready to succeed in the 21st century. This doesn't happen without practice — and a few failures along the way. We aren't doing our jobs as guardians if we don't adequately prepare young people for the road ahead.

Start on the right foot. Internet safety isn't about "don't," "never," or "no." It's about learning how to create an environment to say "yes." "Grandma, I want to start social networking." Answer: "That would be great wouldn't it! Let's figure out how we can make that happen. There are some skills you'll need to learn, and some responsibilities you'll have to master to protect our privacy and respect others. So let's get started."

Effective safety is something families do together. You really can't force people over the age of about 10 to act safely online.

Fortunately, kids have a basic sense of self-preservation most of the time. They don't want to be insulted, ripped off, or abused by a scammer, thief, or criminal. And when they realize their actions may place not only themselves, but their family members or friends, at risk, they are fairly interested in using safety measures.

Here are some steps to help you get started making a safer online experience for the whole family:

➡ Discuss online safety positively with your grandchildren or other minors in your care — especially those who want to go online from your computer(s). Listen to what they want to do, and talk about what it takes to respect each other's safety needs.

➡ Figure out what works for your personal and family values. Treat each child and teen uniquely because there is no one-size-fits-all solution.

➡ Decide which activities they are ready for, and create a plan to help them get ready to take on new activities with the corresponding responsibilities that go with them.

➡ Install safety software (see Norton Antivirus, shown in **Figure 11-1,** for an example), use it unfailingly and always keep it current. (Much of this software is free). Depending on the age and maturity of minors in your care, or using your computer, you may also want content filtering and family safety (parental control) software installed. See Chapter 15 to learn more about technology tools.

➡ Be transparent. Nothing will kill trust and collaboration faster than spying. If you install family safety tools to monitor activity be up front about it and explain why it's there.

➡ Encourage the children in your care to be selective about who they interact with online and which sites they visit.

➠ It may make sense for you to set an access password on your user account so that grandchildren can't go into your files without you expressly granting access. See Chapter 3 for more about choosing passwords. Set up a separate user account for the kids to use to go online and save their own files and programs.

➠ Set boundaries about posting information that can personally identify you, a family member, or friend. Learn more about sharing info safely in Chapter 7.

➠ Teach grandchildren the skills and savvy to avoid opening links or attachments in ads or e-mails that can transmit spam and viruses to your computer.

➠ For the youngest grandchildren, you may want to put your computer and Internet-connected game consoles in a central location. This helps you to keep an eye on what they're doing online.

Figure 11-1

➡ Work together, find out how and where to report abuse on every service your grandchildren use. Create an environment that encourages kids to report any problems to you. Demonstrate to them that acting as a responsible Internet citizen can help stop the illegal activity, harassment, and predatory behavior of online criminals.

➡ Talk about not trading personal information for freebies. Just as in the physical world, if it sounds too good to be true, it probably is. Unwanted software, such as spyware and viruses, often piggybacks on software or other merchandise that's free.

➡ Request information about the safeguards on the computers that your grandchild uses outside the home. This includes computers at school, the public library, and the homes of other family members or friends.

➡ Help your grandchildren choose safe e-mail addresses, IM names, chat nicknames, and other such identifiers.

➡ If you're a full-time care giver, sit down periodically with the kids to review who they communicate with and what they're doing online. Review their safety settings to be sure they are still appropriate, or adjust as needed as they grow.

Help Protect Grandchildren Using E-Mail

Today, kids don't consider e-mail cool, so they don't use it often. However, it's a tool they'll use now and then, so follow this advice for safer e-mailing:

➡ For young children, use a service that enables you to limit your child's contacts to people you know.

➠ Talk to teens about who they communicate with and what they talk about. Set boundaries that match your family's values and your grandchild's age, reassessing these boundaries periodically as your grandchild matures or wants to begin using new services.

➠ Caution them not to list their e-mail addresses publicly or respond to e-mail from people they don't personally know.

➠ Teach them to ignore all sweepstakes and any quiz that asks them to enter their e-mail address They should always guard their e-mail account information.

 Help your grandchild understand that use of any online service, and access to additional features within those services, is a privilege that requires mastery of new skills and a commitment to new responsibilities. Agree upon ground rules for safe use of services prior to expanding your grandchild's venture into new areas or use of new devices. Learn more about e-mail safety in Chapter 5.

Help Create Safe Instant Messaging Experiences

Instant messaging (IM) is primarily done from a computer, although it can also be done through some mobile (cell) phone services. IM allows people to interact online in real time, sending short messages back and forth, something like a text-based phone call. Here are some tips to help keep younger children and teens safer when they use instant messaging:

➠ For younger children, use services that allow you to limit your grandchildren's contacts so that they can send IM or text messages to only people you both know.

- Teach them not to list their IM names publicly, for example on their social networking pages, or respond to IMs from people they don't know personally. Look for options in their instant messaging programs to help them set their profiles to private. (See **Figure 11-2** for such settings in MSN Messenger.)

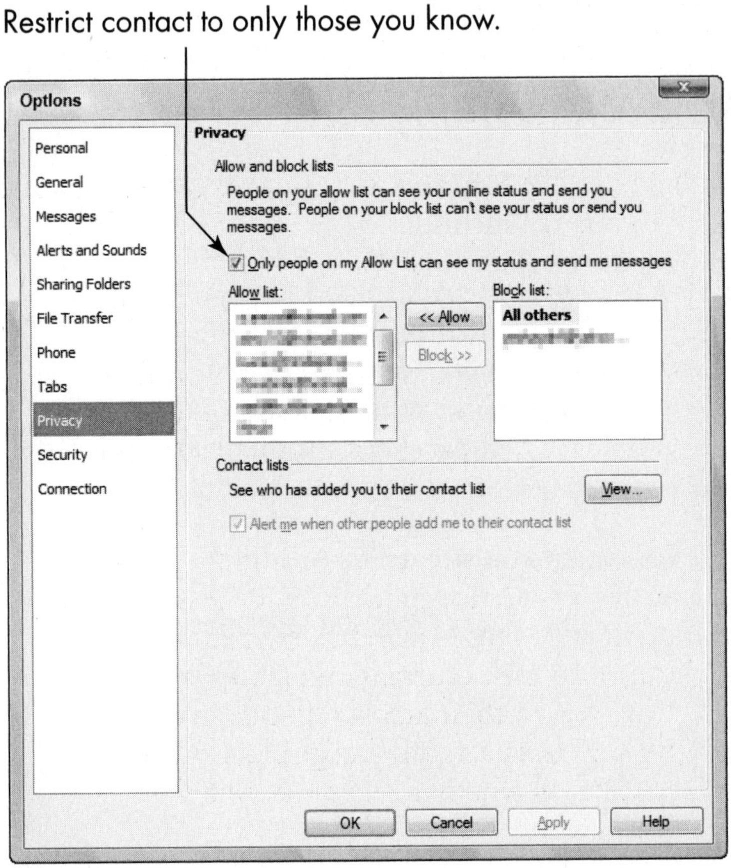

Restrict contact to only those you know.
Options
Personal
General
Messages
Alerts and Sounds
Sharing Folders
File Transfer
Phone
Tabs
Privacy
Security
Connection
Privacy
Allow and block lists
People on your allow list can see your online status and send you messages. People on your block list can't see your status or send you messages.
Only people on my Allow List can see my status and send me messages
Allow list:
Block list:
<< Allow
Block >>
All others
Contact lists
See who has added you to their contact list
View...
Alert me when other people add me to their contact list
OK
Cancel
Apply
Help

Figure 11-2

Some IM programs have an option that allows friends of friends to send instant messages to you. This option is all about connecting people with common interests. However, limiting access to your information is harder using this approach, which is one of the real concerns about adding strangers to your IM buddy list

➡ Familiarize yourself with all the features in the IM program your grandchild wants to use and consider potential risks. IM programs may enable sharing of photos, allow you to give remote access to your computer (which gives a person on another computer access to your files), facilitate group communications, and provide location finders that help someone pinpoint a device's location.

Stay Safer on Social Networking Sites

Two things can help you determine the appropriateness of a social networking site for your grandchild:

➡ **Age restrictions.** Typically, social networking sites provide clear age guidelines. For example, Club Penguin (see **Figure 11-3**) is designed for 6–14 year olds, but it's open to all ages; Webkinz is designed for users 6–13+; MySpace and Facebook require users to be 13 or older.

➡ **Spend time browsing the site and reading the site's safety and privacy protection policies with your grandchild.** Look at the types of interactions and communications that are occurring and compare the site's stated standards to their actual enforcement of standards. Nothing beats actually exploring a site for helping you determine whether it's appropriate for children in your care.

When you're grandchild is ready to sign up, be aware that accepting the service's default settings may expose more information than he or she intended. Children should be especially cautious about exposing too much about their name, age, or location. Here's how to make smart choices when opening a social network account:

➠ Help kids evaluate the questions that services ask in the registration process. There's a clear difference between required information and optional. (See **Figure 11-4**.) The rule of thumb is to enter as little as possible. If, over time, they want to add more, the can do so, but taking information back is far more difficult.

➠ Sites often encourage sharing more information than is required, and they typically position doing so as a way to be more popular, a ploy children and teens fall for more often than adults. Sometimes this information provides them with a more customized experience. Sometimes they simply want it for marketing purposes, or to sell.

Figure 11-3

Sites should state what is required and what is optional

Figure 11-4

➠ Teach them to understand what they share (see Chapter 7 to learn this for yourself). It's often very difficult to remove information from sites, and many have come to regret the amount of information they shared. Future employers, romantic partners, college admissions officials, cyberbullies, and others may search for them online, and early indiscretions can stay up there to haunt them throughout their lives.

Blog Safely

Social networking sites allow users to interact with each other in many ways, and to share their thoughts through blogs (which is short for Web logs). Here are some tips for kids sharing through blogs:

⟼ The site should offer site monitors and tools to help protect user safety, such as a way to control who has permission to see the blog and the ability to block harassing users and turn comments on or off.

⟼ Know who owns the content. Read the terms and conditions of the blog site relative to content. Even some of the most popular blog and social networking sites have clauses that give the service the right to use anything people post in any way they want. Choose a service that respects your grandchildren's right to their own content and retain their privacy.

⟼ If a blog is not set to private, anyone can visit and comment on what the blogger is saying or posting. Kids don't realize that most blog sites default blog posts to being publicly viewable; they have to change the setting to make their blog private. The more personal or identifiable the information your grandchildren share, the fewer people they should share it with. If your grandchildren choose to make their blogs public, they should disclose only what they would want anyone on the Internet to know.

⟼ Periodically review or ask your grandchildren to review who has access to their pages. Friends change over time and once-trusted people may become less trusted. It is particularly important for them to immediately block access to anybody with whom they have had a disagreement. One of the most common causes of cyberbullying is the breakup of a friendship; the content they have on their blog pages becomes the most common ammunition used against them.

➡ Help them protect their real names on their sites, and everyone else's names too. (See an example of what not to do in **Figure 11-5**.) Their friends know their names; nobody else needs to.

- Keep information that puts them on the map out of their blog. Tell them not to mention such details as their addresses, schools, or even their town names (especially if they live in small towns).

- They should protect any information that gives away their actual birth dates (birth year is enough to sign up with services) or year of graduation.

A blog user's alias, but it still reveals her name

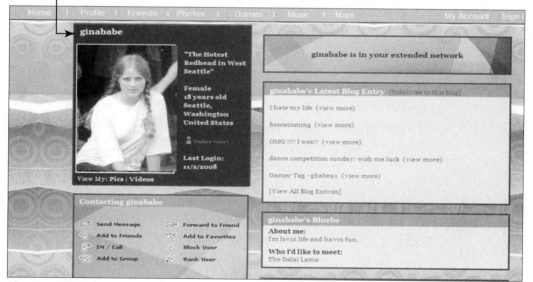

Figure 11-5

⟶ Help them to understand how to really see what information is being shared.

 Most social networking sites show the user's profile photo, even when the user's pages are set to private. See Chapter 6 for more about how to spot risks in photos or videos that you post online.

⟶ Help children in your care to understand the need to be careful about sharing their feelings in a blog because that information is permanent. Explain that they express feelings in a blog in various ways. The moods they show, poems they select, the music they list, the pictures they post, all tell a lot about who they are and how they feel.

⟶ Suggest your grandkids check out what their friends expose about them in their blogs and help them learn to talk to others about respecting their privacy. Friends may accidentally be giving out their real names or information that can locate them, such as the schools they attend. (See **Figure 11-6.**) Perhaps a friend has a photo of friends on her site with a caption indicating who your grandchild is.

⟶ Spam messages on social networking sites often appear as comments. These typically include links to sites, and young people need to avoid these like the plague — they often place malware on your computer or contain offensive content.

 Visit our Web site, www.ilookbothways.com, to use hands-on skill-builder tools to practice spotting risks in text and photos.

Blogs can reveal a wealth of personal information

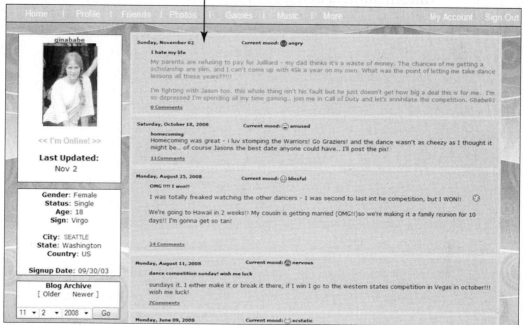

Figure 11-6

Understand Exposure in Quizzes and Surveys

Quizzes and surveys that your grandchildren find online (see **Figure 11-7**), including those on social networking sites, are usually entertaining and may seem like a harmless pastime. But quiz and survey companies are for-profit businesses, and they typically make their money by selling the consumer information they collect. (See Chapter 8 for more about quizzes and surveys.)

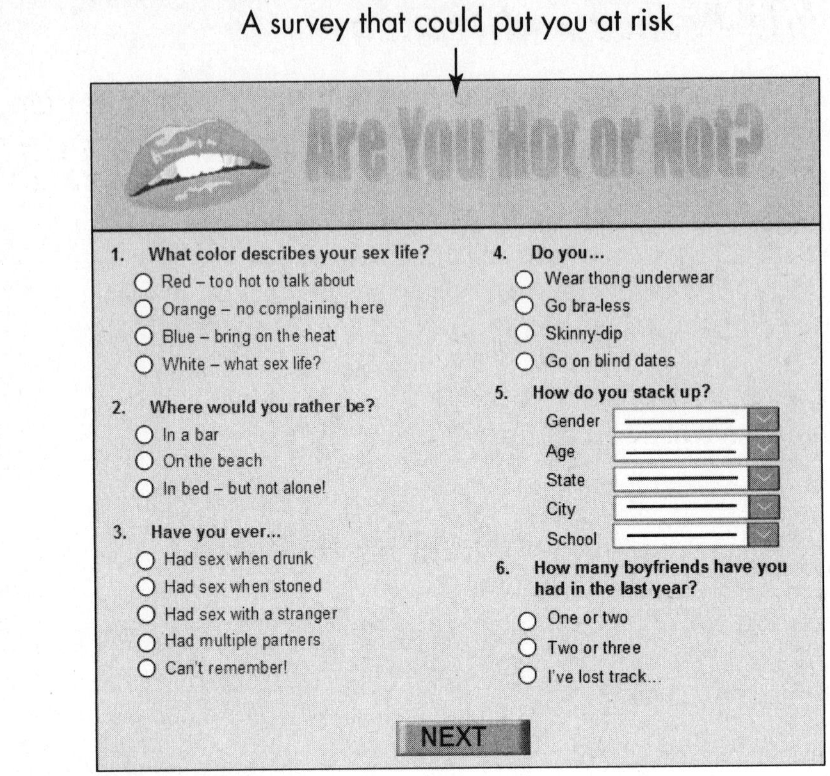

A survey that could put you at risk

Figure 11-7

Teach children in your care to assume that

➡ Information entered in quizzes and surveys is being sold. By reviewing the types of surveys or quizzes your grandchildren take, a company or person may learn a great deal.

➡ Sites that allow users to create their own quizzes and surveys in most cases are making money from selling information about the person posting the survey, as well as selling the answers of responders.

➡ Sometimes people post the quizzes they took on their social networking sites. This is something to help your grandchildren consider carefully, especially if their sites are publicly viewable.

Understand Mobile Phones and Texting

Most mobile (cell) phones today are small computers with rich feature sets. Before you buy a phone for a child or teen in your care, ask yourself what are the features on the phone, and what services do these features enable? Look at the answers from a safety perspective: Which safeguards are in place, along with all those cool features?

Here are some cell phone features to think about before buying:

➠ Does the phone have Internet access? Depending on the age and maturity of a minor, this may or may not be desirable.

➠ Does the phone offer filters that block content that could be harmful to children or offensive to you? Is the filter turned on? If the filter isn't on by default and you think it should be, ask the sales person to turn it on for you in the store and help you set appropriate filter levels.

➠ Which services do the filters cover? If the phone has TV, find out if the service allows you to set ratings restrictions on shows. Find out how this feature treats unrated programs. Are there filters that apply to music services?

➠ Does the phone or device have location (GPS) capability? (See **Figure 11-8**.) You should be able to block this capability or limit it if you choose to, so that your grandchildren can't allow people to track their location.

➠ Does the phone have a camera? The rising image quality in mobile phone cameras documents a lot of poor choices. While most teens use cameras sensibly, others document extreme behavior to look cool for each other, take and swap inappropriate pictures or short videos of themselves or allow someone else to do so. They also snap photos or shoot video humiliating or harming others to post online; they photograph their crimes, and take inappropriate photos of other minors. Some find that embarrassment isn't the only consequence: they may also face criminal charges. Those photographing sexual images of themselves or others may face felony charges for creating and distributing child sexual abuse images.

➡ Can the phone link your child to social networking sites? Social networking sites are seeing huge increases in traffic via mobile phones. Teens in particular use these features to update their statuses and monitor their friends' communications and activities. Spur-of-the-moment posts, whether on the computer or a mobile device, are often done without considering safety. What seems like a good idea to share today may not seem like a good idea in the long term.

➡ Do you know how to report theft of the phone? You may need to provide serial numbers or other information found on the phone itself — usually found under the battery. Ask the sales clerk what information you need in order to report theft. If you don't have this information written down, you surely won't be able to find it after the phone is stolen.

➡ Do you know how to report harassment or bullying? The carrier should have a clear set of procedures that you can use to report any malicious calls. It's best to know these in advance of any trouble. Discuss these procedures and all other issues listed here with any child who will use a phone.

Figure 11-8

Choose Between a Pre-Paid and Monthly Phone Account

Many care givers like pre-paid phone plans because they prevent anyone who uses the phone from exceeding their spending limit. Should they run out of minutes, they can choose to purchase more at any store that sells pre-paid minute phone cards, which includes just about every grocery and convenience store.

However, consider a couple of things before you choose between a pre-paid account and an account that bills monthly. These include the following:

➡ Some companies allow you to review incoming and outgoing calls made on pre-paid accounts; some don't.

An account with a monthly bill shows every phone number called including time of day and helps you understand who your child communicates with. Review their call history with your child and explain that this isn't an invasion of privacy but a way to help keep him or her safe. Especially note unfamiliar numbers from out of your area.

➟ The monthly bill (see **Figure 11-9**) tells you what times of day calls are taking place. If a child's having difficulty getting up for school in the morning or sneaking out at night, look at the child's phone calling and texting history. If calls and text messages are flying in the middle of the night, you may need to take the phone away from the child after a certain time in the evening, setting a time that the family believes is too late for accepting or making phone calls, and returning the phone in the morning.

It's also useful to pay attention to calls and text messages sent during school hours. Most schools prohibit use of cell phones during school, except for emergencies. If a child or teen's phone record shows a lot of calls or text messages placed during school hours (especially to other students) this may indicate a problem with paying attention in class or cheating on tests.

 Sit down with the children in your care to periodically check the content on the phone. Which ringtones are they using? Are the photos they've taken and the photos sent to them appropriate? What other items have they downloaded (games, ads and coupons, and so on)? What services have they purchased? Are the services appropriate, and do they have ongoing monthly fees? You may not find some services appropriate. Does the phone allow them to watch videos? If so, which videos are they watching?

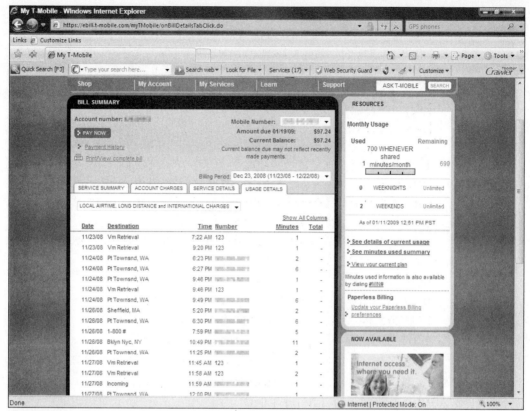

Figure 11-9

Protect Students at School

Official school Web sites, online newsletters, team Web sites, and the like often contain specific information about students, including full names and photos, identifying student council participants, various sports team members (see **Figure 11-10**), and so on. Some classes may also create their own publicly viewable Web sites so that students can post projects and care givers and students can check out homework assignments.

This information automatically associates students with specific school locations, and often contains details about exactly when and where meetings, practices, and events will take place. This is enough for anyone to locate children, know their patterns of going to and from school, and their interests.

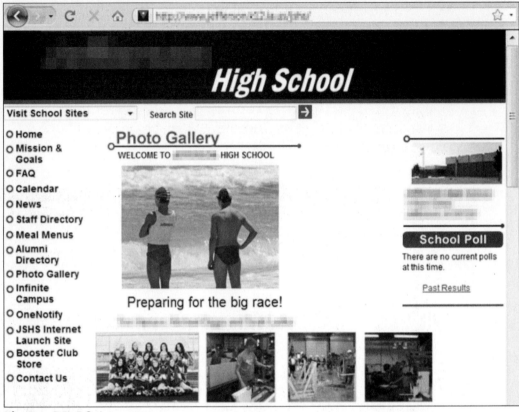

Figure 11-10

If the school your grandchildren attend publicly exposes personal information about students, it's time for the school to do a safety analysis of all online communications to identify and minimize risks. Encourage the school to consider making the information two-tiered: Some is visible to the general public, while some is restricted to the approved list of e-mail addresses that students and parents provide at the beginning of each year.

Play Games Safely

All the advice we give about gaming in Chapter 10 applies to kids and teens as well as adults. Here's a quick rundown of what you should help minors in your care keep in mind:

➟ Choose safe gaming sites by reviewing their policies and evaluating the companies behind them. Gaming sites such as MSN, AOL, and Yahoo! (see **Figure 11-11**), xBox, World Of Warcraft, and Lordsgame are very respectful of people's privacy, won't download malware (malicious software) to computers, and monitor their services for safety, for example. Other sites may not maintain these standards.

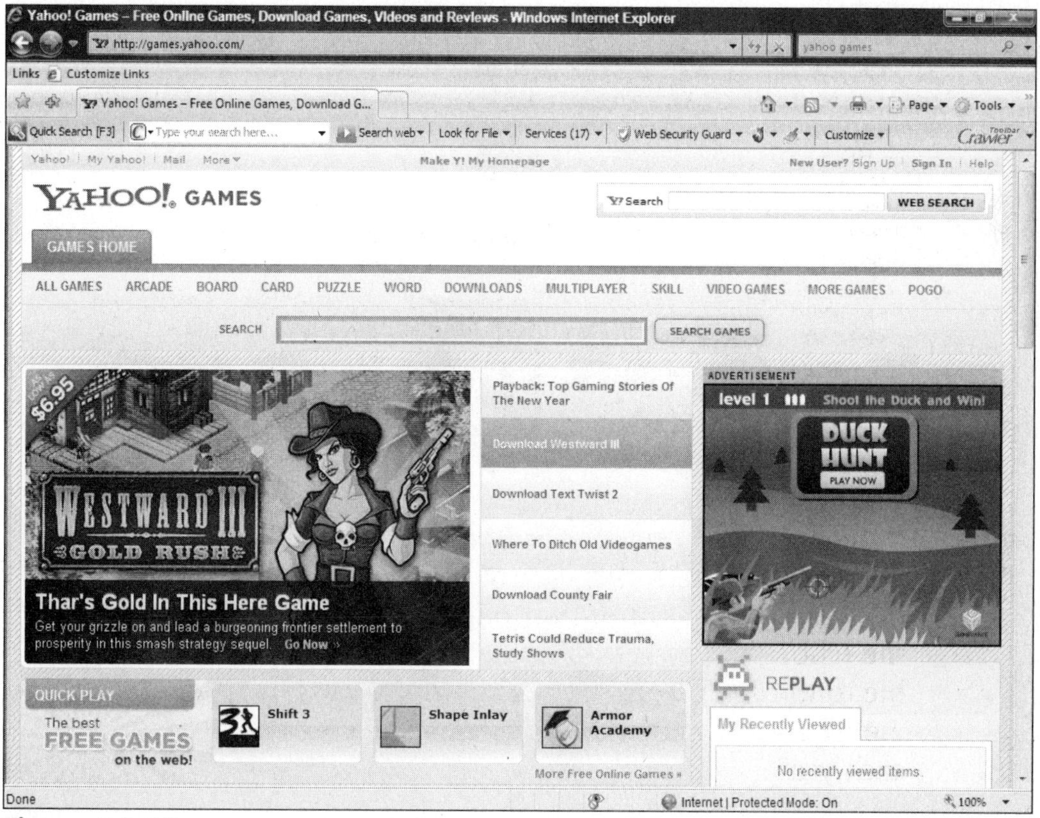

Figure 11-11

➟ Be aware that kids play Internet-connected games on a variety of devices, from game consoles to cell phones, as well as computers in your home or in friends' homes. Discuss which games are appropriate for them to play based on their ages, maturity levels and your family values.

➠ Some people use game environments as a way to bully others. Teach your grandkids that they may never be abusers, and help them report the abuse to the service provider, and block the abuser from contacting them again. Make it clear that retaliating isn't acceptable (and almost always leads to an escalation of abuse).

➠ If a child is bullied or solicited in a gaming site, cutting them off from the game isn't a solution, as their online world is an important part of their support network. Instead, help them to block specific abusers and report the abuse. Encourage children in your care to talk to you or another adult if they're having problems.

Understand the Act of Cyberbullying

All bullying is carried out by malicious attackers seeking implicit or explicit entertainment or profit through the abuse of another person. Cyberbullies just have new tools to use in these attacks. When you add e-mail, blogs, instant messaging, mobile phones, digital images, and other electronic tools, bullying takes on entirely new dimensions.

➠ The Internet allows large numbers of people to witness a bully's abuse.

➠ Taunts and threats are no longer restricted to the school grounds and can occur 24/7.

➠ Cyberbullies can attack victims in their most private refuges through their phones and Web sites.

➠ The accusations cyberbullies hurl may be permanently viewable, haunting the victim for the rest of their lives as people who search for them online come across the malicious content.

➠ Cyberbullies can choose to cloak their actions in anonymity, which may encourage them to act out in vicious ways.

Cyberbullying, also called online harassment and cyber stalking, can involve any of these acts:

➠ Sending mean or threatening e-mails or IMs.

➠ Posting insulting, threatening, or derogatory comments about someone on one or more Web sites.

➠ Spreading rumors about someone through blogs, discussions, or social journals.

➠ Threatening physical harm or verbally intimidating someone.

➠ Stealing and altering photos in damaging ways or adding derogatory comments; they can then post them on social networking sites (such as MySpace) or send them to the victim's friends, family, school, employers, and so on.

➠ Pretending to be the victim by creating fake blogs to start trouble with the victim's friends. Posting embarrassing images under the victim's identity.

 The full scope of cyberbullying is difficult to measure because of real issues surrounding underreporting. However, research indicates that nearly one in six U.S. children grades six to ten (that's 3.2 million students) are victims of online bullying every year (though children of all ages can experience this phenomenon).

Six Steps to Avoid and Prevent Cyberbullying

Have minors in your care follow these steps to avoid cyberbullying:

➠ Keep personal information (address, phone number, and so on), feelings, and personal photos private so that abusing this information is more difficult for a bully to find. Advise the child or teen to immediately restrict access to information from anyone who becomes angry with them.

➥ Use technology tools (see **Figure 11-12**) to block anyone whose behavior is inappropriate or threatening in any way. (If they're younger they'll need help with this.)

➥ Never answer phone calls or read messages, e-mail, or comments from cyberbullies. Do set them aside in case authorities need them as evidence.

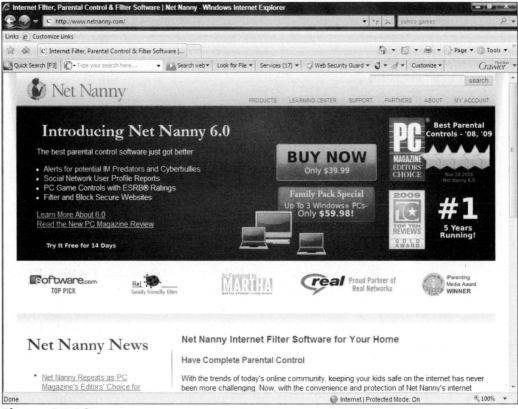

Figure 11-12

Check in with your grandchildren periodically to ask whether they're being bullied, whether in person, on the computer, or on their cell phones.Make sure children know why they should never bully others, and make it clear what the consequences will be if they do. Some parents of bullies tend to minimize or dismiss their children's behavior. They consider such behavior as being "just a phase," or they say that "kids will be kids." Not only does this point of view utterly disregard the tremendous damage done to victims, it also fails to recognize the very dangerous paths bullies walk.

 Those who participate in cyberbullying head down a very negative path. They are far more likely to also become involved in other delinquent behavior online and offline. These problem behaviors include abusing alcohol, cheating on school tests, skipping school, physically assaulting peers or adults, damaging property, shoplifting, drug abuse, running away from home, carrying weapons, and detention or suspension from school. Bullies also have significantly increased risk of imprisonment, failed relationships, and failure to succeed in a work environment in later life. If your grandchild is a bully, find help now.

What to Do If Your Grandchild Is Cyberbullied

Often, young people who are victims of bullying are told they should just ignore it or toughen up. Instead of dismissing them, support them when they speak up about online abuse.

To help kids and teens who are being cyberbullied, follow these guidelines:

➠ Help the victims of cyberbullying understand that the bullying isn't their fault. If you ask most bully victims why they're being bullied, they say it's because they have whatever 'deficiency' the bullies claim — they're too short, have a lisp, are too fat or skinny, or whatever. In reality, bullies choose an easy target and then figure out a justification for the bullying. Too often, victims feel their characteristics caused them to be singled out, and they feel that they're somehow at fault. They aren't.

➡ Teach your grandchild that it's a myth that weaklings tattle. In reality, those who tell are the ones who aren't willing to be bullied. Speaking out and getting help are positive declarations that they deserve to be treated better and are willing to take steps to ensure that they are.

➡ Protect your grandchild from further abuse. This means reacting and acting very carefully to not make matters worse. The biggest fear kids have in telling adults about bullying is that their fears will be dismissed, that they'll be blamed, or that their Internet access will be cut off.

➡ If you feel that you or your grandchild is in any way at risk, call the police. Don't hesitate or wait to see if the abuse will stop.

➡ If you or your grandchildren are harassed or threatened online, report the abuser to the Web service. (See **Figure 11-13.**) If the online services don't provide the support you need, change services and let the provider know why you changed.

➡ Report online abuse to your Internet service provider (ISP) or phone abuse to your cell phone company, and follow any instructions for documenting the problem and taking action against the abuser.

You may want to contact the school for advice, even if the cyberbullying isn't by another student, as schools have to deal with this issue daily.

Report abuse to the Web service

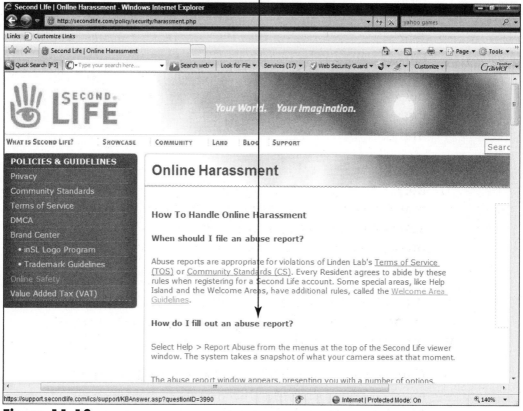

Figure 11-13

Talk to Kids about Sexual Predators

There are sexual predators online — just like offline. But there's a large gap between the sensational way that news reports present facts that make online sexual exploitation of minors seem like an hourly event and reality. For the most part teens know how to deal with sexual solicitation as a crude and dismissable fact of life. That said, you should educate yourself about the tactics of sexual predators, warning signs of children at risk, and candidly discuss these with children in your care.

Certain things, including the following, put some kids more at risk of sexual attention than others:

➡ Internet sexual predators, like offline sexual predators, prey on people of all ages. The group most at risk for online sexual predation is teens between the ages of 13 and 15. Younger kids are less likely socialize online, and older teens are generally a bit more cautious.

➡ Young people with low self-esteem and few friends have significantly increased vulnerability for this type of grooming — they're seeking understanding, they're willing to be extreme, and they've already lost their footing. There are simple steps that you can take to significantly reduce the risk of online sexual exploitation of children in your care.

➡ Don't preach "stranger danger." Sexual predators who use online tools are often not strangers to their victims. Family members, family friends, teachers, coaches, club leaders, and others who want to exploit a minor sexually frequently use the Internet (and cell phones) as grooming tools.

➡ Talk to kids and teens about online sexual predators in the same matter of fact way you talk about other kinds of potential threats they may face.

➡ Sexual predators groom children to establish trust, isolate the victims from their friends and family, and make the victim feel special with gifts and so on.

Teach your kids to question why someone they meet online is actively seeking their trust, sending gifts, or trying to alienate them from their family or friends.

➡ Teach kids to trust their instincts when something feels weird and report it to you.

 Take time to read "Internet Safety Education for Teens: Getting It Right," at `http://depts.washington.edu/hcsats/PDF/factsheets/Internet_Saftey_for_Teens_2-6-08.pdf`, created by the Crimes against Children Research Center. Also, visit our Web site, `www.ilookbothways.com`, and search for the latest information on sexual predators.

If You Think Your Grandchild Is Being Groomed

If you suspect your grandchild is being groomed by a sexual predator, follow these steps:

➡ **Stay calm.** Fear and anger are natural reactions; however they can frighten the child. Never blame, punish, or embarrass a victim.

➡ **Believe your child.** Children don't typically lie about sexual abuse. Believe what you're being told and listen carefully.

➡ **Reassure the victim that this isn't his fault.** Thank the child for telling you. Give positive messages such as, "This isn't your fault," or "You were very smart to tell me about this."

➠ **Allow your child to express feelings but control your own feelings about the situation.** Put your child's feelings center stage and don't confuse them with your own reactions.

➠ **Get back to normal life as soon as possible.** Protect your child, but don't make her feel different or isolated.

➠ **Seek help for yourself.** Care givers often feel angry, guilty, or to blame when they learn their child has been groomed by a sexual predator. Talk to someone you trust, or call a counselor who can help you.

Report Sexual Abuse

To gather evidence and report abuse, follow these steps:

➠ Look at the files and communications on your grand-child's computer, mobile phone and other devices together with your grandchild.

➠ If any of the following occurs, contact the police, and follow their instructions:

• You believe your child is at physical risk.

• Your child or anyone in the household has received child pornography or abusive images.

• Your child has been sexually solicited or receives sex-ually explicit images

➠ Inform your service provider of the abuse on its service.

To report known or suspected child exploitation anywhere in the country, contact the National Center for Missing and Exploited Children (www.missingkids.com; see **Figure 11-14**) at 1-800-THE-LOST.

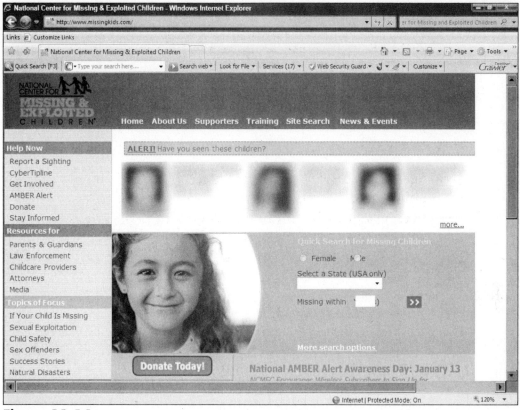

Figure 11-14

Use Software to Keep Grandkids Safer

Chapter 15 is all about how technology can keep your computer safe from threats such as viruses and spyware, but in addition to these programs there are software products you can use to help your grandkids stay safe online. These include the following:

➠ **Content filtering and safety settings (often called parental controls)** Browsers provide some content filtering, to help you set boundaries for the types of sites, text, and images returned in search results. Operating systems, Internet service providers, and Web portals provide safety settings that you can set to filter content based on keywords or categories of content (such as sexually explicit or violent content). You can also use these programs to limit or monitor your child's online activities.

Protect Yourself As Well

Kids sometimes misbehave and get into trouble. Some grandchildren leverage unprotected information to make purchases, empty bank accounts, steal identities, or even cyberbully their grandparents. To protect yourself, take these measures:

➡ Password-protect your user account to protect your own information and privacy before you allow grand-children or anyone else to use your computer.

➡ Set up a user account just for your grandchild (see **Figure 11-15**) On a Windows Vista computer, choose Start➪Control Panel, and click User Accounts and Family Safety to set up new accounts or password protect an existing account.

Click here to set up new accounts and add passwords

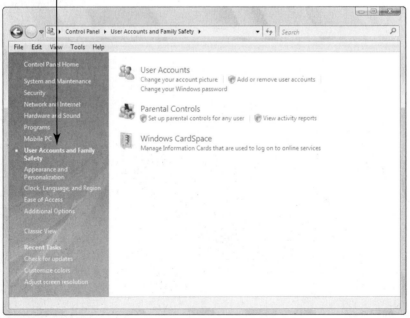

Figure 11-15

Part III

Protecting Your Wealth and Your Health

The 5th Wave   By Rich Tennant

"The first thing you should know about investing online is that when you see the exploding bomb icon appear, it's just your browser crashing—not your portfolio."

Shop 'Til You Drop . . . But Safely

Chapter 12

The convenience of shopping online is wonderful. You can buy just about any product or service online, any time of the day, any day of the week. Return policies are usually generous. (Although you may have to pay for return shipping in addition to the original shipping, which is the online equivalent of the time and gas it costs you to return something to the mall.)

In addition to convenience, online shopping, whether through a store, classified, or auction site, provides a much larger selection than you can find under one roof in a store in town. You also have the ability to learn a lot more about most products, compare brands and features, read the product reviews of other customers and see what kind of experience they had with the store or seller. Another great benefit of online shopping is that it almost always gets you the best prices, out-of-state purchases may be tax free, and shipping is often free or at low cost.

Shopping safely, which we discuss in this chapter, involves knowing who you're doing business with, understanding what information to provide, avoiding scams, and knowing which methods of payment are safest.

Overview of Online Shopping Safety

Getting a great deal online involves considerably more than getting the lowest price. Before buying anything online, consider these points:

➡ You should be sure that the product arrives on time, it's of the quality you expect, and it includes a proper warranty. The seller should also clearly state its return policy and provide support with any questions or issues you have.

➡ Is the offer too good to be true? (See **Figure 12-1** for an example of an offer that looks suspicious.) Avoid buying from any e-store (online store) that promises too much at too low a price. If the price is low, you have to consider whether the merchant came by the items legally, whether you'll ever receive the items, whether the items will work, if you'll be able to return damaged goods, or if the merchant is also generating revenue by selling your financial information.

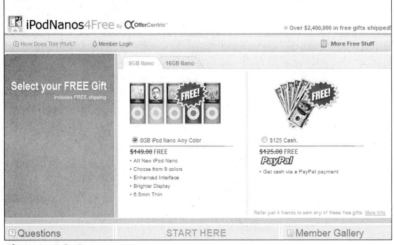

Figure 12-1

➠ Use a payment service or credit card for payment. The U.S. Federal Trade Commission limits your liability for credit card purchases to no more than $50 of unauthorized charges if your financial information is stolen. Don't use debit or ATM cards as in most cases there is no limit to your liability if these get abused and you could find your account emptied. Don't use checks as they have too much of your personal information on them including your bank, your bank account number and your banks routing number for transferring money out of your account. Any seller that asks for a cashier's check, wire transfer, or money order is almost always a scam, and once the money is sent, you have no way to get it back.

➠ Use payment services (such as PayPal shown in **Figure 12-2**) that allow you to register with them and pay companies through them without ever exposing your credit card number or personal information to the seller.

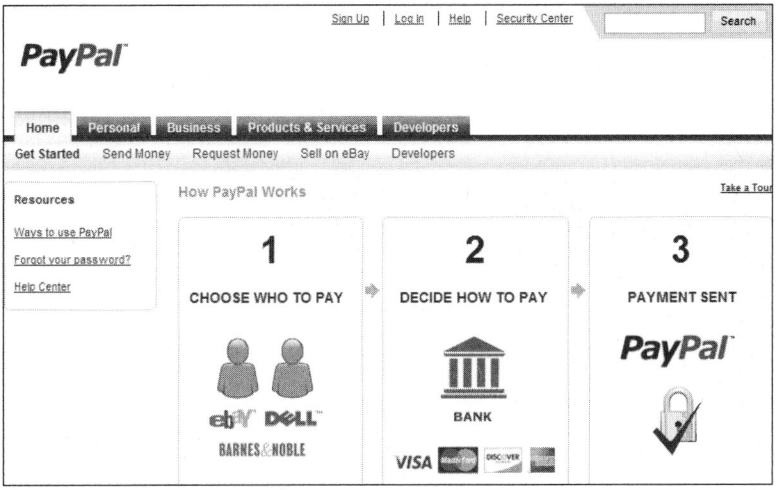

Figure 12-2

➡ It's wise to create a dedicated e-mail account for online shopping and transactions to reduce the risk of getting more spam into your primary e-mail account. We also recommend using one credit card exclusively for online transactions. If that card is compromised, you can quickly shut it down quickly without disrupting any other accounts.

➡ Review the company's shipping methods. Understand which carriers they use, their shipping rates, their tracking tools, and insurance coverage.

 Disreputable stores frequently run an absurdly low-price offer and then, claiming the item is out of stock, try to sell you something else; this is a classic bait-and-switch technique.

Choose Safe Sites

The fundamental safety consideration when shopping and performing transactions online is the same issue Internet users have to consider when sharing personal information: trust. Learning how to determine which companies, institutions, and individuals are worthy of your trust when it comes to your financial information is a critical life skill. Consider the following:

➡ **Do you know the store from the brick-and-mortar world?** If the Web site is owned by a store you already do business with and where you can physically return any item, or you have experience with their level of service and trustworthiness, you're probably in very good hands.

➡ **What is the site's reputation?** The really big, well known online brands work hard to maintain their reputation and should give excellent service and support if there are questions. On less-known sites, if you know others who have had consistently positive experiences with the online store, you can be reassured of the site's quality.

➡ **Doing your own background check.** Found a great price but it's from a store you don't know? Check it out on sites dedicated to reviewing e-stores, such as Epinions (www.epinions.com), BizRate (www.bizrate.com), and the Better Business Bureau (www.bbb.org). If you can't find any (positive) review for the store, think hard before shopping there. Another Web site to consider is The National Fraud Information Center (www.fraud.org; shown in **Figure 12-3**) which watches out for shady Internet dealings and offers consumer tips on its Web site.

Welcome to **www.fraud.org**
Home of the National Consumers League's Fraud Center

Think you've been a victim of fraud?

Help us fight con artists by reporting suspicious activity on our **online complaint form**.

With your support, NCL's Fraud Center has helped millions of consumers avoid scams.

Keep us going strong!

learn to avoid fraud with these **Fraud Center** resources

Frequently Asked Questions
what the Fraud Center does, what happens when you report, etc.

Telemarketing Fraud
consumer tips and Fraud Center trends

Internet Fraud
consumer tips and Fraud Center trends

Scams Against Businesses
tips for business owners targeted by con artists

Figure 12-3

➡ **Is the Web site secure?** Legitimate online merchants offer secure transactions. Look for two assurances to see if you're on a secure site. The URL should show

https**s**: (note the addition of the s at the end of
http) when you're making a purchase. Also, you
should see a lock symbol in to the right of the Web
address bar. (See **Figure 12-4**.)

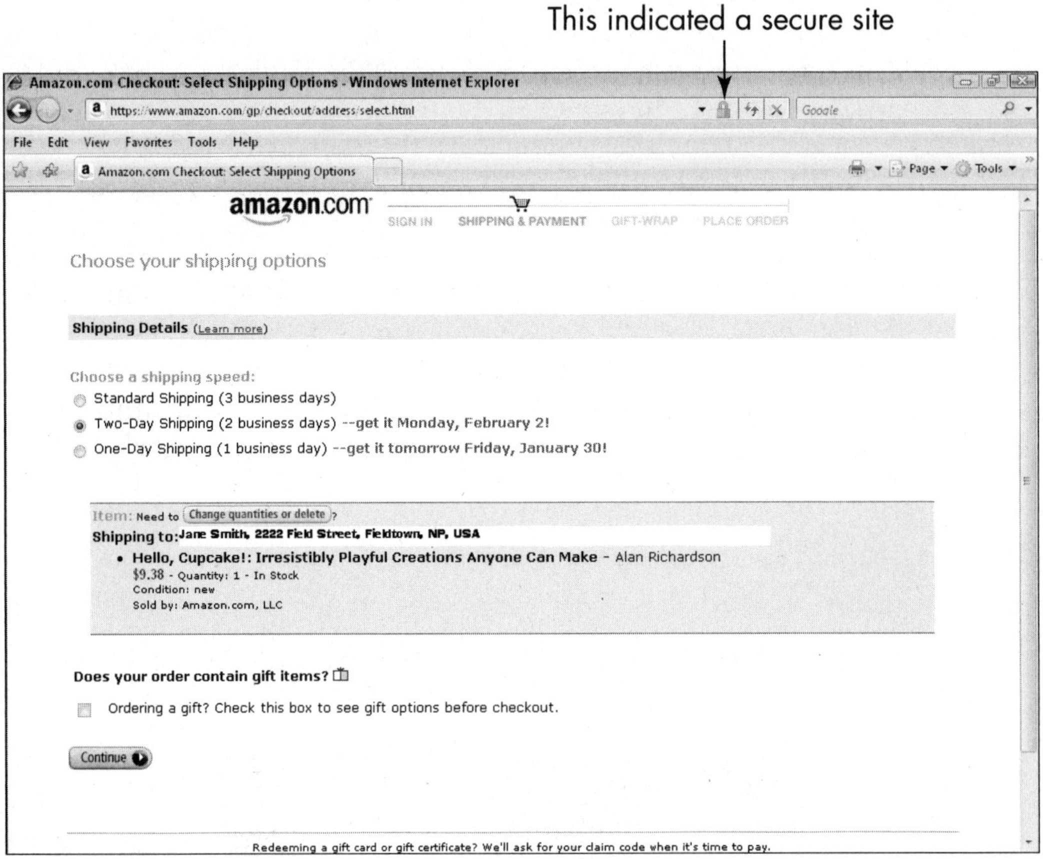

This indicated a secure site

Figure 12-4

➡ **Does the merchant collect more information than is
necessary to complete the sale?** You'll need to provide some method of payment, an address, and a telephone number, but that should be all. If, for example,
if a merchant requests your social security number or
driver's license number, *never* provide it. Some reputable companies ask additional questions about your
interests to enhance their service. These questions
should always be optional. Remember, your information is a commodity, and you should feel that you're

getting appropriate value in return and understand how the information will be used (will it be resold to others?) before providing your information.

Make Online Purchases

Although every site is slightly different, making a purchase online usually involves these steps:

1. Browse the site using links or their search feature until you find an item you want to buy.

2. Click the button called something like **Buy** or **Add to Cart** or **Add to Shopping Bag.** (See **Figure 12-5.**) Some sites have shopping carts, some shopping bags, some checkout carts or shopping baskets — but they fulfill the same function, and it's pretty easy to figure out where to put your purchases.

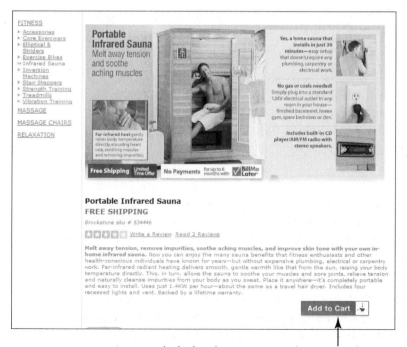

Click this button to make a purchase

Figure 12-5

3. You're then usually taken to your shopping cart, which shows the item you just put in it. You can go back to shopping. (Some sites offer a **Continue Shopping** link you can click to go back to the previous page, or you can just click the site logo to go to the home page or a link to shop a category of items.)

4. When you finish putting all the items you want to buy in your cart, click the link called **My Shopping Cart** (or **Checkout**, or **My Shopping Basket**, or whatever the site calls it).

5. At this point, you may want to look for discount coupons. Even when the company's Web site isn't displaying coupons, they may well have some, and the product manufacturer may also provide coupons. The best way to look for these is to open a new browser window so you don't lose your place in the store. Search using the company name and the word coupon to find any coupon codes or promotional codes that you can use. Enter these into the promotional code field on the store's purchase screen. Repeat the search using the name of the product and the word coupon. If you are lucky, you may get more than one discount to apply. *Note:* there are also Web sites that specialize in providing discount coupon codes for thousands of online stores. Search on the term coupons, (be sure to only use Web sites that are reputable), and see what you find.

6. When you've added any promotional/discount codes, review your purchases and quantities to make sure they are correct. When you're sure they are, continue the checkout sequence, which will involve:

- Entering your billing and shipping addresses

- Choosing a shipping method, such as standard or express

- Entering payment information (usually your credit card information, but some sites take PayPal)

- Reviewing and authorizing the purchase

7. When the purchase goes through, the seller sends an e-mail to you, confirming the purchase and providing a way to track the items as they're processed and then shipped to you. (See **Figure 12-6.**) Save the e-mail as both a receipt and to track or dispute (if it becomes necessary) the purchase.

➜ **Victor the Florist - Order Confirmation - VICORD200807152**
orders@victortheflorist.com sent it to me on **Jul 15, 2008, 7:07 PM**

| Reply | Reply All | Forward | ▾ | Trash | Spam | More actions ▾ |

Thank you for placing an order with Victor the Florist. Below are the details for your online order.

Order Totals	
Item Subtotal	$47.00
Delivery Total	$10.95
Tax Total: State/Province	$4.49
Total	$62.44

Order Information	
Order Number	Order Status
	Pending Shipment
Order Date and Time	IP Address
07/15/2008 07:04:57 PM	

Billing Information	
Billing Address	Email Address
	Telephone Number

Items	
TF57-1 - Spring Delight	Delivery Information
Date for Delivery: July 16, 2008; Card Message: Hope you're foot and spirits are fine. Love you! Nancy & Earl; Add a Balloon: No Balloon; Add a	

Figure 12-6

Sell on Classified Sites

Selling items through an online classified site is a much better option than using newspaper classifieds. Far more people will see the ad, it's usually much cheaper to place, and you can include lots more information. (See **Figure 12-7.**) Follow a few safety tips to have the best experience:

➟ When describing the item for sale, limit the personal information you give. For example, don't include in photos anything that pinpoints your location or identity, such as a house number, your child, other possessions, or identifying information that isn't relevant to the item being sold.

➟ Only give a general location, such as the name of your city, not a specific address, in your ad.

➟ Only deal with local people who you can meet face to face. The further away a buyer (or seller) is, the higher your risk of fraud. Out-of-area buyers are almost always fraudulent.

➟ Never accept payment in the form of a cashier's check, wire transfer, money order, money transfer, or escrow services. These are scams. You will end up without the item you "sold" and without payment. To add insult to injury, you may also get stuck paying the bill for the check or wire! You want cash at the time of the transaction or through a reputable payment service. (See the section "Payment Services" later in this chapter).

➟ Be wary of suspicious behavior. If someone offers to pay more than the asking price, he's committing fraud. If someone asks for your checking account information so she can transfer funds, the transaction isn't legitimate. Providing this information will put the money in your bank account at high risk of theft.

➟ Never send an item before payment in the form of cash or a transfer of funds into a PayPal (or similar service) has been received.

➟ Scammers often use hard-luck stories to get you to give them the item for free. No matter how sad the story sounds, it's likely a scam.

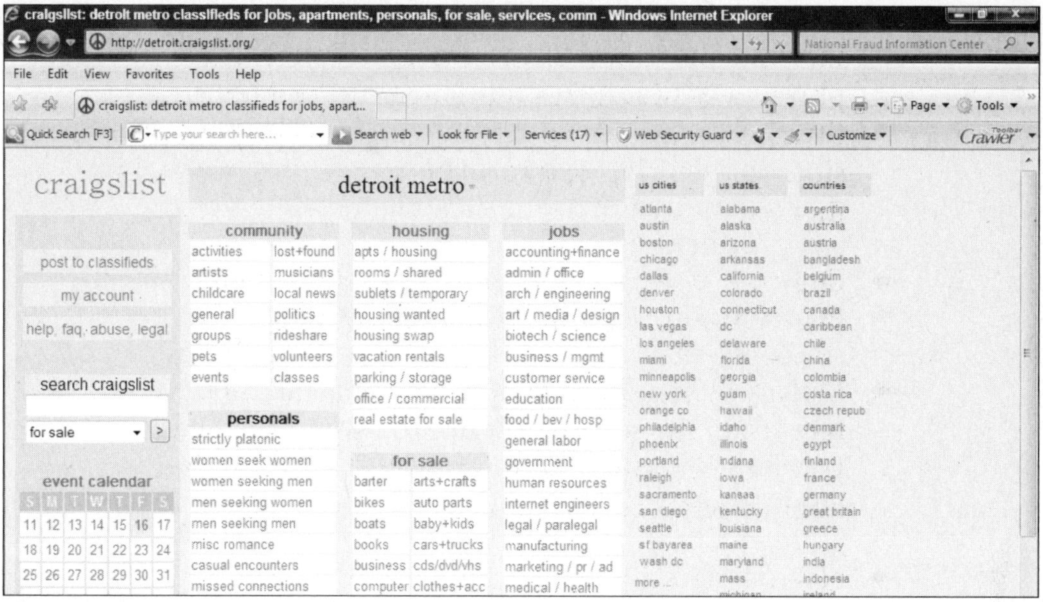

Figure 12-7

➡ Unless the item is too big to easily transport, always bring the item to a public place to show potential buyers rather than having the buyer come to your home. Don't invite trouble to your doorstep.

➡ Never meet buyers alone. Always have someone with you, even if you're meeting the buyer in a public place.

➡ If you're selling a device such as an iPod or PDA through a classified or auction site, consider what content is on the device. Strip off all personal information and make sure that it doesn't contain copyrighted content that isn't yours to sell.

Buy on Classified Sites

Online classifieds have great deals on all kinds of items, and a few smart safety precautions will help you have a positive experience. Advice for buyers is similar to that for sellers (see the previous section), but from a buyer's unique perspective. Here are safety tips for online classified site buyers:

➡ Before buying or selling anything on a classified site, read the site's Terms and Conditions, understand its abuse reporting procedures, and any safety tips the site provides.

➡ When creating an account on a classified ad site, use a separate e-mail account (not your personal e-mail account). Many sites provide an e-mail account for you, but if the site you choose to use doesn't, create a new e-mail account for yourself for your classified transactions. You shouldn't share your personal e-mail account with strangers.

➡ Don't ever include a personal phone number in your profile or when responding to an ad.

➡ Only deal with local people who you can meet face to face. The further away a buyer or seller is, the higher your risk of fraud.

➡ Research the item carefully before purchasing and be wary if the asking price is unrealistically low. Check other ads for the same item on the same or another classified or auction site.

➡ Check the item carefully before releasing payment. For example, if it's an electronic gadget, plug it in or turn it on to be sure it works.

➡ The best way to pay for items is with cash or with a secure payment service. (See the next section.) If the seller asks you to pay more than the original price and offers to give you a check for the difference, say no — it's a scam. Don't pay with a personal check, as they show your address, full name, and sometimes your phone number, along with your bank account and routing number.

➡ Avoid going to someone's house to view an item
unless it's too large to expect the seller to transport.
Ask to meet in a busy public place. Always bring
someone with you.

➡ Report any abuse to the classified service provider (see
Figure 12-8), and law enforcement, if necessary.

 If you are the victim of a scam, report it though the
Internet Crime Complaint Center at www.ic3.gov/
default.aspx.

---

craigslist
online community

about > help > abuse

harassment, publication of personal information

If your personal information has been posted in a craigslist ad:

- use our online form to report the issue
- choose "harassment" from the drop-down menu.
- put 911 in the subject field.
- provide as much information as possible, including the posting ID number, keywords that might appear in the ad, and the specific craigslist city and category in which the post appears.

abusive email

If you receive an abusive email response to one of your posts, forward the information to the "abuse" address for the sender's email account provider.

In addition, it may help to set up a block against the sender's email address in your email client.

general complaints about abusive posts

Please flag abusive posts.

Still have questions? try our help desk discussion forum or send us a note.

Updated:
Sep 15th 2008 04:29 PM

Figure 12-8

Payment Services

A great way to protect your financial identity when shopping online is
to use an online payment service. There are several payment services,
the most common are PayPal, Yahoo!, and PayDirect (see **Figure 12-9**).
Payment services enable you to use a third-party service so you never
expose your credit card or bank information to online companies or

individuals. Typically you have three basic options: you can put cash into your account on their service, link your account on their service to your bank account, or you can have them securely store your credit card information. Then, when you buy something, the service holds your payment until a buyer confirms the purchase is complete and releases the payment. The seller only sees Paypal's transaction information. This offers buyers an increased level of protection from a fraudulent seller.

Proprietary payment services may increase a buyer's protection by providing another avenue for complaints, and they may also screen out fraudulent sellers because of the reduced anonymity of the transaction. However, the degree of protection for a defrauded buyer may be limited, depending on the particular features of the payment service.

Figure 12-9

Online Auctions

Online auctions sites such as eBay continue to increase in popularity as consumers participate from computers and mobile phones. These sites are a great way to pick up good deals and unusual items (see **Figure 12-10**), and with a few simple safety precautions you can have great experiences both buying and selling in auctions. Reputable services go to great lengths to monitor their services for any scams or abuse, but you still need to stay alert and use some common sense.

Figure 12-10

Here are some things to keep in mind when participating in online auctions:

➠ Auction sites provide buyer and seller reputation ratings. Always look at the reputation of the seller (or buyer if you are selling an item). Your chances of a positive experience are far higher when dealing with individuals and companies with sterling reputations.

➠ Be particularly careful if buying 'antiques' or expensive name brand items through auction sites. Unless you are happy with knockoffs, you want to be able to verify authenticity of the items.

➡ Some auction scams tempt victims to send money for promised items and then deliver nothing — or items far less valuable than the promised items.

➡ Another ploy is overpaying for an item. In this scenario, a criminal buys an item from you with a check for a larger amount than the item's value and asks you to reimburse the difference. It's only after you've shipped the goods and refunded the difference that you discover the check bounces and the criminal gets away with your property and your cash.

➡ Be particularly careful with international sellers. If something goes wrong in one of these transactions, there's very little that can be done to help you get your funds or goods back.

Watching Your Pennies Online

Many people are worried about conducting any part of their financial lives online. They worry that the danger of having their accounts broken into or their identity stolen is somehow greater online than offline.

In fact, the greatest risk of ID theft is still that someone might take mail from your mailbox or discarded documents from your trash. With a good understanding of creating and using strong passwords (see Chapter 3), some savvy about avoiding e-mail scams (see Chapters 5), protecting yourself against downloaded spyware (see Chapter 15), and the specific advice we provide about online investing, banking, and bill paying in this chapter, you can go a long way towards avoiding ID theft and enjoy the convenience of safely managing your financial life online.

Invest Online

Online investing and investment tracking is fast, efficient, and often less expensive than using an offline broker. The Internet also makes it very easy to check the value of any stock you are interested in. Many online companies such as E*TRADE and Charles Schwab let you place your own orders for a small fee.

No matter where you invest, do your research. The types of investment fraud seen online mirrors the fraud perpetrated over the phone or through the mail.

For example:

➡ Hundreds of online investment newsletters offer seemingly unbiased information, free of charge, about featured companies or recommended stock picks. While legitimate online newsletters can help investors gather valuable information, many simply offer useless information for a fee. If an investment newsletter comes unsolicited to you, it's probably a scam.

➡ Criminals may use a combination of Internet tools to help them look legitimate. They may build sophisticated Web pages, send newsletters, post fake news on investment Web sites and more. Then they may reference these and urge you to visit them as a way of verifying that you've checked several sources.

 To invest wisely and steer clear of fraud, get the facts from the U.S. Securities and Exchange Commission's Web site at www.sec.gov.

➡ E-mail phishing scams (see **Figure 13-1**) may attempt to get you to divulge your account numbers or passwords. No legitimate financial institution will ever ask you for sensitive information via e-mail — or notify you of a problem with your account via e-mail. Discover more about phishing in Chapter 5.

 While bank accounts are protected by government insurance programs from theft, investment accounts (online or offline) aren't. Be particularly protective of your investment accounts, and consider spreading investments into several accounts so that your entire nest egg isn't put at risk from a single scam.

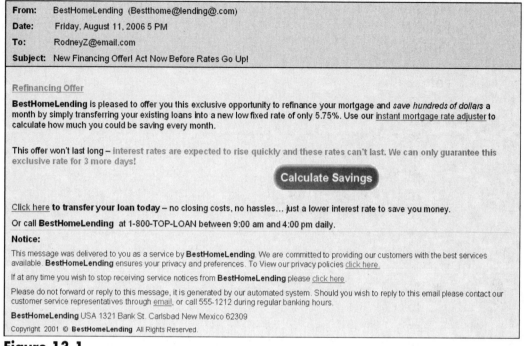

From:	BestHomeLending (Bestthome@lending@.com)
Date:	Friday, August 11, 2006 5 PM
To:	RodneyZ@email.com
Subject:	New Financing Offer! Act Now Before Rates Go Up!

Refinancing Offer

BestHomeLending is pleased to offer you this exclusive opportunity to refinance your mortgage and *save hundreds of dollars* a month by simply transferring your existing loans into a new low fixed rate of only 5.75%. Use our instant mortgage rate adjuster to calculate how much you could be saving every month.

This offer won't last long – interest rates are expected to rise quickly and these rates can't last. We can only guarantee this exclusive rate for 3 more days!

Calculate Savings

Click here to transfer your loan today – no closing costs, no hassles... just a lower interest rate to save you money.

Or call **BestHomeLending** at 1-800-TOP-LOAN between 9:00 am and 4:00 pm daily.

Notice:

This message was delivered to you as a service by **BestHomeLending**. We are committed to providing our customers with the best services available. **BestHomeLending** ensures your privacy and preferences. To View our privacy policies click here.

If at any time you wish to stop receiving service notices from **BestHomeLending** please click here.

Please do not forward or reply to this message, it is generated by our automated system. Should you wish to reply to this email please contact our customer service representatives through email, or call 555-1212 during regular banking hours.

BestHomeLending USA 1321 Bank St. Carlsbad New Mexico 62309

Copyright 2001 © **BestHomeLending** All Rights Reserved.

Figure 13-1

Bank Online

Banks go to great lengths to safeguard your information and online transactions and there are protections in place to shield consumers in the event of banking fraud. (See **Figure 13-2**.)

Banking and paying bills online is convenient, and it can be safer than banking and bill paying in the physical world, where lost and stolen mail and having discarded statements stolen from your trash are concerns. Online account access allows you to check balances, transfer funds between accounts, view statements, and pay bills online.

You can also choose to use a software product such as Quicken from Intuit (see **Figure 13-3**) to manage your budget and bill paying and synchronize with your bank records and pay bills online.

In most cases, the weakest link in online banking is the consumer. This is good news because it means that you can control your online risk by educating yourself.

Challenge Questions help prevent banking fraud

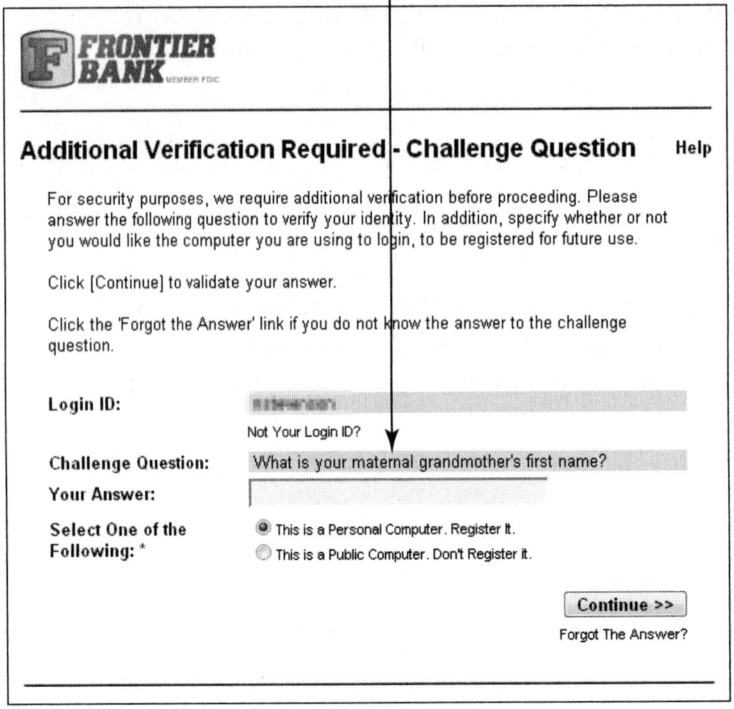

FRONTIER BANK
MEMBER FDIC
Additional Verification Required - Challenge Question
Help
For security purposes, we require additional verification before proceeding. Please answer the following question to verify your identity. In addition, specify whether or not you would like the computer you are using to login, to be registered for future use.
Click [Continue] to validate your answer.
Click the 'Forgot the Answer' link if you do not know the answer to the challenge question.
Login ID:
Not Your Login ID?
Challenge Question:
What is your maternal grandmother's first name?
Your Answer:
Select One of the Following: *
This is a Personal Computer. Register It.
This is a Public Computer. Don't Register it.
Continue >>
Forgot The Answer?

Figure 13-2

Quick Survey
Quicken
Help Me Choose
Products & Services
Support
Sign In
Order Status
Cart
keyword
Sign In
Help Me Choose
Compare Products
Free, Easy Money Management Online!
Free Quicken Online brings together ALL of your financial information online, so you can easily manage your simple personal finances.
Start Now
Learn more
Automatically downloads and categorizes your transactions, so you know where you're spending
See all your bank and credit card accounts in one place, with one password
You can even access your personal finance information from your cell phone*
Free Quicken Online
Simple Personal Finances
FREE Quicken ONLINE
Deluxe
Maximize Your Savings
Just $59.99
Premier
Optimize Your Investments
Just $89.99
Home & Business
Personal & Business in One
Just $99.99
Rental Property Manager
Personal & Rental Property in One
Just $149.99
All Your Accou
in One Place
Save Where
You Shop

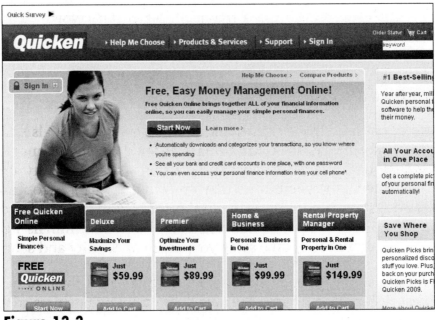

Figure 13-3

Follow these steps to stay safer:

➠ Make sure your computer has up-to-date versions of anti-virus and anti-spyware software, and continue to install all updates you receive from the software.

➠ If you open an account with an online-only bank, confirm that the bank is legitimate and that your deposits are insured.

➠ Create strong passwords (see Chapter 3 for information about how to do this) for accessing your account, and keep personal information private and secure.

➠ Never conduct financial transactions from a public computer because you don't know if these computers are infected with malicious programs that may be stealing your information.

➠ Always type your bank's Web address into your browser yourself or use your bookmark. (See Chapter 4.) You can find the Web address on your statements or by searching for your bank's Web site using a search engine.) If you click a link provided in an e-mail, you may land on a site that looks legitimate, but isn't.

Protect Your Identity Online

Identity theft is a serious crime, and it occurs when criminals steal and use your information to commit financial fraud or other crimes. These actions can have a serious impact on your financial credibility and security. Thieves or cyberbullies may use your information to ruin your reputation, steal and sell your medical records, obtain loans in your name, or misuse images of you. Whatever else these criminals steal and do, at a minimum they take away your sense of security and safety.

The total cost of identity theft is astounding. In 2007, the cost in the U.S. was $45 billion dollars. Business loss drives up business costs, so consumers pay this portion as well, just indirectly. The average victim spends hundreds of hours trying to restore his or her identity. Although most victims are discovering the abuse earlier (and quick action is key in reducing the time it takes you to clean your records up), it now takes longer on average to eliminate fraudulent transactions from credit reports and other sources than ever before.

Stay alert to avoid this kind of attack, and take the following actions wherever you roam online:

→ Be conservative with personal information online, whether it's on your social networking page, dating site, discussion board, survey, quiz, or somewhere else. ID thieves look to accumulate information about you.

→ *Never delay.* If you see a questionable charge on an account, check it out. The sooner you identify and begin to solve a case of identity theft, the easier it is to clean up.

ID theft may also be very emotionally distressing. Most victims feel violated and frustrated, particularly because they don't know how or from where the information was stolen. If you're a victim of ID theft, get help from the Identity Theft Resource Center at www.idtheftcenter.org.

If one family member's identity is compromised, it increases the risk to other family members. If your child or grandchild is a victim, for example, some of your information may make its way into criminal hands. Don't assume that youth is any protection from ID theft. Some children's identities are stolen even before they're born if parents announce the child's name and expected birth date in a public way. If something happens to anybody in your family, take all the steps given here to monitor your credit reports, financial accounts, and medical records to spot irregularities.

Understand Medical ID Theft

It's important that seniors know about medical identity theft because it can have very serious consequences. Financial ID theft can threaten your finances and reputation. Medical ID theft can threaten your life.

Those who use your identity to gain access to medical care or services may introduce changes to your medical records to get what they are after. For example they may want drugs for resale. To accomplish this they may alter your records to show you have conditions that require the drugs. This can put you at real risk in an emergency when a decision is based off false information.

It can be very difficult to identify and to undo those changes. Discovering medical identity theft can be harder to detect than financial identity theft and you may have to hunt to unearth it. Some people discover medical identity theft when medical bills they aren't responsible for show up in the mail. Sometimes an insurance investigator alerts victims, or doctors notice errors in patients' medical files.

Based on some of the cases of medical identity theft that have come to light, here's some advice from www.worldprivacyforum.org:

➡ Closely monitor any "Explanation of Benefits" sent by an public or private health insurer.

➡ Pro-actively request a listing of benefits from your health insurers.

➡ Request a copy of current medical files from each health care provider.

➡ File a police report.

➡ Correct erroneous and false information in your file.

➡ Keep an eye on your credit report.

➡ Request an accounting of disclosures.

Online Personal Health Records

There is a push by the government, doctors, and insurance companies to get all medical records online. The benefits are obvious: records could be combined to provide the best overall medical history of a patient, there could be instant access to critical information in emergencies, and so on.

But placing your medical records online also leaves you extremely vulnerable if the database holding your records is compromised. There is a lot of conjecture about how secure these records will be, but the reality is we have significant data breaches of all types of secure records and databases, even in the most sensitive military and national security records.

You may have received a letter from Health and Human Services inviting you to sign up with a company that provides PHR (Personal Health Record) services, stating that the companies will guarantee your privacy. Be very cautious.

The quotes below are from the Department of Health and Human Services brochure at www.medicare.gov/phr.

➡ "Since you will have a unique user ID and password, only you will be able to view your record. Most companies that provide PHRs offer a secure site to protect and keep your information safe."

➡ "Most health care providers and Health Plans who offer PHRs must give you a Notice of Privacy Practices, which tells you how they keep your personal information private and safe."

The use of the word "most" in these statements is very concerning, because this clearly means "not all." If you choose to register for a Personal Health Record, understand that these records may be compromised and your sensitive medical history could then be in the hands of criminals.

Understand the Risk of Identity Theft by Age

As a senior, you may feel particularly at risk for ID theft and financial scams. In fact, 18–29-year-olds are most at risk because they most likely haven't yet damaged their credit, are less likely to check their credit, are more likely to share too much information online, move frequently — so records go to others — and are more likely to apply for credit cards without reading the fine print or considering the source. (See **Figure 13-4**.)

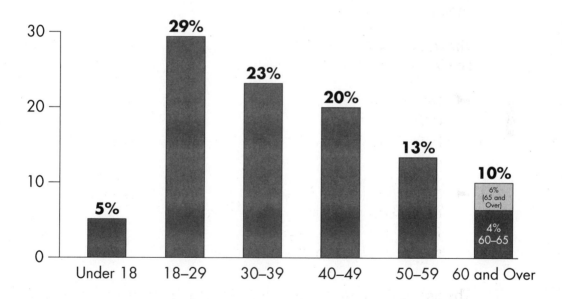

Identity Theft Complaints by Victim Age[1]
January 1 – December 31, 2006

[1]*Percentages are based on the total number of identity theft complaints where victims reported their age (225,532). 94% of the victims who conracted the FTC directly reported their age.*

Figure 13-4

Some people believe that if they have little money in their bank account, there's nothing to steal. Unfortunately, what matters isn't just how much you have in your bank account; it's how far in debt the thief can place you by using your information to apply for loans or purchase expensive items on your credit. In fact, a criminal may leave the money in your checking account untouched and drive up debt so that it takes longer for you to be alerted the problem.

 There's a useful Identity Theft Risk Assessment Quiz from Rutgers University to help you learn better habits to prevent ID theft. Try it out at `http://njaes.rutgers.edu/money/identitytheft/`.

Get Your Free Credit Reports

All people over the age of 14 or so need to be monitoring their credit score, as this is one of the quickest ways to spot ID theft. Here are some important facts about obtaining your credit reports:

➠ You have the right to one *free* credit disclosure in a 12-month period from *each* of the three national credit reporting companies — TransUnion (`www.transunion.com`), Experian (`www.experian.com`), and Equifax (`www.equifax.com`).

➠ The easiest way to get these reports is through AnnualCreditReport.com (see **Figure 13-5**), a service created by these three credit institutions specifically to help consumers get free annual reports. Simply go to this site, answer some questions to verify your identity, and submit your request. As of this writing, all three agencies allow you to submit this request online. (You may see offers that charge you for reports, but why pay when you can use this site to get them for free.)

➠ You can also pay for credit monitoring services to watch your credit for you. (See **Figure** 13-6.)

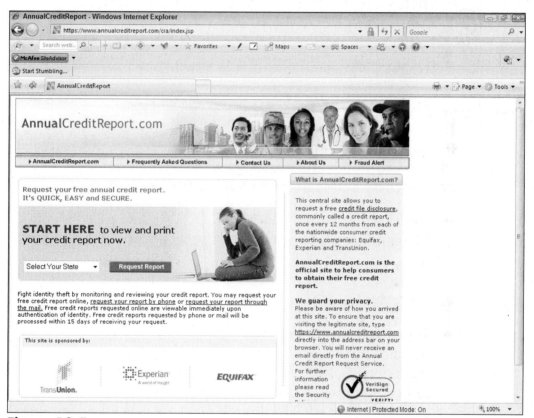

Figure 13-5

Figure 13-6

Freeze Your Credit

You may hear the terms *security, credit freeze,* and fraud alert. Here's what they mean:

A *security* or *credit freeze* is a request to a credit bureau to stop sharing your credit file with potential creditors or insurance companies. You, too, can't open new credit while a freeze is in place. Individuals can request that the credit bureau temporarily lift the freeze for the purpose of obtaining new credit, although there may be a fee involved to do so. A freeze is not 100 percent safe because some creditors issue credit without pulling a credit report. Companies with whom you have an existing relationship can still pull a report despite the freeze, and your information may be given out for the purpose of prescreening you for credit offers. Credit freezes cost about $10, unless you've been a victim of ID theft — in which case, they're free. Placing a freeze on your accounts is an excellent safeguard.

A *fraud alert* is a less restrictive option that can help prevent fraud. An alert doesn't block new credit, but it does insert a comment on your history that indicates that you may be a victim of fraud. Call the toll-free fraud number of any one of the three major credit bureaus to place a fraud alert on your credit report for 90 days. The other two credit bureaus are automatically notified to place fraud alerts. All three credit reports are then sent to you at no charge.

Continue Protecting Your Identity Online

After an identity theft, even when you've gone through all the steps to restore your identity and financial standing, you remain at increased risk of a recurrence because much of your identity doesn't change.

You can change your credit card account number, close your bank account, and fix a manipulated credit history, but your birth date, birth place, mother's maiden name, names of past employers, and other personal information never changes.

This information is likely to remain in criminal databases, and it has the potential of being reused many times. Once you've been a victim, you'll need to be extra diligent in monitoring your identity forever.

You can take many significant steps to protect yourself, but there's no silver bullet or magic solution, especially as you may not be the one exposing your information. Publicly available property tax records, court records, and housing records all make finding information about you easier.

Follow these steps to keep yourself safer from ID thieves:

➠ As discussed elsewhere in this chapter, everyone above the age of 14 needs to actively monitor his credit history by obtaining credit reports at least three times a year.

➠ Consider if you want all, part, or none of your information viewable in online phone directory searches. It usually costs money to keep your information private (often referred to as a privacy tax), but the few dollars it costs may be well worth it to you.

➠ Check your county Web site for your property records to be sure these do not also show your loan papers, social security numbers or other information that is not required by law. Check to see if birth, marriage, and death certificates are available online, and if so, how much information these contain. Demand that sensitive information be removed.

➠ If your identity is stolen, contact your bank(s) and other financial institutions immediately. Contact local law enforcement and file a report. Contact your medical insurance company. Freeze your credit with the three credit reporting companies. (Ideally, you freeze this now and leave it frozen to avoid the fraud.)

➠ If you're a victim of identity theft, go to the FTC's Identity Theft Web site (www.ftc.gov/bcp/edu/microsites/idtheft; see **Figure 13-7**) to get information about additional steps you may need to take.

➠ Identity theft victims should alert their friends and family. Your identity theft means friends and family may also be affected, depending on the information stolen or abused.

Figure 13-7

Healthcare That Makes You Feel Better

Getting the best information about your health and the health of your family members (including pets) is important. So where do you go for advice?

Sixty percent of consumers now turn to the Internet for medical advice, according to research conducted by the Opinion Research Corporation in the Fall of 2007. Alarmingly, 54 percent follow online advice even when they don't believe it!

In this chapter, we look at how you can take advantage of the great information online related to healthcare, both from Web sites and others like yourself who share their thoughts and experiences. We explore the convenience and pitfalls of buying drugs online. Finally, we give you a rundown of various types of abuses, including medical ID theft and medical scams, so that you can navigate the world of Internet health resources safely.

Chapter 14

In this chapter . . .

Connect with Others with Similar Concerns

When you have a medical condition, it's great to talk to someone else who's gone through the same experience. Although it's no replacement for your doctor's advice, sharing with others may help you through a stressful time. Here are some things to keep in mind when connecting with others about health-related topics:

➡ People with serious medical conditions often share a great deal of information about themselves that can lead to identity theft. To stay safer when sharing information about a health-related issue, talk about the illness but refrain from sharing personally identifying information.

➡ Always take others' comments with a grain of salt. These people aren't experts, may be self-diagnosing inaccurately, may not share the same condition you have, or may have had unique responses to drugs or treatments. Ask your doctor the same questions you ask others online so that you get a balanced perspective.

➡ Sites that are primarily medical information sites, such as WebMD (www.webmd.com), host forums and message boards on a wide variety of health topics. Choose a reputable site for participating in discussions.

➡ Some social networking sites provide ways to interact with other members over health-related issues. However, you should always be cautious about sharing health information if you're identifiable, for example, from information in your social network profile.

➡ For those with addictions like alcoholism, there are sites such as SoberCircle (www.sobercircle.com; shown in **Figure 14-1**) and DailyStrength (www.dailystrength.org), where the encouragement of others can help you with recovery.

Welcome to the new SoberCircle   Recovery Lives Here

Sign Up | Log In   Search

It's never too late
Get Help Now!
Strictly Confidential

sober circle

Home   Browse   Inbox   Blogs   Community   Media   Addons   Resources   Get Help

Blog Results

Blog Home

Search Blogs

--Select Member Type--

Submit

Category

12–Step (42)
Announcements (51)
Creative Writing (27)

Results for Announcements

Member	Type	Blog Post Subject	Views	Date
	In Recovery	I finally got my van!!... As many of you know, I have been wanting to get a van with a raised roof for years. My little Pammy is in a wheelchair because she has cerebral palsy. She weighs 90 lbs. & it's difficult to lift her into the front seat. Her wheelchair is not as heavy as she is–LOL! What I WANTED was an Astrovan, and I was blessed...	1/16/2009 9:11 AM	
	In Recovery	1 year of sobriety... Here I am– 1 year later– and I am still sober!! Life still has alot of ups and downs(i think it always will), but I refuse to use alcohol to help me get thru them! As my sponsor told me...I	1/14/2009 7:31 AM	

Figure 14-1

➠ Some sites focus on emotional support for people with specific serious diseases. One example is PatientsLikeMe (www.patientslikeme.com; shown in **Figure 14-2**), a social networking health site with communities for ALS, MS, Parkinson's Disease, HIV, and mood disorders such as depression and bipolar disorder, progressive supranuclear palsy, multiple system atrophy, and Devic's disease.

➠ If you find the behavior or comments of anyone you meet in a health-related discussion online to be rude, aggressive, or invasive, stop the communication and report the person to the site immediately.

 A site to check out if you're dealing with cancer is ChemoCoach (www.chemocoach.com), which covers several types of cancer in its discussion forums.

Figure 14-2

Be Wise about Using Online Medical Advice

There are very reputable medical Web sites that provide a wealth of information about a broad spectrum of medical conditions. On the other hand, there are also plenty of quack sites that dispense entirely spurious medical "advice." So how can you tell the difference?

Here's some advice about online medical advice sites:

➡ It may seem obvious, but one of the best resources for advice on good medical sites is your doctor. Ask your health professional if he recommends a Web site for your specific condition.

➡ Look for the Health on the Net Foundation (HON) seal of approval. (See **Figure 14-3**.) This seal is given to only those sites that are accredited against a strict set of principles. If you don't see this seal on the site, search for sites that have it.

➡ A company called URAC gives accreditation to health-related sites. A committee of experts regularly reviews accredited sites for accuracy and quality.

The Health On the Net Foundation seal

Figure 14-3

➡ Remember that the nomenclature .org at the end of a site name denotes a non-profit organization rather than a commercial business. A site such as Mayo Clinic.org (www.mayoclinic.org; shown in **Figure 14-4**), focused on research and education, won't bombard you with advertisements for healthcare products, and visiting the site may be less likely to result in spam.

 Your health and the health of those you love is not something to take chances on. Although qualified medical Web sites provide a wealth of information that can help you understand symptoms and illnesses, no source will provide you with better or more reliable information than a well-trained medical specialist who knows you, your family members, or your pet. Before treating yourself based on information you find online, always consult with your medical advisor.

 Remember many medical Web sites are for-profit businesses, and as such are there to make money. This isn't a bad thing per se, but you do need to be aware of how they make their money, and if their recommendations are biased towards their own products. You also need to be clear about how they treat any information you disclose about yourself, as they may sell information to drug and medical companies. It's critical that you're aware of the terms and conditions and privacy rights to make informed choices about what information you share.

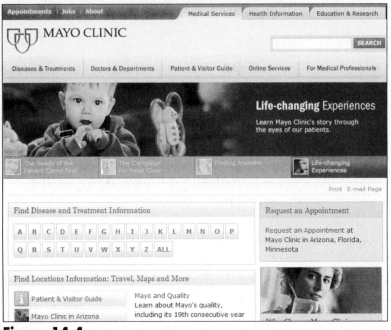

Figure 14-4

Discount Drugs and Online Prescriptions

Buying drugs online can be private and convenient, but you have to make sure you're dealing with a reputable pharmacy. The U.S. Food and Drug Administration (FDA) recommends using only Web sites of U.S.–based pharmacies licensed by a state's board of pharmacy. Check out the Web site of the National Association of Boards of Pharmacy (NABP; www.nabp.net), which can tell you how to get in touch with your state's board. This site also offers a list of online pharmacies that have been accredited through its Verified Internet Pharmacy Practice Sites (VIPPS) program. (See **Figure 14-5**.) If you live in a country other than the U.S., check with your regional authority to get similar guidance.

Also, according to the U.S. FTC, avoid sites that

➠ Don't require a prescription or prescription medications.

➠ Don't have a licensed pharmacist available to answer your questions.

➡ Don't provide their physical business addresses and phone numbers.

➡ Are based outside the U.S. or aren't licensed by the state board of pharmacy where they're based. Regarding buying drugs from online sites not based in the U.S., the U.S. FDA has stated this: "The FDA, due to the current state of their regulations, has taken the position that virtually all shipments of prescription drugs imported from a Canadian pharmacy by a U.S. consumer will violate the law."

Don't gamble with your health. The money you save could cost you dearly. Disreputable sellers may send drugs that are fake, expired, mislabeled, or the wrong dosage. The drugs may contain dangerous ingredients, or may not be stored or shipped correctly. If the site is based outside the U.S., there's very little that the U.S. government can do if there is a problem.

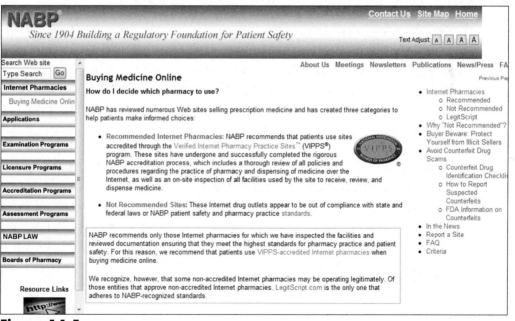

Figure 14-5

Keep in mind that drug prices vary, so you may want to shop around. Sites such as PharmacyChecker.com for Canadian citizens and Consumer Reports in the United States (www.consumerreports.org) help you compare drug prices. Rxaminer (www.rxaminer.com) provides information on generic substitutes for common drugs that might save you money, if your doctor approves them for your use.

Medical Identity Theft

With the increase in personal medical records being stored online, medical ID theft is of great concern. People with serious medical conditions may be more willing to provide information that leads to identity and financial theft. Just because you share information about a health-related issue online doesn't mean you have to share personally identifying information.

Medical ID theft may result in your medical records becoming inaccurate, as insurance claims for conditions you don't have go into your file. You may end up paying thousands of dollars for deductibles or treatment of uncovered conditions. Your credit could be damaged, and insurance cancelled.

Medical ID theft is a lucrative business. Your medical coverage can be leveraged or sold in a variety of ways:

➥ Using your insurance and your identity someone with no health coverage can buy prescription drugs online or get medical treatment charged to your insurance policy.

➥ Your information can be used to submit false claims to insurance companies, and the criminal collect the payments.

Vigilance is your best defense against Medical ID theft. Always review any medical bills and insurance notices for charges that seem suspect. Online, there are a few key principles to follow. (See Chapter 13 for more detailed information on ID theft.)

➡ Don't personally identify yourself if discussing your health online, either in your own blogs, or in discussion forums; this includes making sure your screen name does not give you away.

➡ Make your blog private if you intend to publish any health-related information.

Never take online health quizzes or forward e-mails with such surveys or quizzes.

➡ Never provide information such as your insurance policy number, doctor's name and location, or medicare/Medicaid policy numbers to anyone online. Not in e-mail, IM, or any other online communication tool. You may need to provide some pieces of this information when logging into your insurance company's or doctor's Web site, but be extremely cautious to ensure you are on their legitimate site.

➡ Check your health insurance provider's Web site (see **Figure 14-6**) for advice on avoiding medical ID theft.

 Unlike credit information, which is held by the three credit reporting bureaus, medical records are often scattered all over, in doctor's offices, insurance companies, and pharmacies, so it's hard to track false information. Under HIPAA (Health Insurance Portability and Accountability Act), the federal law that addresses medical privacy, you're entitled to a copy of medical record documents, although you may have to pay for it. If there's an error, you can add a correction to the record, but you can't have information deleted.

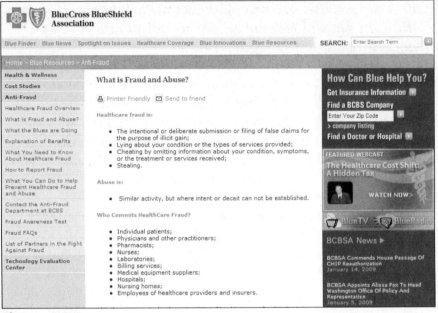

Figure 14-6

 There are several outcomes of medical ID theft, which can be harder to undo than financial ID theft. Stay vigilant, and challenge any questionable charge immediately. If you suspect fraud, have a notice placed on your account so the insurance company double-checks before paying claims.

Warning Signs of Health Fraud

Health-fraud con artists use the same tactics and phrases repeatedly. Learning to spot them can help you avoid scam sites and offers.

Health-fraud red flags, according to the FTC, include

➡ Web sites that offer quick and dramatic cures for a wide variety of ailments. A site may claim that a treatment is beneficial in treating cancer, ulcer, prostate problems, heart trouble, and more, for example.

➡ Statements that suggest the product can treat or cure diseases. You might see claims that a product shrinks tumors, cures impotency, and the like.

➡ Promotions that use words like *scientific break-through, miraculous cure, secret ingredient,* and *ancient remedy.* (See **Figure 14-7**.)

➡ Text that uses impressive-sounding terms like *hunger stimulation point* and *thermogenesis* for a weight-loss product. These terms are sometimes plucked out of scientific journals, but they may have nothing to do with the disease or condition you have — let alone legitimize the cure you're being peddled.

➡ Undocumented case histories or personal testimonials by consumers or doctors claiming amazing results. "After eating a teaspoon of this product each day, my pain is completely gone." Most are made up, and others are hearsay. Some patients' recoveries may be due to a remission of the disease from previous or concurrent treatments.

➡ Limited availability and advance payment requirements. *Hurry! This offer will not last,* for example.

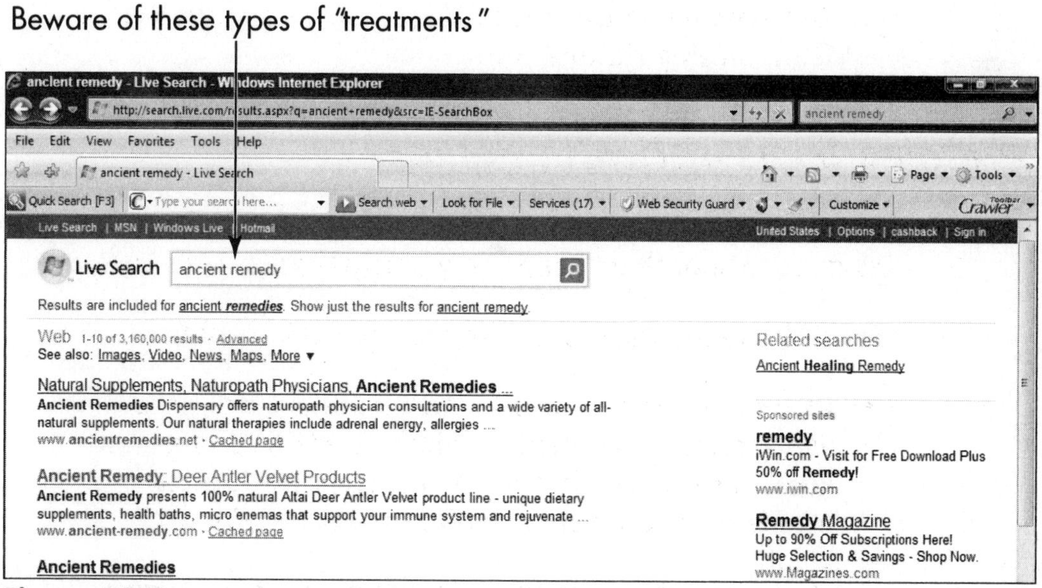

Beware of these types of "treatments"

Figure 14-7

➡ Promises of no-risk money-back guarantees. *If after 30 days you have not lost at least four pounds each week, your uncashed check will be returned to you,* and the like.

➡ Promises of an easy fix. For many serious diseases, there are no cures, only therapies to help manage them.

➡ Paranoid accusations — suggesting that healthcare providers and legitimate manufacturers are in league with each other to suppress this miracle cure.

 Look closely at the vocabulary that these Web sites use. The words *in days* can mean any amount of time. The term *rapid* is ambiguous.

 Beware of products offered as a *Free Trial! — You pay only shipping and handling*. In these cases, the charges levied for shipping and handling are exhorbitant and one way scammers make money. Think about it: If the pills cost them 45 cents and the mailing costs them two dollars, but they charge $19.95 in shipping and handling, they still earn $17.50 from every customer. If they can scam ten thousand consumers, they earn $175,000 dollars.

Surveys on Health Can Make You Sick

Quizzes and surveys you find online (such as the one shown in **Figure 14-8**), including those on social networking sites, are usually entertaining and may seem like a harmless pastime. But quiz and survey companies are for-profit businesses. Because consumer information is a commodity, you should assume that information you enter in quizzes and surveys is being sold. (Chapter 8 provides more information about quizzes and surveys.)

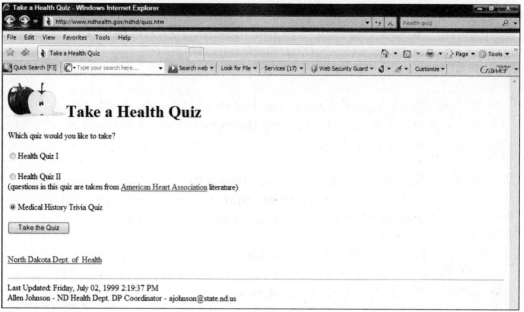

Figure 14-8

Here are some things to keep in mind if you're tempted to take online quizzes:

➡ Seniors especially need to be careful about taking health-related surveys. For example, the information from a medical quiz may be passed directly to pharmaceutical companies, online drugstores, or insurance companies. The medical quiz shown above for example asks extremely detailed questions — clear down to how often do you eat processed meats in a week — and routes all this sensitive information instantly to CVS Pharmacy, that uses it to push its products based on your responses.

➡ Your quiz and survey information may be used to limit coverage of preexisting conditions, deny coverage and more. The ramifications of this do not end with you, the information may also impact the insurance coverage of your children and grandchildren.

⟶ Make sure you understand the reputation, privacy policies, and terms of use of the site creating or hosting the quizzes. Our recommendation is clear: NEVER take an online medical quiz or survey. If you choose to do so, at least consider the answers to the following questions:

- Why did the company create this quiz?

- What will the company do with the information?

⟶ Could taking a quiz impact my medical coverage or the coverage of family members?

Miracle Medicine For Sale

One of the most loathsome forms of online fraud is perpetrated against people struggling with serious illnesses who are eager for a cure from any quarter, no matter how unlikely. Consider the following:

⟶ Internet health fraud is a growing problem. The FDA describes health fraud as offering "articles of unproven effectiveness that are promoted to improve health, well being, or appearance."

⟶ Scammers' products run the gamut — from miracle drugs (see **Figure 14-9**) to medical devices, foods, and even cosmetics. Whether offered in the form of a fruit juice, a vitamin pill, salve, or inhalant, the companies that offer these products provide jargon and hype with amazing claims of success to particularly vulnerable people.

⟶ Many victims of health fraud suffer from a variety of illnesses and conditions, including cancer, AIDS, heart disease, diabetes, herpes, obesity, and sexual dysfunction.

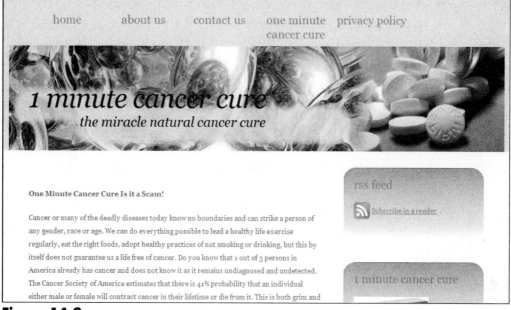

home   about us   contact us   one minute   privacy policy
                                              cancer cure

1 minute cancer cure
the miracle natural cancer cure

rss feed

Subscribe in a reader

1 minute cancer cure

One Minute Cancer Cure Is it a Scam!

Cancer or many of the deadly diseases today know no boundaries and can strike a person of any gender, race or age. We can do everything possible to lead a healthy life exercise regularly, eat the right foods, adopt healthy practices of not smoking or drinking, but this by itself does not guarantee us a life free of cancer. Do you know that 1 out of 3 persons in America already has cancer and does not know it as it remains undiagnosed and undetected. The Cancer Society of America estimates that there is 41% probability that an individual either male or female will contract cancer in their lifetime or die from it. This is both grim and

Figure 14-9

People with these and other conditions should be aware of several problems with online offers for alternative drugs and cures.

➠ The goal of these scams is to steal money by selling hope. At best, patients are purchasing placebos where only their pockets incur damage — some end up throwing their life's savings, even incurring debt in their pursuit of health.

➠ These products may be contaminated, diluted, ineffective, out of date, or have harmful side effects. Any product, synthetic or natural, potent enough to work like a drug is potent enough to cause side effects, and any treatments you use without a prescription can have adverse reactions, particularly in conjunction with medications you're already taking. Many struggling with illnesses are paying for products that abbreviate rather than prolong their lives.

➡ Beyond the direct risks of damage from spurious cures, there's an indirect risk: Taking these instead of proven treatments could mean that patients get sicker.

➡ Don't be fooled by the term *natural* (see **Figure 14-10**) — it doesn't equate to *safe.* Many natural ingredients are lethal — cyanide, for example, is found in many common plants. Conversely, 60 percent of over-the-counter drugs and 25 percent of prescription drugs are based on natural ingredients. Alternative cures have no exclusivity on the use of natural ingredients.

How rampant is health fraud online? Consider the results for some health cures from a recent Google search:

➡ 44,800 results for *black salve,* a cancer treatment which claims to draw cancer out through the skin but in reality burns healthy skin tissue and causes severe scarring.

➡ 11,100 results for *Hoxsey cancer treatment,* an unproven herbal remedy that the FDA has tried to get rid of since the 1950s.

➡ 3,150,000 results for *diabetes cures*. (Diabetes can't be cured, just managed.)

➡ *Weight loss* gets a whopping 70,300,000 results. Weight-loss pills alone commands 2,120,000 links. There just isn't a guaranteed weight-loss supplement that the five o'clock news and your doctor missed, although there are several that can cause serious harm.

 Although many search results on health cures lead to scholarly articles, a great many more lead to fraudulent sites. It's easy to create a slick site and pose as a medical practitioner online and make wild claims that link to a variety of fraudulent supporting medical studies.

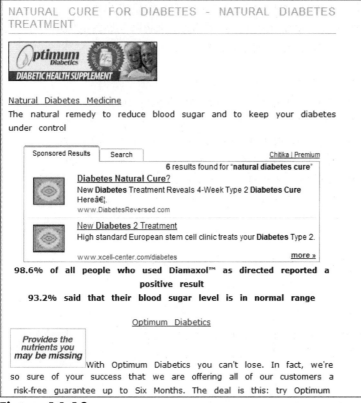

Figure 14-10

Products that cure serious diseases are widely reported in the media, not discovered on obscure Web sites.

The older you are, the more heavily targeted you are likely to be for these types of scams so be especially vigilant.

To check out a health product you encounter online, the FDA suggests that you take these steps:

⟹ Talk to a doctor or other health professional whom you trust, and follow their advice.

⟹ Check the source. If you are looking for prescription drugs, follow the advice listed above for finding certified pharmacies. If you are looking for other types of health products, make sure the company is based in your country by calling their phone number and verifying their address. If you're a United States citizen, for example, you can file complaints against U.S. companies, but there is little than can be done if you don't get what was promised from a foreign-based company.

➡ Check with the Better Business Bureau or your attorney general's office to see if complaints have been lodged against the company.

➡ Check with a relevant professional medical group such as the American Heart Association or National Arthritis Foundation to see if they endorse the Web site or product.

➡ Contact your local FDA office (find the number in the blue pages of your phone book, or go to `www.fda.gov/default.htm`, shown in **Figure 14-11**) to find out if they've taken any action against the product or its marketer.

➡ Report fraud to the service provider where the ad was posted, to the Better Business Bureau, and to the FDA.

Here are some good resources for helping you avoid medical scams and fraud:

➡ `www.quackwatch.org`

➡ `www.scamshield.com`

➡ `www.scambusters.org`

➡ `www.healthfinder.gov`

FDA | U.S. Food and Drug Administration | U.S. Department of Health and Human Services

FDA Home Page | Search FDA Site | FDA A-Z Index | Contact FDA

Contact FDA

If you want to communicate your comments, questions or suggestions to FDA through the Internet, please start by selecting your area of concern:

Select a Topic ▼ [Go]

Need Information About the Registration of Food Facilities:
Submit questions to the Help Desk.
Phone: 1-800-216-7331

Have a comment/question about the Website? We'd like to hear it. Please let us know if you need assistance with a broken link, a page loading incorrectly, or other technical problems. Please provide the URL (address) of the troublesome page. You can report these problems or let us know what you think about our Website by using our Website Feedback form.

Contact Us by Mail or Telephone

If you have comments or questions you can also contact us by mail:

Food and Drug Administration
5600 Fishers Lane
Rockville, Maryland 20857

or by telephone:

- 1-888-INFO-FDA (1-888-463-6332) -- main FDA Phone Number (for general inquiries)

Where to Look for Answers

- Website Index
- Search FDA Website
- Site Map
- How to Report Problems with FDA-regulated Products
- Frequently Asked Questions
- Getting Information from FDA
- FDA Field Offices
- FDA Job Information
- About FDA

Information For:

- Consumers
- Patients
- Health Professionals
- State/Local Officials
- Industry
- Press
- Women
- Español
- Kids

Figure 14-11

Part IV
Being Proactive

The 5th Wave   By Rich Tennant

"Face it Vinnie-you're gonna have a hard time getting people to subscribe online with a credit card to a newsletter called, 'Felons Interactive'."

Using Technology to Keep You Safer

Your computer contains software and files that can be damaged in several different ways. One major source of damage is from malicious attacks that are delivered via the Internet.

➡ Some people create damaging programs called *viruses* specifically designed to get into your computer hard drive and destroy or scramble data.

➡ Companies might download *adware* on your computer, which causes pop-up ads to appear, slowing down your computer's performance.

➡ Spyware is another form of malicious software that you might download by clicking a link or opening a file attachment. *Spyware* sits on your computer and tracks your activities, whether for use by a legitimate company in selling you products or by a criminal element to steal your identity.

Microsoft provides security features within Windows Vista that help to keep your computer and information safe, whether you're at home or traveling with a laptop computer.

In this chapter, we introduce you to the major concepts of computer security and cover Windows Vista security features that allow you to do the following:

➡ Understand computer security and why you need it.

➡ Run periodic updates to Windows, which installs security solutions and *patches.* (Essentially, patches fix problems with the operating system.)

➡ Enable a *firewall,* which is a security feature that keeps your computer safe from outsiders and helps you avoid several kinds of attacks on your data.

➡ Work with Windows Defender, which is new in Windows Vista. Windows Defender is a built-in solution for managing all your security settings centrally.

➡ Set up Windows Defender to run automatically.

➡ Set up trusted Web sites so that Windows doesn't display alerts when you try to go to those sites. Make settings so that sites you trust are displayed and sites you don't trust are blocked.

➡ Protect your network with an encryption key.

➡ Discover how to use cell phones more safely.

Understand Computer Security

When you buy a car, it has certain safety features built in. After you drive it off the lot, you might find that the manufacturer slipped up and either recalls your car or requests that you go to the dealer's service department to have a faulty part replaced. In addition, you need to drive defensively to keep your car from being damaged in daily use.

Your computer is similar to your car in terms of the need for safety. It comes with an operating system (such as Microsoft Windows) built in, and that operating system has security features. Sometimes that operating system has flaws, and you need to get an update to keep it secure. And as you use your computer, you're exposing it to dangerous conditions and situations that you have to guard against.

Threats to your computer security can come from a file you copy from a disc you insert into your computer, but most of the time, the danger is from a program that you download from the Internet. These downloads can happen when you click a link, open an attachment in an e-mail, or download one piece of software without realizing that *malware* (malicious software) is attached to it.

You need to be aware of these three main types of dangerous programs:

➠ A *virus* is a little program that some nasty person thought up to spread around the Internet and infect computers. A virus can do a variety of things, but typically, it attacks your data, deleting files, scrambling data, or making changes to your system settings that cause your computer to grind to a halt.

➠ *Spyware* consists of programs responsible for tracking what you do with your computer. Some spyware simply helps companies you do business with track your activities so that they can figure out how to sell you things; other spyware is used for more insidious purposes, such as stealing your passwords.

➠ *Adware* is the computer equivalent of telemarketing phone calls at dinner time. After adware is downloaded onto your computer, you'll get annoying pop-up windows trying to sell you things all day long. Beyond the annoyance, adware can quickly clog up your computer. Its performance slows down, and it's hard to get anything done at all.

To protect your information and your computer from these various types of malware, you can do several things:

➠ **You can buy and install an anti-virus, anti-spyware, or anti-adware program.** It's critical that you install an anti-virus program, such as those from McAfee, Symantec (see **Figure 15-1**), or Trend Micro, or the freely downloadable AVG Free. People are coming up with new viruses every day, so it's important that you use software that is up-to-date with the latest virus definitions and protects your computer from them. Many anti-virus programs are purchased by yearly subscription, which gives you access to updated virus definitions that the company constantly gathers throughout the year. Also, be sure to run a scan of your computer on a regular basis. For convenience, you can use settings in the software to set up automatic updates and scans. Consult your program's Help tool for instructions on how to use these features.

➠ **Install a program that combines tools for detecting adware and spyware.** Windows Vista has a built-in program, Windows Defender, which includes an anti-spyware feature. (We cover Windows Defender tools covered later in this chapter.) If you don't have Windows Vista, you can purchase programs such as Spyware Doctor from PC Tools.

➠ **Use Windows tools to keep Windows up-to-date with security features and fixes to security problems.** You can also turn on a *firewall,* which is a feature that stops other people or programs from accessing your computer without your permission. We cover these two features in this chapter.

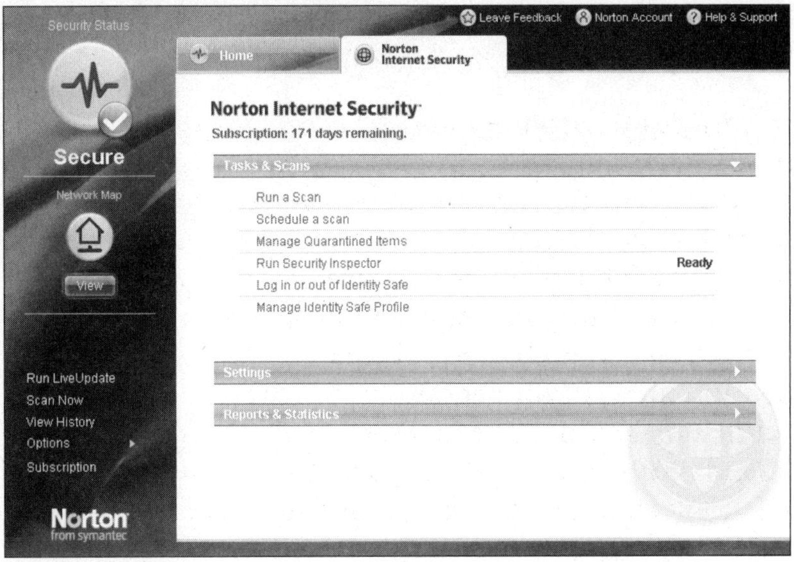

Figure 15-1

Understand Windows Update Options

When a new operating system like Windows Vista is released, it's been thoroughly tested; however, when the product is in general use, the manufacturer begins to find a few problems or security gaps that it couldn't anticipate. For that reason, companies such as Microsoft release updates to their software, both to fix those problems and deal with new threats to computers that appeared after the software release.

Windows Update is a tool you can use to make sure your computer has the most up-to-date security measures in place. You can set Windows Update to work in a few different ways. Here's how:

1. Choose Start⇨All Programs⇨Windows Update.

2. Click the **Change Settings** link on the left side of the Windows Update window.

3. In the resulting dialog box (see **Figure 15-2**), check the option you want from among these settings:

- **Install Updates Automatically:** With this setting enabled, Windows Update starts at a time of day you specify, but your computer must be on for it to work. If you turn off your computer, the automatic update will start when you next turn on your computer, and it might shut down your computer in the middle of your work to complete the installation.

- **Download Updates But Let Me Choose Whether to Install Them:** With this setting enabled, Windows Update downloads updates and notifies you (through a little pop-up message on your taskbar) when they're available, but you get to decide when the updates are installed and when your computer *reboots* (turns off and then on) to complete the installation. This is our preferred setting because we have control and won't be caught unawares by a computer reboot.

- **Check for Updates But Let Me Choose Whether to Download and Install Them:** With this setting enabled, you neither download nor install updates until you say so, but Windows notifies you that new updates are available.

- **Never Check for Updates:** You can stop Windows from checking for updates, and you'll want to check for them yourself, manually. (See the next section.) This puts your computer at a bit more risk, but it's useful for you to know how to perform a manual update. For example, you might discover that a new update is available, and you might need that update to proceed with a task (such as getting updated drivers or a language pack.)

4. If you want to have Windows recommend updates for your system, select the **Recommended Updates** checkbox.

Making your Windows Update settings

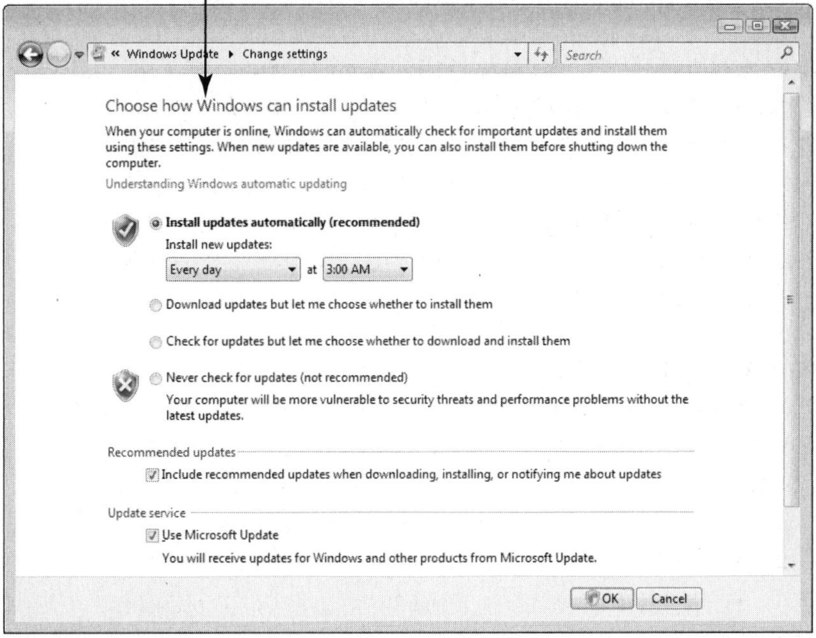

Figure 15-2

5. Be sure the **Use Microsoft Update** checkbox is selected.

6. Click **OK**.

Run Windows Update

No matter which Windows Update setting you choose (see the preceding section), you can run a manual update at any time. To do so, make sure you have an active Internet connection and follow these steps:

1. Choose Start⇨Control Panel⇨Check for Updates.

2. In the resulting Windows Update window, click **Check for Updates**. Windows thinks about this for a while, so feel free to page through a magazine for a minute or two.

3. In the resulting window, shown in **Figure 15-3,** click the **View Available Updates** link.

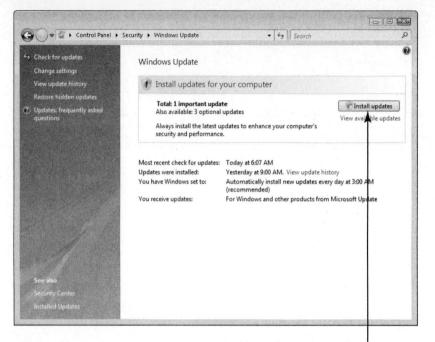

Click this link to check for updates

Figure 15-3

4. In the resulting window, which shows the available updates (see **Figure 15-4**), select the check boxes for the updates you want to install. (It usually doesn't hurt to just accept all updates, if you have the time to download them all.) Then click the **Install** button.

5. A window appears, showing the progress of your installation. When the installation is complete, you might get a message telling you that it's a good idea to restart your computer to complete the installation. Click the **Restart Now** button.

 You can set up Windows Update to run at the same time every day. Click the **Change Settings** link in the left pane of the Windows Update window (refer to **Figure 15-3**) and choose the frequency (such as every day) and time of day to check for and install updates.

Choose the updates you want to install

Total available: 4 updates

Name	Type	Published
Windows Vista (4)		
☑ Windows Malicious Software Removal Tool x64 - September 2008 (KB890830)	Important	9/9/2008
☐ Broadcom - Network - Broadcom 802.11b/g WLAN	Optional	Yesterday
☐ Conexant - Audio - Conexant High Definition SmartAudio 221	Optional	9/15/2008
☐ CXT - Network - HDAUDIO Soft Data Fax Modem with SmartCP	Optional	9/19/2008

Total selected: 1 update

Install   Cancel

Click this button

Figure 15-4

 If you set Windows Update to run automatically, be forewarned that when it runs, it might also automatically restart your computer to finish the update installation sequence. Although it displays a pop-up message warning that it's about to do this, it's easy to miss. Then you might be startled to find that whatever you're working on shuts down and your computer restarts when you least expect it. Pick a time to check for updates when you know the computer will be on but not likely to be in use (for example, two in the morning if your computer is always on).

Enable the Windows Firewall

A *firewall* is a program that protects your computer from the outside world, preventing others from accessing your computer and stopping the downloading of dangerous programs such as viruses. With a firewall on, if you try to access sites or download software, you're asked whether you want to allow such access. Be aware, however, that you must turn on your firewall before you connect to the Internet for it to be effective. Follow these steps to turn on the firewall in Windows Vista:

1. Choose Start⇨Control Panel⇨Check This Computer's Security Status.

2. In the Windows Security Center window that appears (see **Figure 15-5**), verify that the Windows Firewall has a status of On. If it isn't, click the **Windows Firewall** link in the left pane of the window and then click the **Change Settings** link in the resulting dialog box. Note that you have to have a user account with administrator permissions to change these settings. You can control this through the Control Panel under the User Accounts and Family Safety settings.

If the Firewall is off, click this link to enable it

The current Firewall status

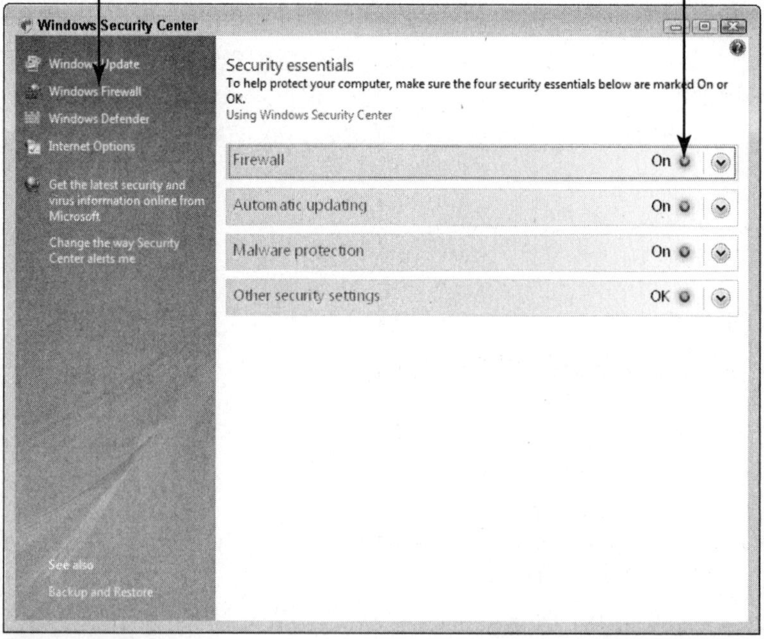

Figure 15-5

3. In the resulting Windows Firewall Settings dialog box (see **Figure 15-6**), select the **On** option and then click **OK**.

4. Click the **Close** button to close Windows Security Center and the Control Panel. Your firewall is now enabled and should stay enabled unless you go in and change the setting.

 Anti-virus and security software programs might offer their own firewall protection, and they might display messages asking whether you want to switch. Check their features against the Windows Firewall features and then decide. (Usually, most firewall features are comparable. The important thing is to have one activated.)

Select On to enable the Firewall

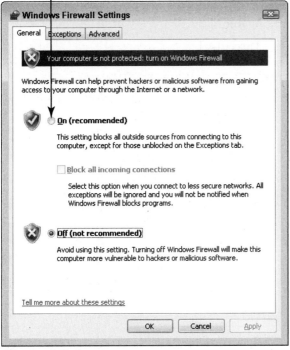

Figure 15-6

Turn On a Firewall On a Mac

1. Click the **System Preferences** icon.

2. In the resulting System Preferences window, click **Security**.

3. In the Security dialog box, click the **Firewall** tab (see **Figure 15-7**) and choose from these settings:

- **Allow All Incoming Connections:** Essentially disables the firewall feature.

- **Block All Incoming Connections:** Stops any site or service from connecting to your computer.

- **Limit Incoming Connections to Specific Services and Applications:** Allows you to specify which services and applications can connect to your computer.

4. Click the **Close** button to close the dialog box and save your settings.

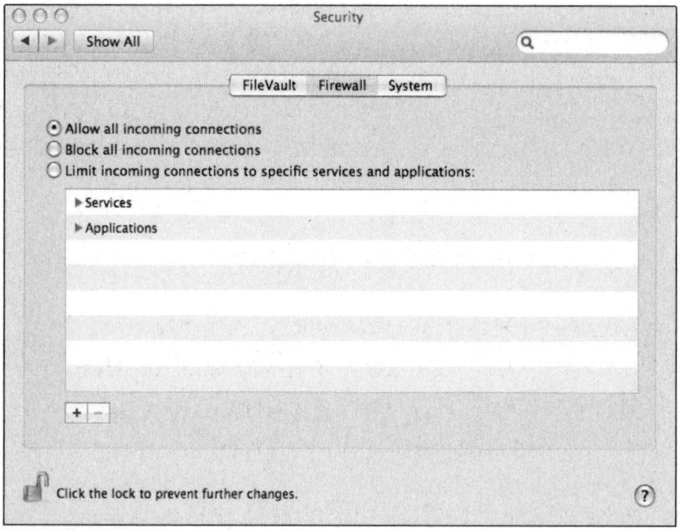

Figure 15-7

If you want to stop anybody else from making changes to your firewall settings, click the lock symbol in the bottom-left corner of the Security dialog box shown in Figure 15-7. To unlock the settings, click the lock symbol again and enter your user authentication information (username and password).

Run a Windows Defender Scan

Spyware and adware cause pop-up ads to appear on your screen or track your online activities. With the amount of spyware and adware attempting to download to your computer, an anti-spyware/adware program is a must-have security tool. If you don't guard against these, those annoying pop-ups will be the least of your problem. Eventually, these programs will slow your computer performance to a crawl.

Several good free programs are available, or use your operating system's tools (such as Windows Defender, in Windows Vista). With some programs, you may need to purchase a subscription to get automatic updates. As with anti-virus software, you can set up anti-spyware/adware to run scans automatically at a specific time.

If you use Windows Defender to detect spyware, you must run a *scan* of your computer system on a regular basis, which searches your computer for any problem files. You set Windows Defender to run scans automatically, or you can manually run a scan at any time. To adjust these settings, follow these steps:

1. Choose Start➪All Programs➪Windows Defender.

2. In the resulting Windows Defender window, click the **down-pointing arrow** on the Scan button (if you click the Scan button itself the scan begins). (See **Figure 15-8.**) In the resulting menu, choose one of three options:

- **Quick Scan:** This runs a scan of the likeliest spots on your computer where spyware might lurk. In many cases, this quicker scanning process finds most, if not all, problems and is good choice for a daily automatic scan.

- **Full Scan:** This scan checks every single file and folder on your computer and gives any currently running programs the once-over. However, be aware that during a Full Scan your computer might run a little more slowly.

- **Custom Scan:** This scan allows you to customize where to scan. This is helpful if you suspect that a particular drive or folder harbors a problem.

3. If you choose Quick Scan or Full Scan, the scan begins immediately. If you choose Custom Scan, you can click the **Select** button in the Select Scan Options dialog box that appears. Then, in the Select Drives and Folders to Scan dialog box (See **Figure 15-9.**), select drives, files, and folders to scan. Click **OK.** Back in the Select Scan Options dialog box, click **Scan Now.**

Click the down-pointing arrow on the Scan button

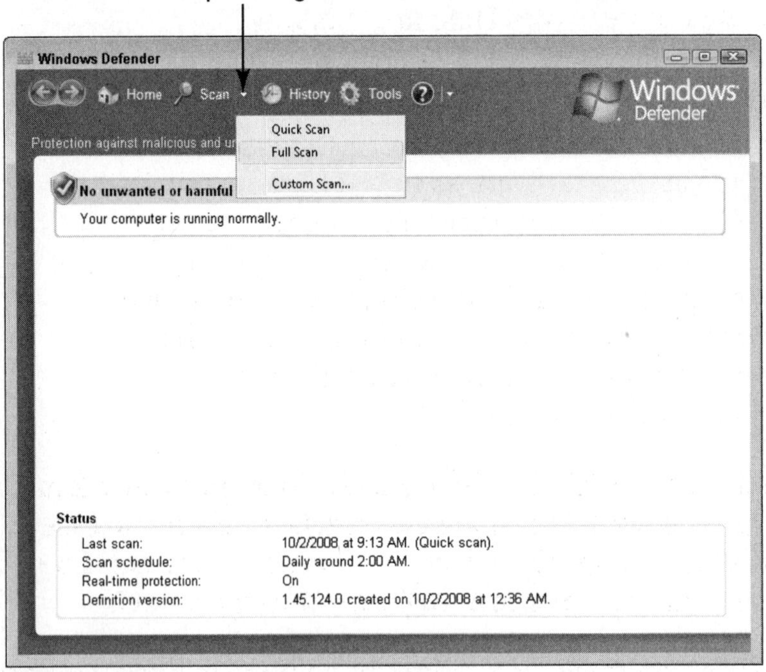

Figure 15-8

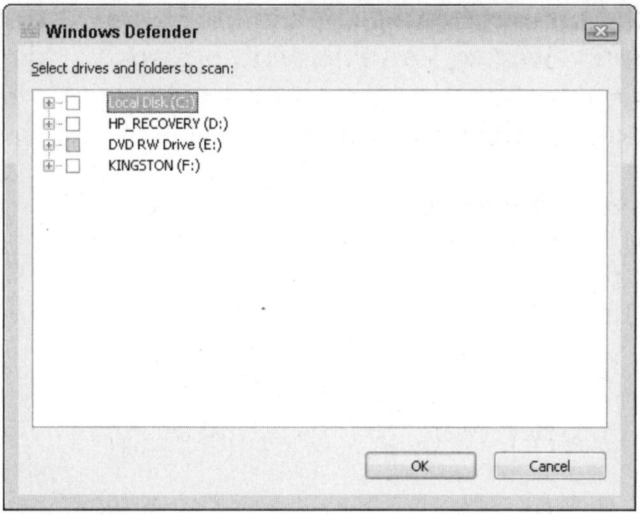

Figure 15-9

4. When a scan is complete, a dialog box appears, listing any instances of spyware that were found and deleted or informing you that no spyware was found. Click the **Close** button to close the Windows Defender window.

The History button in Windows Defender reviews Windows Defender's activities and actions. This is especially useful if you choose to run scans manually and don't remember whether you ran one recently. In that window, you can also view your settings for Microsoft SpyNet. By default, Windows Defender sets you up with a basic membership in SpyNet so that your computer automatically reports actions to remove spyware to Microsoft.

An advanced membership is also available. Like the basic membership, it doesn't cost you anything. It alerts you when new threats are detected and also provides Microsoft with more data about your computer — and some personal information might get through as well.

Allowing reports on spyware activity can help Microsoft prevent or stop such threats; however, if you don't want to report issues with your computer and spyware to Microsoft, you can choose not to join Microsoft

SpyNet by clicking the **Change Settings** link in the History dialog box and clicking the **I Don't Want to Join Microsoft Spynet At This Time** radio button.

Set Up Windows Defender to Run Automatically

If you prefer to have Windows Defender run on its own so you never miss a scan (which is a good idea, by the way), you can set it up to do so.

1. Choose Start⇨All Programs⇨Windows Defender.

2. In the resulting Windows Defender window, choose Tools⇨ Options.

3. In the Options dialog box that appears (see **Figure 15-10**), select the **Automatically Scan My Computer** check box (if it isn't already selected) and then choose the **Frequency**, **Appoximate Time** of day, and **Type** of scan from the drop-down lists.

Select this option for automatic scans

Figure 15-10

4. To ensure that your scan uses the latest definitions for *malware* (a kind of spyware with malicious intent), select the **Check for Updated Definitions before Scanning** check box.

5. Scroll down to the bottom of the Options dialog box (see **Figure 15-11**) and make sure that the **Use Windows Defender** check box is enabled (selected) to activate the program.

6. Click **Save** to save your settings.

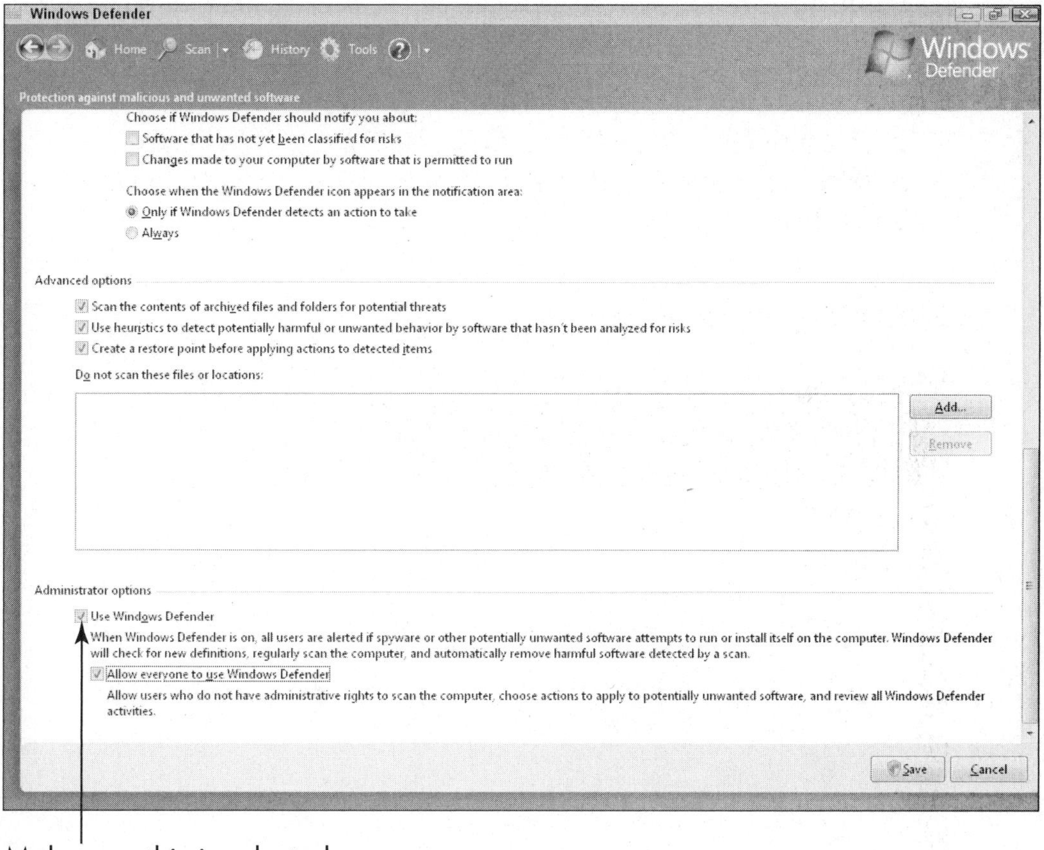

Make sure this is selected

Figure 15-11

If you want to exclude certain files or locations from the regular scans, you can use the **Advanced Options** in the Windows Defender dialog box. Click the **Add** button and browse for the location or file you want to exclude.

Set Up Trusted and Restricted Web Sites

1. Choose Start⇨Control Panel⇨Security.

2. In the resulting Security dialog box, click the **Internet Options** link.

3. In the resulting Internet Options dialog box, click the **Security** tab. (See **Figure 15-12**.)

Click the Security tab

Then click the Trusted Sites icon

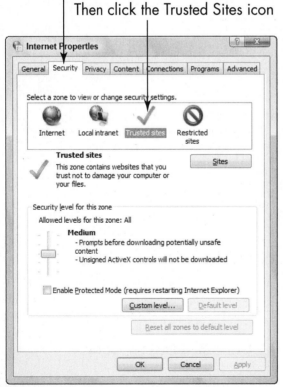

Figure 15-12

4. Click the **Trusted Sites** icon.

5. Click the **Sites** button.

6. In the resulting Trusted Sites dialog box (see **Figure 15-13**), enter a URL for a *trusted Web site* (one that you visit regularly and have determined to be safe) in the Add This Web Site to the Zone text box.

 Note that if the Require Server Verification (https:) for All Sites in This Zone check box is selected in the Trusted Sites dialog box, any Trusted site you add must use the `https:` prefix, which indicates that the site has a secure connection.

Enter the Web address here

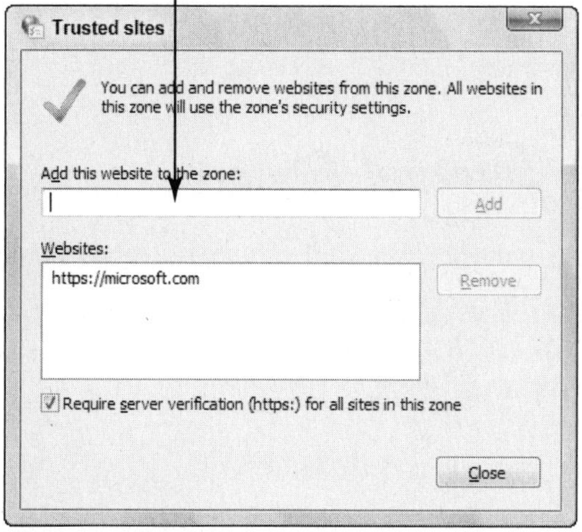

Figure 15-13

7. Click the **Add** button to add the site to the list of Web sites.

8. Repeat Steps 6, and 7 to add more trusted sites.

9. When you're done, click **OK** twice to close the dialog boxes.

To add sites you do *not* trust, you use a similar procedure. Complete the previous Steps 1–3. Then click the Restricted Sites icon and add the Web addresses.

You can establish a Privacy setting on the Privacy tab of the Internet Options dialog box to control which sites are allowed to download cookies to your computer. *Cookies*, tiny files that track your online activity, recognize you when you return to a source site. For example, when you go to an online shopping site, such as Amazon.com, to shop, cookies keep a record of what you're looking at. Then when you return to the site later, the site uses cookies to provide you with information on similar products. *Trusted sites* are the ones that you allow to download cookies to your computer, even though the privacy setting you've made might not allow any other sites to do so. *Restricted sites* can never download cookies to your computer, no matter what your privacy setting is.

Change Privacy Settings in Internet Explorer

Your browser should help you monitor your browsing experience, but you have to make certain settings to get the level of monitoring you prefer. For example, in Internet Explorer (IE) you can choose Tools⇨ Internet Options to set security and privacy preferences.

1. With IE open, choose Tools⇨Internet Options and click the **Privacy** tab, as shown in **Figure 15-14.**

2. Click the slider and drag it up or down to adjust your browser to different levels of security settings.

3. Read the choices and select a setting that suits you.

Click the Privacy tab to make privacy settings

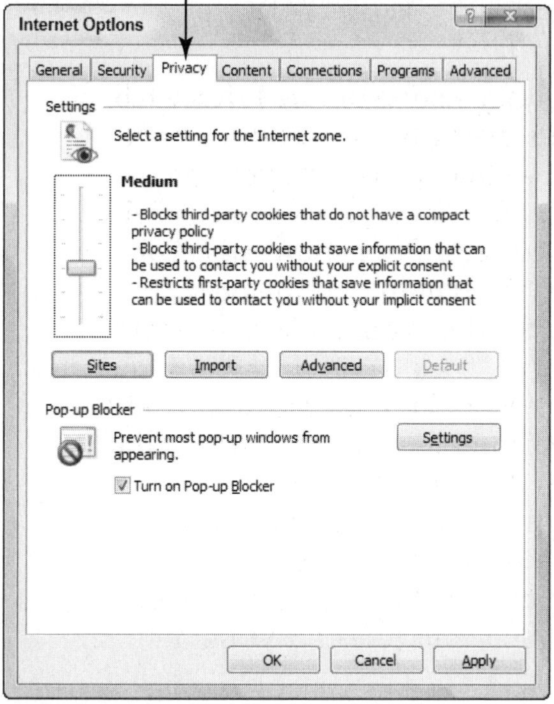

Figure 15-14

4. Click **OK** to save your settings.

 The default Privacy setting — Medium — is probably a good bet for most people. To restore the default setting, open the Internet Options dialog box (choose Tools⇨Internet Options), click the Privacy tab, and either click the Default button or move the slider back to Medium.

Browser settings provide a small measure of content filtering. To comprehensively filter content so you don't see unwanted materials or sites, you may want to purchase filtering software. This helps you set boundaries for the types of sites, text, and images you and your family are exposed to.

Change Privacy Settings in Firefox

1. Choose Tools⇨Options.

2. In the resulting Options dialog box, click the **Privacy** tab. (See **Figure 15-15**.)

Figure 15-15

3. You can make the following modifications here:

- **History:** Modify these settings if you don't want people who access your computer to view your browsing history.

- **Cookies:** Modify these settings to limit or block cookies (small files that track your online activity) from being downloaded to your computer. Use the Exceptions button to allow only certain sites to download cookies, and the Show Cookies button to see what cookies currently reside on your computer.

- **Private Data:** If you want to clear various private data, including saved passwords, browsing history, and cookies when you exit Firefox, use these settings.

4. When you finish adjusting settings, click OK to save them.

 If you simply can't wait and want to clear all your private settings right away instead of when you exit Firefox, open the Options dialog box (choose Tools⇨ Options), click the Privacy tab, and click the Clear Now button.

Enable Content Advisor

Many ISPs (Internet service providers) and Web portals provide content-filtering tools. You can set these up to filter out content that you don't wish to see based on keywords or categories of content (such as sexually explicit or violent content). You can also use these programs to limit or monitor your grandchild's online activities. Contact your ISP for instructions on how to use these tools.

If you don't find your ISP's tools adequate, you can search online for products that provide various levels of content monitoring.

Some Internet browsers provide content-filtering tools as well. Here's how settings work in Internet Explorer (IE).

1. With IE open, choose Tools⇨Internet Options.

2. In the resulting Internet Options dialog box, click the **Content** tab to display it.

3. Click the **Enable** button. (*Note:* If you don't see an Enable button, you should see Disable and Settings buttons instead. That means that Content Advisor is already enabled. Click the **Settings** button to see the options and make changes if you wish.)

4. On the **Ratings** tab of the Content Advisor dialog box (see **Figure 15-16**), click one of the categories of content such as Language, Depiction of Alcohol Use, or Content that Creates Fear, Intimidation, etc.. Use the slider to set the site-screening level that's appropriate for you.

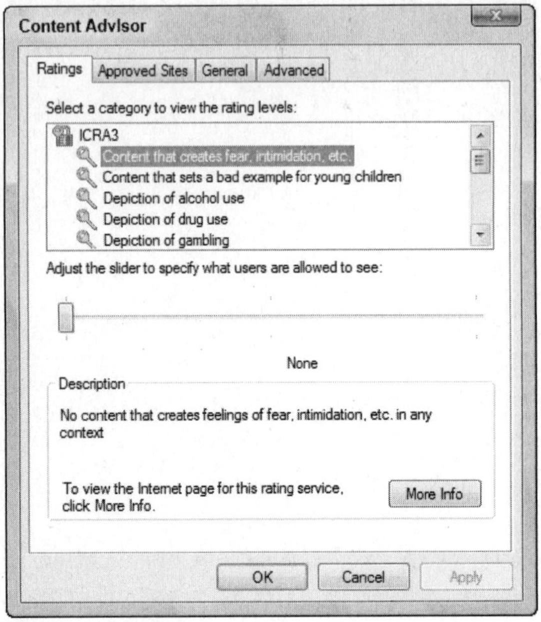

Figure 15-16

5. Repeat Step 4 for each of the categories.

6. Click the **Approved Sites** tab (see **Figure 15-17**) and enter the name of a specific site (or select it from the list of Web sites) that you want to control access to.

7. Click either of the following options:

- **Always:** Allows users to view the site, even if it's included in the Content Advisor screening level you've set.

- **Never:** Means that nobody can visit the site, even if it's acceptable to Content Advisor.

Content Advisor

| Ratings | Approved Sites | General | Advanced |

You can create a list of websites that are always viewable or never viewable regardless of how they are rated.

Allow this website:

[   ]   [Always]

                                                [Never]

List of approved and disapproved websites:

    ✅ amazon.com   [Remove]
    ⊖ craigslist
    ✅ microsoft.com

                    [OK]   [Cancel]   [Apply]

Figure 15-17

8. When you finish adjusting your settings, click **OK** twice to save them.

 If you want to view sites that you don't want others to see, you can do that, too. Open the **Content Advisor** dialog box (follow the previous Steps 1–3) and click the **General** tab. Make sure that the **Supervisor Can Type a Password to Allow Viewers to View Restricted Content** check box is selected. Then click **Create Password**. In the dialog box that appears, enter the password, confirm it, enter a hint, and click **OK**. Now if you're logged on as the system administrator, you can get to any restricted site by using this password.

If you don't feel that you can set up your computer's security, it may be well worth hiring a computer technician from a reputable company to review your security settings and fix any problems you may have. Make sure that you check the company's reputation through the Better Business Bureau, and make sure that whoever comes to your home is fully licensed and bonded.

Protect Your Wireless Network

If you set up a wireless router but didn't set up security passwords or activate encryption, chances are good that your network and your computer aren't protected. But you can correct that fairly easily by following the instructions provided by Microsoft or Apple. (**Note:** Doing this means that when you want someone to access your wireless network from another computer, she will have to get the password or key from you before she can go online.)

To protect an existing Windows Vista wireless network, follow these steps:

1. Choose Start⇨Control Panel.

2. Click the **Network and Internet** link.

3. In the resulting dialog box click the **Network and Sharing Center** link.

4. In the Network and Sharing Center window in the left pane, click the **Set Up a Connection or Network** link.

5. In the next window, click **Set Up a Wireless Router or Access Point**.

6. In the resulting Set Up a Wireless Router or Access Point window, click the **Connect to a Network** link.

7. In the resulting Connect to a Network window (see **Figure 15-18**), right-click your network and choose **Properties.**

8. In the resulting Wireless Network Properties dialog box (see **Figure 15-19**), choose an Encryption Type. This is typically **WEP**. When you select WEP, a security key appears.

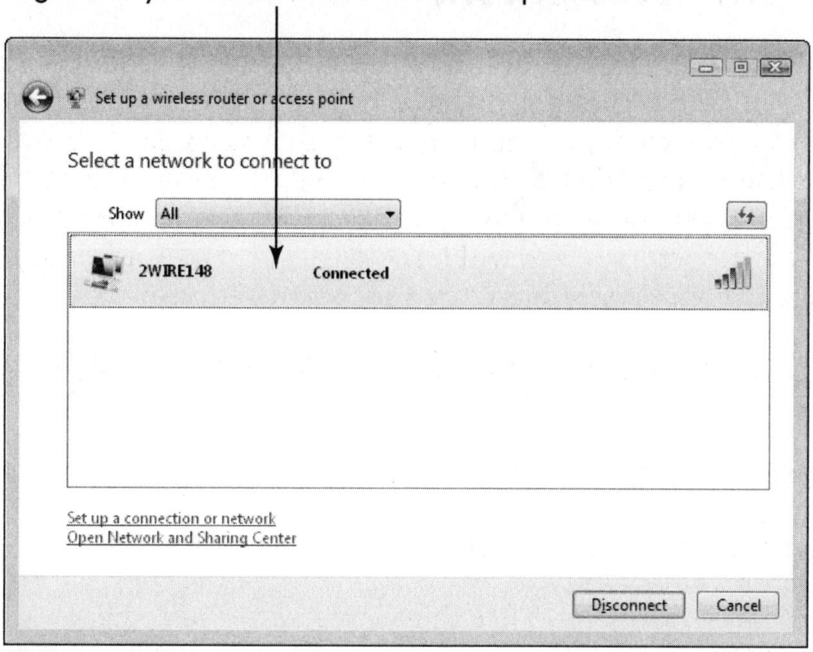

Right-click your network and choose Properties

Set up a wireless router or access point

Select a network to connect to

Show | All | ▼

2WIRE148   Connected

Set up a connection or network
Open Network and Sharing Center

Disconnect   Cancel

Figure 15-18

9. Click the **OK** button to save your settings, then click the **Close** button twice to close the open windows.

 If you've caught the RV bug, you might want a smart phone that allows you to check your e-mail from the road. If you prefer having Internet access from your computer, consider a service such as WiFiRV. Using such a service, you can access so-called *hotspots* (areas with wireless Internet service) around the country — if your computer has a wireless card installed. Go to www.WiFiRV.com to read about this service and look up RV parks that provide access to hotspots. See Chapter 4 for more about Internet safety.

Select your encryption type

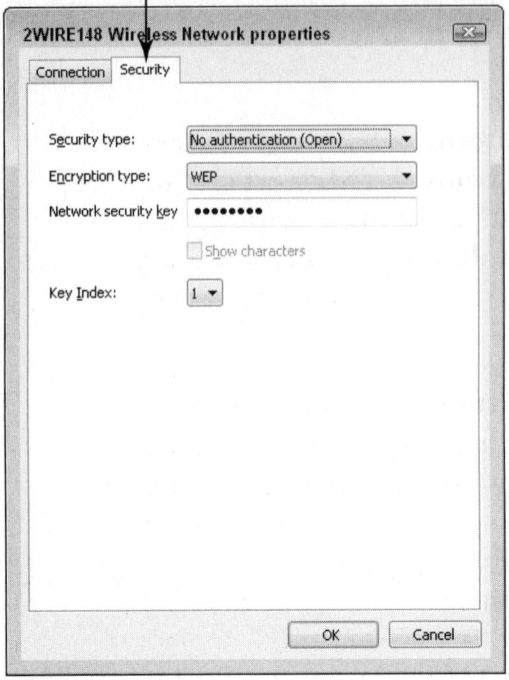

2WIRE148 Wireless Network properties

| Connection | Security |

Security type: | No authentication (Open) ▼ |

Encryption type: | WEP ▼ |

Network security key | •••••••• |

☐ Show characters

Key Index: | 1 ▼ |

OK | Cancel

Figure 15-19

For establishing a new wireless network on the Windows Operating System (first time setup), refer to the very detailed instructions found at `http://windowshelp.microsoft.com/Windows/en-us/help/76174f4a-7522-425a-9424-324dd299265e1033.mspx`. For establishing a new wireless network on the Apple Operating System (first time setup)refer to the very detailed instructions found at `www.apple.com/support/panther/network/`.

Protect Yourself on the Go: Cell Phone Safety

For most people, it's hard to imagine how we managed before we had mobile (cell) phones. Most cell phones today are actually small computers with rich feature sets. Before you buy a phone for yourself or your grandchild, ask these questions:

➡ **Does the phone or device have Internet access?** If you want to check e-mail or use the Web to look up restaurants or directions when you're on the road, you need Internet access.

➡ **Does the phone with Internet access offer filters that block content that could be harmful to children or offensive to you?** Is the filter turned on? If the filter isn't on by default, ask the sales person to turn it on for you in the store and help you set appropriate filter levels.

➡ **Does the phone or device have location (GPS) capability?** GPS allows you to let your phone's location be tracked. This is useful for emergencies, such as a car accident when you can dial 911. If the phone doesn't have GPS capability, 911 may not be able to identify your location. If you need to, you should be able to block this capability or limit it so that your grandchild can't grant access to predators who are trying to track your location.

➡ **Is the phone or device Bluetooth enabled?** Bluetooth is a technology that allows a mobile phone to seek, discover, and talk to other Bluetooth-enabled devices in the area. This capability is available in some cars so that you can talk hands-free while driving, which is, in fact, required by law in many states. However, with Bluetooth enabled, nearby devices can access information on your phone. When Bluetooth functionality is turned off, other devices can't detect the phone, pull information from it, or send information to it.

Here are some additional cell phone safety tips:

➡ **Know how to report theft of the device.** You may need to provide hardware information found within the device, under the battery. If you don't have this information written down, you surely won't be able to find it once the phone is stolen.

➡ **Know how to report harassment or bullying.** The carrier should have a clear set of procedures you can use to report any malicious calls. It's best to know these in advance of harassment.

When buying a cell phone and/or signing up for cell phone service, consider whether you should get a pre-paid account or an account that bills charges monthly. Depending on your phone usage, it may be more economical to get an account where you buy minutes, rather than paying a monthly fee and taxes whether you use the phone that month or not. If you use the phone only when you go on trips, for example, a pre-paid plan such as one offered by Tracfone (find this at www. tracfone.com, shown **Figure** 15-20) makes sense.

Figure 15-20

Knowing Your Rights and Making a Difference

Chapter 16

You are part of the brave new world of the Internet. This is a frontier in which laws, ethical standards, and common-sense approaches to daily behavior are still evolving. The way you behave, the way you treat others, the way you allow yourself to be treated, and how you hold companies and governments responsible for their behavior will help to shape this world.

In order to hold up your end, you have to understand what your rights are and what you should demand of others — both individuals and companies. In this chapter, we explore those rights, the recourse you have if you're the victim of certain types of abuse, and what you can and should demand of online entities to leave your mark on this world for yourself and future generations.

It's Never the Victim's Fault

In any crime, the predator bears the entire blame.

➡ Predators frequently try to make a victim believe that the abuse was the victim's fault. If that person feels stupid, guilty, or ashamed, he or she will be much less likely to report it.

➡ Predators who use emotions to help achieve their goals — whether their aim is financial or sexual — often try to convince their victims that the interaction was something they wanted. People who are lonely or have low self esteem are particularly susceptible to this tactic.

➡ If you're victimized online or offline, don't blame yourself. Preserve whatever evidence you may have — e-mails, instant messages, purchases, and so on — and report the abuse to both the service provider and your local law enforcement agency. It doesn't matter where the criminal says he is, you always report crimes against you to local law enforcement, and they will contact other jurisdictions if needed. Your actions may help to save another person from the heartache that you've experienced.

 There's no such thing as consensual sex between adults and minors. Sexual acts with minors are illegal and exploitive. As a society, everyone must be committed to protecting minors — even when the minor acts against his or her own best interests. Whether you are a caregiver, grandparent, uncle or aunt, or friend of a young person, you owe it to the minor to learn how to protect her. See Chapter 11 for more about how to do this.

ID Theft Victims' Rights

If you're a victim of ID theft, you may have months of work ahead of you to clear up your records, but if you know your rights, you can move forward more confidently. Although state regulations may vary (see **Figure 16-1**), here are some of the provisions you should check into:

➠ **Limitations imposed on collection agencies:** A collection agency may not call a debtor more than one time in 180 days in order to collect on debts associated with an identity theft, as long as the victim forwards information regarding the alleged theft. A victim must provide the following:

- A written statement describing the nature of the fraud or theft and identifying the documents and/or accounts involved.

- A certified copy of a police report. According to the FTC, "In your report, you should give as much information as you can about the crime, including anything you know about the dates of the identity theft, the fraudulent accounts opened and the alleged identity thief." Detailed information should specifically identify the relevant financial institutions, account numbers, check numbers, and so on.

- A copy of a government-issued photo identification card dated before the date of the identity theft, such as your driver's license or passport.

- A statement that a debt is under dispute as the result of identity theft. Collection agencies are prohibited from calling consumers about transactions that are identified as fraudulent.

Figure 16-1

 Under certain limited circumstances, a collection agency may not be liable for repeated contact with a debtor, even contacts that would otherwise violate the statute. This is the case if it acts in good faith and the contacts are covered by any one of several exceptions. Visit www.ftc.gov/bcp/edu/microsites/ idtheft/consumers/defend.html for more about ID theft victim rights and recourses.

➡ **Limitations imposed on reporting agencies:** Within thirty days of receiving proof of a consumer's identification and a copy of a filed police report verifying the claim of identity theft, a credit reporting agency must

- Permanently block information from a credit report that may be the result of identity theft.

- Tell the entities furnishing information covered by the report that the information has been blocked.

- Under certain circumstances, such as errors or consumer misrepresentation, the consumer reporting company or the company providing information can call off the block.

Your Rights Regarding Spam

The federal CAN-SPAM Act (see **Figure 16-2**) went into effect on January 1, 2004. Federal lawmakers created The CAN-SPAM Act (Controlling the Assault of Non-Solicited Pornography and Marketing Act of 2003) to help stop the onslaught of spam. The CAN-SPAM Act preempts all state law that regulates commercial e-mail, except with regard to how state law prohibits falsity or deception.

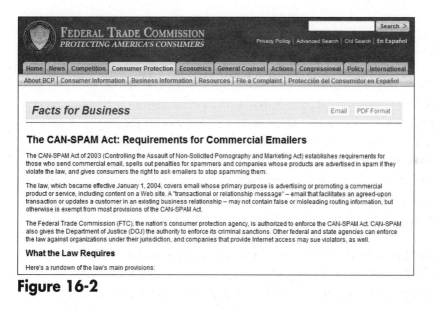

Figure 16-2

The federal statute

⟹ Requires that senders of commercial e-mail allow people to opt out of receiving more e-mail.

⟹ Requires e-mail to be identified as an advertisement or commercial e-mail.

➡ Requires sexually-oriented e-mail to be labeled as such in the subject line.

➡ Requires the physical address of the sender to be included in the e-mail.

➡ Creates criminal penalties for those who violate the law.

 If you would like to file a complaint under the CAN-SPAM Act, send an e-mail to the FTC at spam@uce. gov. The FTC also provides more detailed information about spam issues and the CAN-SPAM law on the FTC Web site (www.ftc.gov/bcp/conline/edcams/spam/index.html).

Your Internet Safety Bill of Rights

Everyone's sense of safety and content-appropriateness varies somewhat, depending on their own moral compass, the country they live in, their social peer group, and the situations they find themselves in.

Risk aversion or risk tolerance thresholds, like morality-based filter options, should be easy-to-set clear choices. Unfortunately, all too often, no choice is provided, or default choices are assumed.

The first step to take charge of your Internet experience is to know your rights as a user.

All Internet users have the right to a safe Internet experience. Your safety and the safety of your family on the Internet should not be left to features a company adds at the last minute (add-ons) or those you have to pay extra for. You can't buy a new car without safety belts or air bags; you shouldn't have to settle for Internet products or services that fail to offer safety in the same basic way.

In a nutshell, we believe every online consumer has these rights:

➡ **You have the right to an informed online experience.**

- You should know in advance about any potential risks in Web programs and services such as Internet dating services, social networking or blogging sites, or instant messaging programs, so that you can appropriately respond and make safe choices.

- You have the right to complete information about every safety feature in a product or service (see **Figure 16-3**), and safety recommendations by feature should be easy to discover. At the bare minimum, you should be able to find safety information in the Help section that specifically covers how to apply every feature. Ideally, however, the program would give safety advice at key points, such as when you type in information or before you post a picture.

- When services are upgraded, you have the right to be informed of new features or changes to existing features and their impact on your safety. You should also have a clear way to opt out of any features you're uncomfortable with. For example, if changes are made to a subscription you've paid for and you want to cancel, you should be able to get a refund for remaining time.

➡ **You have the right to set your own terms for your online experience (within the constraints of the law).**

- You have the right to get content that matches your values and blocks content you don't wish to see, no matter what your age.

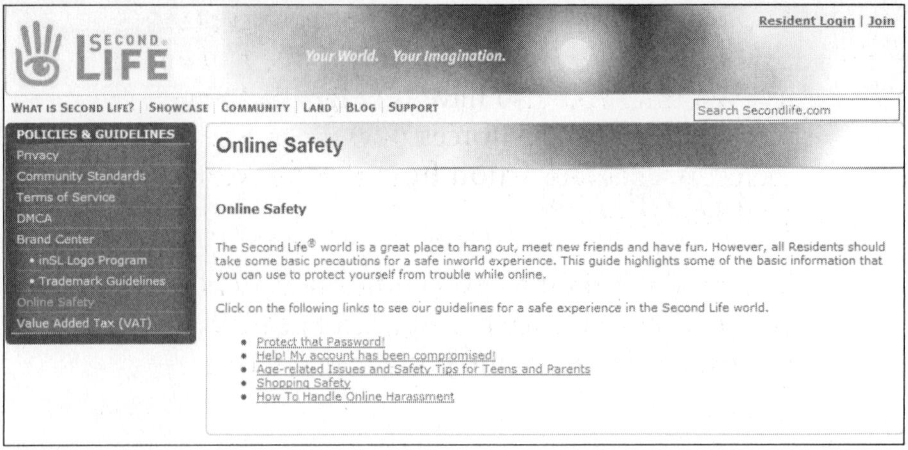

Figure 16-3

- You have the right to set boundaries so that you're exposed to only the level of potential risk you're comfortable with, whether you're more willing to take risks or more risk averse. This includes being able to manage the online experience of minors in your care.

- You have the right to know if you're being monitored online and how you're being monitored — such as which of your activities is being tracked and to whom it's reported, whether it's to companies or other individuals. Your children have this right, too.

➥ **You have the right to expect online products and services to guard your safety.**

- You have the right to feel confident that products and services won't be released to the public without undergoing rigorous safety, privacy, and legal reviews and testing.

- You have the right to know the privacy and safety policies of online products and services. (See **Figure 16-4**.) These should be easy to find and written in terms that are easy to understand.

- You have the right to easily report abuse of the products or abuse through the products of you or a loved one. You also have the right to know how well the company enforces its policies and to expect immediate action from the company if a problem arises.

- You have the right to expect the equivalent of a product recall notice if a significant safety risk is discovered in an online product or service.

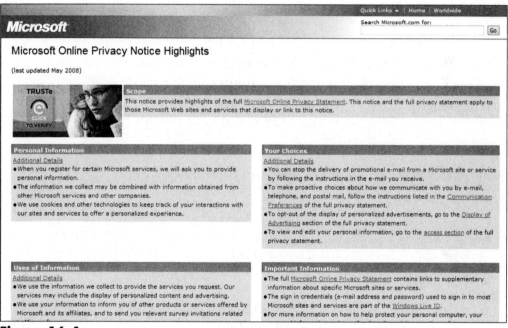

Figure 16-4

 As a consumer, you can — and should — vote with your feet if the experience you're having on a service doesn't meet your expectations. You can make a difference. Your safety rights won't be established in Internet programs and services overnight. But if you let companies know what you think, they'll surely be delivered faster.

Demand More from Online Companies

Just as not every person is trustworthy, not every company is worthy of your trust in equal measure. This is why it's important to choose which information we provide to various businesses in the brick-and-mortar world. What information you provide to a grocery store clerk differs from the information you share with your bank manager. This ability to select what companies know about you is at least as necessary online.

However, in addition to taking the time to identify reputable online companies that will respect your information, we aren't hearing enough about the responsibility of companies to build safer products. Our background is in the Internet industry. We love technology. But the industry as a whole hasn't taken enough steps to design or provide a safer consumer experience.

➡ In most cases companies simply provide people with access to products and urge them to have fun. These products hurtle consumers through cyberspace at warp speed but don't provide the equivalent of a user's manual, let alone a driver's education.

➡ Most online services fail to build basic safety measures equivalent to the brakes, locks, or airbags that are built into your car, and even fewer adequately test their products for safety.

➡ Companies provide terms of use and codes of conduct on their sites, but most fail to take the responsibility to enforce their policies and ensure reasonable safety for users on their sites. *In their own online environments, service providers must be the first line of safety and enforcement.*

➡ Companies have a responsibility to inform consumers about changes to their products that have an impact on safety. Many adult IM users are surprised to discover that IM has steadily upgraded far beyond the real-time e-mail service they thought they knew.

➡ As companies rush to add great new features, such as rich profiles, avatars, extended networking (friends of friends), video and music players, bots, gadgets, buddy searches, and shopping and location tools, they cut corners on hardening the products against a variety of online crimes and abuse, leaving consumers at risk.

➡ In the race to be first with a new feature, or to catch up with a competitor, tradeoffs are required. All too often, the first features cut and the last features reluctantly added are safety related, such as filters for images and text, safety information within products, the ability to turn off or restrict access to high-risk features, as well as tools that specifically help users manage their exposure, and tools to help companies track abuse behind the scenes on their services.

Service providers will continue to innovate, and this is good news for everyone. However, consumers have the right to be informed about each new feature that affects their exposure to risk, and we should be able to determine whether the risk potential is appropriate for us and our families. Automatic upgrades without safety messaging bears a strong resemblance to the old bait-and-switch tactics when consumers aren't given the right to choose. The Internet industry has for years promoted self-regulation of online tools and services, but it's consistently failed to deliver adequate safeguards for consumers.

 Use your common sense when dealing with online services. Most Internet services and products are businesses. They're for-profit organizations, not philanthropic endeavors. Building safety into products costs money, may slow development, and probably restricts the number of users (like restricting users under a certain age, or filtering content prior to exposing it on the site) which in turn reduces their revenue.

It's important to remember that many free sites aren't free; the companies might make their money by selling advertisers access to their users, so more users equals more money. It isn't usually in a company's financial interest to restrict access even to those users with a history of bad behavior, as it restricts ad revenue. Nor is it in the immediate best interest of the companies to build safety tools unless consumers or regulations demand it.

The great news is that you have tremendous power in this financial model. When companies make money by having lots of users, they lose money when users leave their sites — and they become very concerned *and responsive* if users threaten to leave their sites because of poor policies, lack of safety, and so on. If you and others act, you can make a tremendous difference.

Hold the Government Accountable for Your Privacy

Some safety precautions, such as crossing the street safely or locking your house when you go out, are your responsibility.

Other safety measures aren't. We don't ask consumers to build public roads, ensure that the roads meet quality standards, or require consumers to enforce speed limits. In the same way, we can't place the full burden of online safety on consumers.

These three key responsibilities lie firmly in the domain of government:

➡ Establishing minimum safety standards for companies and their products and services so that consumers can use technology without fear of harm.

➡ Monitoring companies' compliance with established safety standards and penalizing companies that fail to meet them.

➡ Enforcing the law. Fighting criminals isn't a job for ordinary citizens; it leads to fear and vigilantism (as we've seen in the vigilante efforts of ordinary citizens to trap predators online).

There are several areas where current government response is lacking and where you need to demand improvement.

⟶ Society has tasked government with ensuring the dissemination of public safety messages such as the health warnings on cigarette packaging. Regrettably, holistic Internet safety messaging is still lacking — and much of the current Internet safety messaging fails to provide useful, actionable information. Safety messaging must explain both potential risks and how to evaluate risks so that you can determine your own comfort level.

⟶ Governments and courts need to set age boundaries, establish the dividing line between legal and illegal content, and between safe and unsafe product quality. It should support these laws by

- Creating and enforcing minimum safety standards to restore consumer confidence in online tools and services.

- Passing legislation that enables law enforcement to arrest criminals and get convictions for crimes that aren't covered by existing laws.

- Making funds available for equipment, training, and additional officers. Mandates without funding aren't priorities; they're merely political lip service.

Let your elected officials know that you demand regulations that require consumer protection in online services and products and the development of laws that will allow law enforcement to arrest and prosecute online criminals.

 If you have grandchildren you should know that a Texas judge's ruling determined that parents own the primary responsibility for protecting minors online, as he dismissed a lawsuit filed by the parents of a young teen girl against MySpace. According to the Los Angeles Times, Judge Sparks' specific comment was "If anyone had a duty to protect Julie Doe, it was her parents, not MySpace."

This statement is on par with claiming that parents are primarily responsible for traffic deaths of their teens. If someone hands a 14-year-old keys to a faulty car and says "go have fun" down a poorly maintained freeway that doesn't warn of steep curves, would society blame the parents for the ensuing crash?

What Law Enforcement and Government Agencies Must Do

Law enforcement has primary responsibility to monitor society's safety, prevent crime, and bring to justice those who break the law. Yet, this is a tall order when adequate laws and regulations are missing to facilitate enforcement, adequate safety features weren't built into the products to minimize the potential for exploitation, and even so-called public sites are owned and run by companies, not society. Crime has always enjoyed better funding than law enforcement, but without assurances of basic safety, the public can't fully realize the tremendous opportunities the Internet has to offer.

No government's intent has ever been to abet criminals or expose consumers to crime. Unfortunately, intent doesn't deter crime; actions do. Law enforcement and government agencies must work hand in hand to

⟹ Clearly indicate in government-sponsored public messaging the government role in exposing consumers to risk.

⟹ Thoroughly evaluate and justify all information they make public about individuals.

➡ Do a comprehensive review of the implications of the existing practices around the Freedom of Information Act. (See **Figure 16-5**.) Changes must swiftly be made to protect individuals while safeguarding the public's right to know about government actions, policies, and so on.

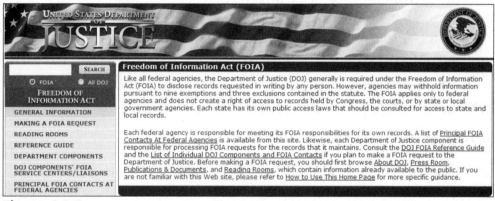

Figure 16-5

➡ Establish a timeframe to require all government agencies to remove sensitive information about individuals.

➡ Find the funding to educate law enforcement staff and empower them to enforce laws and regulations.

 Something you can do is to watch for news about proposed and pending Internet safety, privacy, and policy legislation and speak out. Contact your local, state, and national representatives, and let them know that this matter is important to you.

Glossary

A

adware: A type of malicious code that displays unsolicited advertising on your computer.

anti-virus software: Computer software designed to block malicious programs, code, and software (called *viruses* or *malware*) from your computer.

B

blog: A diary or personal journal posted on a Web site, usually updated frequently. A blog may be set as private or available to be viewed by the general public.

bots: Computer programs that automatically perform repetitive tasks, such as searching through Web sites or indexing information.

browser: Software, such as Firefox, Safari, and Internet Explorer, used to navigate and search the Internet. Most browsers have several security and privacy settings built in.

buddies (buddy list): A list of friends you interact with online through various services such as instant messaging.

buddy search: When two (or more) Internet users search the Web together; both users see the search results at the same time.

C

chat room: An online site used for socializing with others, usually based on a topic or theme.

content filter: A program that allows you to block certain types of content from being displayed on your computer screen. Some of the things you can screen for include coarse language, nudity, sex, and violence. In addition, many Internet browsers have parental controls to help protect your grandchildren from stumbling onto inappropriate sites. You can often choose separate levels of security for yourself and each child based on ages and maturity levels.

cookie: A small piece of code that is downloaded to computers to keep track of the user's activities or preferences. Cookies may simply help a site enhance it's service for consumers, or may be used by criminals to track personal information.

cybercriminals: People who commit criminal activity that targets computers — or people who leverage computers and online information to find real-world victims.

cybersex: Also called *computer sex, Net sex,* and *hot chat.* People can have virtual sexual encounters through text, images, voice, and/or video.

D

discussion board: Also called *Internet forums, message boards,* and *bulletin boards.* This feature of some Web sites allows users to post comments on a particular topic and respond to each other.

download: Transfer of material from a server or remote computer to your computer, mobile device, or game console.

E

e-mail: A message initiated in an e-mail program, such as Outlook, that is sent to another e-mail user electronically via the Internet.

e-mail signature: A block of text added to the end of e-mail messages, usually automatically. A signature might contain your full name, your job description, location, phone number, and an inspirational quote.

emoticons: Small graphic symbols (such as smiley faces) used to indicate emotional state, opinion, or response. Emoticons are useful when no body language provides clues to feelings.

F

file sharing: The ability to store files either in a central place that one or more people can share. Files can be stored on the Internet or on any computer that provides access to other computers. File sharing allows those who have permission to access shared files to modify or download them.

firewall: A security system, usually made up of hardware and software, that is used to block hackers, viruses, and other malicious threats to your computer. It is delivered through a network such as the Internet. Installing or activating a firewall feature on your computer is one of the most important actions you can take to help protect your computer and information.

for-pay items (winks, avatars): Low-cost add-on products that allow users to customize their experiences on cell phones or other instant messaging devices. These may be cartoon-like images (called *avatars*) or animated cartoons (called *winks*) that you receive or send to others.

G

game console: A machine that is specifically designed for playing video games (although it might also play movies), often hooked up to a TV or computer monitor for viewing. Not all game consoles are capable of Internet connections, but if they are connected, they allow users to play games with others remotely.

gamer tag: The nickname that a user is identified by when playing interactive games.

gaming: Playing or participating in online games.

grooming: The systematic way in which sexual or financial predators manipulate their victims into trusting and depending on them. Sexual predators groom with the goal of meeting a contact in person. Grooming usually involves invoking sympathy, using subtle techniques to alienate the victim from others, and flattery. Grooming might also involve money or gifts.

GSM (Global System for Mobile communications): A digital cellular telephone technology. This system is used mainly in Europe, Australia, and the Middle East, and it is now becoming popular in the United States.

H

handle: (as in *blog handle*) A nickname that an Internet user chooses to display to others online.

I

identity theft (ID theft): Stealing someone's identity in order to impersonate him/her, usually for financial gain.

instant messaging: A real-time, text-based communication used on desktop computers, cell phones, and other devices to send short messages between individuals.

interactive gaming: The act of playing games online, interacting with other players. The term covers a broad spectrum of activities, from children's games to online gambling.

Internet: The large network of computer servers that host and enable the transmission of information via computer connections.

K

keystroke logging: A legitimate way for software developers to understand what is happening as they write code. This technique is also used to track a user's activities online to either monitor or spy on (depending on motivations) what users type and which sites they visit. This type of program can also be downloaded onto your computer without your knowledge by a cybercriminal, who then can gain information about your online activities and even steal your account numbers and passwords.

L

location application: A program that enables you to locate anybody logged onto the Internet physically using a variety of devices (such as a cell phone).

M

malware: Malicious software. This includes any type of harmful code (Trojans, worms, spyware, adware, and so on) that infiltrates a computer without the user's consent. Malware is designed to damage a computer, collect information, or allow the computer to be taken over and used remotely to send spam.

Multimedia Messaging Services (MMS): A method for sending messages that may include audio, video, or images from mobile phones.

mobile computing: Use of a portable device that provides computer functions and can usually connect to the Internet when such access is available.

P

parental controls: Products or services that offer options to parents and other caregivers to help restrict their child's experiences with media or filter media content. These restrictions are currently applied to television services, computer and video games, and Internet access.

peer-to-peer: A method of sharing files directly over the Internet from one Internet-enabled device to another (computer, mobile phone, and so on). This is often done with music files, for example, which might violate copyright laws if the people involved make copies of the material without permission.

persona: The person an Internet user chooses to appear to be, rather than using his true identity. For example, a 65-year-old man might assume the persona of a 12-year-old girl to meet other 12-year-old girls on a social networking site.

personal digital assistant (PDA): A small, handheld computing device typically used to track appointments, contacts, and e-mail.

phishing: The practice of scamming someone into divulging confidential information that she normally would not provide to a stranger. The lure is typically via e-mail that brings the user to a scam Web site. The purpose of phishing is to gather information needed to steal a victim's money or identity.

posting: Uploading information to the Web.

predator: Anyone who preys on others.

R

remote access: The ability to access somebody's computer from another location. Remote access is often used in technical support as a way to fix problems, as it provides full access to the information stored on the computer through a data link.

S

scam: To con, cheat, trick, swindle, sting, or rip off others. Online scams may take the form of deceptive e-mails or other communications via instant messaging, blog comments, and so on, designed to part you from your money or identity.

search engine: An Internet service that allows you to search for information and documents on the Web.

smart phone: A handheld device that incorporates features of a mobile phone, with PDA functions such as a calendar or contact database. Smartphones allow you to install additional features.

SMS (Short Message Service): A form of text messaging used on cell phones, sometimes used between computers and cell phones.

social networking: A category of Internet applications used to help connect friends, business associates, or others using a variety of communication tools.

spam: Unsolicited e-mail messages that attempt to sell you something. Also known as *junk e-mail.*

spim: Spam sent via instant messages.

splog: Spam sent via blogs.

spyware: Software that collects information about you without your knowledge or consent and sends it back to whoever wrote the spyware program. Spyware might look for your bank account numbers, personal information, and so on. Spyware is illegal and pervasive.

Subscriber Identity Module (SIM card): A small card used in most cell phones that holds your identity, authentication, address book, and so on.

surfing: Similar to channel surfing on television, Internet surfing involves users browsing around various Web sites, following whatever interests them.

T

text messaging: A method of sending short messages (also called *SMSes*, *texts*, or *texting*) between mobile phones, other computing devices, and even some landline phones.

U

URL (Uniform Resource Locator): A unique Internet address of a file or destination. To find a particular site or document online, type the URL into the address field of a browser and press Enter.

upload: To post content on the Internet.

username: The name a person chooses to be identified by, for example on a computer within a network, or in an online gaming forum (also called a *nickname* or *gamer tag*).

V

videocams: Also called *Web cams*, these video cameras are attached to or built into computers. Web cams are used to send a video images to others while communicating online.

virus: A self-replicating software program that spreads by sending copies of itself to other devices hidden in code or attached to documents. Viruses are often deliberately destructive to any device that becomes infected, often destroying data or disabling the device's operating system.

Voice over Internet Protocol (VoIP): Use of an Internet protocol to transmit voice communications. VoIP allows you to hold voice conversations over the Internet.

W

Web browser: See browser.

Web site: A collection of documents called Web pages.

Web hosting: A service that provides individuals, organizations, and businesses with online storage space to store and share information, images, blogs, video, or any other content accessible through the Web.

Wiki: A collaborative tool which allows users to contribute information and ideas on a Web site.

World Wide Web (Web): The system of documents stored online, which you can locate using a Web browser such as Internet Explorer.

 **Index**